Hand-Me-Down Genes and Second-Hand Emotions

Hand-Me-Down Genes and Second-Hand Emotions

Stephen Arterburn

THOMAS NELSON PUBLISHERS
Nashville

Copyright © 1992 by Stephen Arterburn.

All rights reserved. Written permission must be secured from the publisher to use or reproduce any part of this book, except for brief quotations in critical reviews or articles.

Published in Nashville, Tennessee, by Oliver-Nelson Books, a division of Thomas Nelson, Inc., Publishers, and distributed in Canada by Lawson Falle, Ltd., Cambridge, Ontario.

Signs and symptoms of depression in infants, toddlers and preschoolers, and adolescents and older teens from *Depression Hits Every Family* by Grace Ketterman (Oliver-Nelson Books: Nashville, 1988). Used by permission.

Unless otherwise noted, the Bible version used in this publication is THE NEW KING JAMES VERSION. Copyright © 1979, 1980, 1982, Thomas Nelson, Inc., Publishers.

Scripture quotations noted NRSV are from the New Revised Standard Version of the Bible. Copyright © 1989 by the Division of Christian Education of the National Council of the Churches of Christ in the United States of America.

Verses marked TLB are taken from *The Living Bible,* copyright 1971 by Tyndale House Publishers, Wheaton, IL. Used by permission.

Printed in the United States of America.

Unless specifically identified as factual, all names and events have been fictionalized for protection of privacy.

Library of Congress Cataloging-in-Publication Data

Arterburn, Stephen, 1953–
   Hand-me-down genes and second-hand emotions / Stephen Arterburn.
    p.   cm.
   ISBN 0-8407-9137-2 (hard)
   1. Compulsive   behavior—Religious   aspects—Christianity.   2. Depression, Mental—Religious aspects—Christianity.   3. Suicide—Religious aspects—Christianity.   4. Obesity—Religious   aspects—Christianity.   5. Alcoholism—Religious aspects—Christianity.   6. Compulsive behavior—Genetic aspects.   I. Title.
BV4598.7.A77   1992
248.8'6—dc20   92-38925
                                             CIP

1 2 3 4 5 6 — 97 96 95 94 93 92

To my grandmother, "Mother Art," who continues to live alone after ninety-two years on the earth. She handed down to me genes full of her strength, stamina, perseverance, and drive. She also taught me how to love and see the best in people. She is one remarkable lady, whose encouragement and kisses were a source of inspiration to me in all that I attempted.

For I the LORD your God am a jealous God, punishing children for the iniquity of parents, to the third and the fourth generation of those who reject me, but showing steadfast love to the thousandth generation of those who love me and keep my commandments.

—Exodus 20:5–6 NRSV

You can't heal a wound by saying it's not there!

—Jeremiah 6:14 TLB

CONTENTS

PREFACE

People can be classified in many ways, but one of the simplest is this: there are those who create problems, and there are those who solve them. Isn't it amazing how some people can take a very small problem and turn it into a major disaster, while there are others who face insurmountable difficulties and figure out a way to resolve them? In personal life it is no different. Some people come out of mildly dysfunctional homes, and they spend the rest of their lives in a self-destruct mode, crashing and burning in flames of blame and shame. Others come out of homes so sick that it seems no one could survive, yet they do. These courageous survivors go on to conquer the problems from the past and lead healthy, productive lives. A large part of the success of individuals who solve and overcome problems is the insight they develop into the problems and the attitude they use in trying to stop the cycle of abuse and personal failure. All problems require insight and an attitude that says people do not have to let the patterns of their past or their parent's past become predictors of the future. Problems *can* be resolved rather than reproduced.

I have picked four problems to address in this book that I believe haunt more people than any others—four problems that connect and interact in complex and powerful ways. Consider depression. By age sixty-five, seven out of ten women and four out of ten men will experience a major depression. Depressed people often medicate their depression with alcohol or food. Depression also often leads to suicide. In fact, those who go through depression are ten to twenty times more likely than the general population to attempt suicide. Alcoholism has reached epidemic proportions: over twenty-two million of today's adults grew up in an alcoholic home. As staggering as it may seem, there are almost fifty million practicing alcoholics in America. The only thing we do more than drink is eat. Obesity is the nation's number one health problem. It puts millions at risk for high blood pressure, diabetes, cancer, respiratory disorders, and many other major health problems. As vast as these problems are, though, they can be solved. We do not have to sit around and wait for our generation to succumb to the same disorders as our parents. But first we must look at why each of these problems affect us the way they do.

I hope you have picked up this book because you are a problem solver and you think this book will help you solve some problems of your own and perhaps those of someone you love. It is to this end—helping us solve problems by gaining insight into ourselves—that this book is written. Without insight we wander through the wilderness of our emotions making less than educated guesses about why we do what we do and why we feel the way we feel. With personal insight we have the opportunity to resolve problems and bring closure to unresolved issues from the past.

Some of the insight we need will come as we look at our wounds and the source of the wounds, thereby avoiding a self-inflicted sentence of a lifetime of woundedness. Wouldn't it be sad for us to live an unexamined life, hiding behind fears that prevent the acquisition of insight that could lead to personal growth?

Not all of the insight we need about ourselves, however, comes from studying problems. Each of us is uniquely and wonderfully made. We don't suffer equally from the same problem, we don't react identically to the same situation, and our bodies don't respond to the environment in the same way. One person takes a drink and spins off into a tragic life of alcoholism. Other people take a drink and find it so unappealing they never touch the stuff again. Some people can eat anything and never gain an ounce. I resent these people since everything I eat one day, I wear as weight the next. The fact is, metabolism varies, and not everyone who is thin is free from an obsession with food or the compulsive addiction to eating all the time.

I was in Gallup, New Mexico, having breakfast before a speaking engagement, and I overheard a conversation among some women. One person said she cannot drink coffee after lunch because it will keep her up all night. Another woman said she can drink a cup just before bedtime, and it doesn't bother her at all. We are all created with different bodies that react differently to food, chemicals, and even life events. To assume that we are all wired the same emotionally is naive. Insight into ourselves will lead us to accept the reality of who we are. I must accept that I am a person who cannot eat whatever I want whenever I want. Others have to accept that they cannot consume one ounce of alcohol. And still others must accept that because of early childhood abuse, sex in a marital relationship will be a different experience for them unless they finally heal the wounds of abuse.

Insight does not come from just the way we were raised or the choices we made. There is a growing amount of evidence that some of the things we do and feel come from the very physical core of who we are. Many are able to accept the idea of environmental predisposition, which says that the environment in which people are raised greatly affects later life. Some understand that there is also a spiritual predisposition, that the sins of one generation actually do affect generations to come. But too often we have been afraid to look at genetic or biological predisposition out of a fear that someone might use it as an excuse to fail or be irresponsible. My experience has been that anyone who will use biological predisposition as an excuse for problems will find some other excuse if that one is not used. Most of us, however, will use the insight into our genetic and hereditary predisposition to help us overcome our problems and prevent them in future generations. In this book, I will introduce you to the results of some fascinating research—evidence that may motivate you to expand your insight.

When people look into their past to find an excuse for failure or a scapegoat, all they do is inflict pain on the scapegoat and delay any possibility for something wonderful to come from early pain. This unhealthy obsession with the past produces a bunch of crybabies who are focused on their past and cannot relate to the real world in the present. It is a means of escaping responsibility for today by focusing too much on the past. It produces an imbalanced life of repeated failure and problems passed down from one generation to another.

To obtain balance in our lives, we must look at three dimensions. We are body, mind, and soul all in one. Often preachers want to talk about the soul and pay no attention to the body in which it lives or the mind that directs it. Most psychologists and psychiatrists have been trained to work with the mind and not to deal with issues of the soul. They have been trained to separate the spiritual from the psychological. Then there are those who look only at the observable physical realm. They see each human as a reactor, and most of the time a predictable reactor. They see each individual living out a deeply ingrained pattern from which there is little choice. None of these perspectives is balanced. As uncomfortable as it might be, we have to move beyond our bias, or the area we are comfortable with, and see if additional information might lend balance and insight into solving personal problems.

Because we often ignore the possibility that genetic and environmental predispositions might be factors contributing to our problems, I will focus on them in this book. And as I said earlier, of all possible contributing factors, genetic predisposition is the one we fear most and understand least. So I will give it the most attention. Despite this intentional imbalance, though, please remember that my hope is that you will approach problems from a balanced perspective, considering all insight that might help. I hope also that you will not be afraid to look at the wounds of your past in order to heal them, and that you will refuse to focus so much on them that they entrap you and those in your family who follow. This book is about resolution and restoration. It is a journey into the depths of your soul that will leave you with a fuller, richer life, dependent on God for your strength. It is also an extremely personal book that takes you through some of my journey to freedom from the past. I am glad you have decided to take this journey, and I pray that when it is over, you will find the peace in your heart you have longed for.

ACKNOWLEDGMENTS

My deepest gratitude to Linda Christiansen and Connie Neal for the research and development they did for this book. And thank you to Brian Hampton for turning a rough piece of writing into a real book.

THE JOURNEY FOR TRUTH

THE SANTA CLAUS SAGA

I had asked for a bicycle from Santa Claus. I was nine, and it was time for me to take my place among the other youngsters in the neighborhood as a vehicle owner. I could see myself riding up to Janet's house, just a few doors down, swinging my leg over the seat, kicking down the kickstand, and swaggering up to the porch where she would be sitting, totally enthralled at the sight before her. I would ask her if she wanted a ride. Of course she would say yes, and then I would whisk her away on the shiny steel handlebars of my vehicle. I could not wait for the day when that bicycle would come and transport me both physically and mentally into a new world of freedom, where I could go fast and stop quick. That Christmas meant a lot to me because Santa promised that he would bring my special present.

Santa's promise did not come by way of my sitting on his lap in some mall. I don't even think they had malls back then. Besides, all those dirty-looking Santas out on the street and in stores were not the real thing. Mom and Dad informed me that few people knew it, but those men were not Santa. That was why you could go to six different stores and see six amazingly unique-looking, fat, sweaty men claiming to be Santa. I thought I had the inside track on the Santa scheme. They told me those big, stinky, clumsy people, who sometimes smelled like they had walked out of a brewery, were just Santa's *helpers*. A helper was like an elf—

only bigger. He needed the big helpers so he and the elves could just keep right on making the toys up until the second the sleigh was loaded. But I had not talked to some helper, some "Santa wanna be"; I had talked to the real thing.

I was at home eating dinner with my mom and two brothers when the call came in. I was greatly saddened that Dad was not there with me to witness the incredible life event. Mom told me to come to the phone because someone wanted to talk to me. When I put the receiver to my ear, all I heard was a big "Ho! Ho! Ho!" Santa went on to tell me he was coming to see me as usual. He thanked me for all the times I had left him milk and cookies, and then he asked me what I wanted him to bring me. That's when I told him about my lifelong desire to be the proud owner of a shiny red bicycle. He assured me that due to the fine reports on my behavior from my mom and dad, he would deliver the shiny red bicycle of my dreams. I think that was when I told him he "kinda sounded like my dad." When I hung up, I was thrilled that I had talked to the real Santa Claus at the North Pole and that he had assured me of a beautiful two-wheeler.

That was one of the last positive thoughts I ever had about Santa. On Christmas Eve we drove to my grandparents' house, just like we normally did. Only this time, due to my father's need to work late, we drove at night. In the middle of the trip, we boys settled in for a nap. My oldest brother slept on the seat, and my other brother slept on the floorboard. That left the shelf under the back window for me, the youngest. Of course if we had a wreck, I would have been hurtled forward at seventy miles an hour through the front windshield and out onto the highway into the path of an oncoming truck, but folks didn't think about those things back then.

In the middle of our nap Dad woke us up to tell us he had just heard on the radio that Santa was nearby. Then my father interrupted himself to tell us to all look out the window and up into the stars, and we could see Santa flying overhead. He claimed he could even see Rudolph's red nose. I looked and looked through that sloped-down back window, but I couldn't see a thing, except about a million stars. Of course my big-shot brothers both claimed that they could see Santa. And once again, little brother couldn't measure up and felt left out. Although I was disappointed in not having an authorized Santa sighting, I was thrilled that he was in the neighborhood and had my bike in the sleigh.

We arrived at my grandparents' house about an hour later, and after all the slobbery kisses were completed, we had a few snacks of hogshead cheese, pickled okra, and root beer floats. Then we went to bed, begging God to make the night go quickly. It did. The next morning we woke up and ran into the next room where I expected to see an incredible red shiny bicycle. Instead, I found some lesser items, such as dumb fruit, a watch, and a note from Santa. I can still see the message of doom that ruined my whole Christmas Day. In the note Santa told me how sorry he was, but the paint was still wet on the bicycle, and it would be a few days before he could get it to me. I was shocked and hurt and couldn't believe I wasn't going to spend the rest of my day riding around on that great machine.

All of my previous doubts about the existence of Santa came flooding in on that day. I didn't believe one bit that the hand-me-down story about Santa was true. I embarked on my first journey for truth to get the straight scoop on Santa. I was determined to find out if it was all made up like some of the kids at school had said, or he had made an honest mistake and used a slow-drying paint. I approached every aunt and uncle and every older cousin in an effort to find the truth. I begged them to tell me what they knew and when they knew it. My big question was, "Did Santa really write this note?" My first quest for the truth ended in everyone supporting the belief that Santa had actually written the note, he really did exist, and soon his sleigh would deliver a shiny red bicycle. I was satisfied because in a million years I could not imagine that so many adults would lie to one little boy.

A week passed, and there was still no red bicycle. A month, two months, and still nothing arrived. I begged my parents to get Santa on the phone and let me discuss the situation with him. Some days I would lie in my bed, crying, waiting for that bicycle to show up. Three months after Christmas a Red Ball freight truck showed up out front with a tall, narrow cardboard box. The truck driver unloaded it onto the driveway and explained to my mother that the merchandise she ordered had somehow gotten lost on the way from the factory. They found it in a warehouse in New York after doing many tracers on it. He apologized and jumped back up in the truck and left. I ran into the house, tears stinging my eyes.

The truck driver revealed the biggest cover-up and deception plot of my life. Santa hadn't sent the stupid bicycle; my parents ordered it, and someone lost the order. And the worst thing of all, when it didn't come after one week or one month or two months, they still didn't tell me the truth about Santa. I begged them for it, and they withheld it. I asked them over and over if there really was one, and they stuck with their story. I felt like a fool. I hated that bicycle and everything it stood for. Every time I saw a Red Ball freight truck after that, I was reminded of that terrible time. Just a sign with the name Red Ball on it would make me intensely sad. Out loud I would tell people how angry I was that they delivered my bicycle so late. It was easier to lash out at a freight company than admit I was furious with my mom and dad for not putting me out of my misery.

I think most children who believe in Santa Claus learn the truth and are grateful their parents played the masquerade with them. I think most children never give it much thought after learning the truth. That wasn't the case for me. It was traumatic for me. It caused me to question the truth about everything. When I heard a story, I didn't know if it was the truth or the true truth—or if it was a lie, a lie that might protect me, yet a lie. A Red Ball truck, a red bicycle, and a man in a red suit caused my world to be a place I could not trust. I became suspicious that what I was being told might not be the whole truth and nothing but the truth. Years later I discovered that my suspicions were correct.

HIGH-SCHOOL REVELATIONS

The Santa secret was not the only secret that my family kept from me. The second one was revealed to me quite casually over dinner with my brother. We had gone to Clayton's Restaurant because it was close and the food was about as good as you could get at that time in Bryan, Texas. I was a senior in high school, and Terry was attending Texas A&M. We were eating several packs of crackers and putting mounds of butter on each one. In the middle of our cholesterol feast my brother told me that in one of his classes he learned that butter can cause a heart attack because it clogs everything up. I responded with the question: "I wonder if it was butter that caused our grandfather to have his heart attack?" That was when the bombshell hit.

Terry retorted quickly, "What makes you think your grandfather died of a heart attack?"

"That's what I've always been told. That's what Mother told me. Well, didn't he?"

Terry fired back, "Of course he didn't die of a heart attack."

"Then how did he die?" I asked.

"He committed suicide."

Santa in a red suit, a truck with Red Ball written on the side, and a red bicycle went whizzing through my mind. I fell back in my chair just long enough to let it sink in that there had been another plot to deceive me, to hold back the *true* truth. But since I was still in some disbelief, I asked my brother for details. In the revelation of details I could figure out if he was lying or if my mother and dad had lied. He shocked me with the story of a man who had a lot of stress and couldn't handle it, a man who placed a shotgun in his mouth and pulled the trigger.

Learning that at age eighteen made me feel like an outcast, like I had never been a full family member. I was deeply hurt and confused. I left there determined to confront my mother about the big cover-up. That night I told her how angry I was to learn that I had been "protected" from the real cause of death of my grandfather. I wanted to know facts, and I wanted to know why. She began to cry immediately as she went to the front closet to pull out some old newspaper clippings and photos.

She showed me pictures of my grandfather and articles about his funeral. The church was overflowing due to the love and respect he had from people who knew him. Mother told me of the stress he had experienced working for the gas company. He was in charge of installing large tanks of gas that, if done improperly, would kill many people. He had a large crew, and the stress was immense.

He had horrendous bouts of depression. His behavior became erratic, and the longer he lived, the worse the situation became. It caused colossal problems between him and my grandmother. Those problems deepened his depression. It became so bad that he was admitted to a psychiatric institution in Dallas, Texas. His depression was so severe that ECT, electroconvulsive therapy, was recommended.

In those days little was known about ECT, and the methods by which it was delivered were quite barbaric. They did not anesthetize the patient, so all of the electrical current that surged through his body and brain was felt down to the last convulsive volt. They did a series of the torturous treatments and then released him to go home. As was the case for many clinically depressed people, when nothing else had worked, ECT did seem to improve my grandfather's ability to function. His mood lightened, and Mother said he seemed to almost be his usual self again.

It didn't last long. Once again he started the deep dark spiral back into depression. He fought to control it but to no avail. He was lost and in need of help. After coming out of the institution in Dallas, he made a vow to the family that no one took seriously. It was a statement that anyone might make innocently, expressing relief to be out of an unpleasant environment. He said, "I'll kill myself before I ever go back into that place again and allow them to run electricity through my body like that."

At the time, no one knew just how serious he had been. Suicide had such a stigma then. Since my granddad was a Christian, the family figured he would never consider something so terrible. They didn't realize how severe his pain was. He meant what he said, and rather than undergo further ECT, he blew away the pain.

Mother tried to explain that when the subject first came up, I was only six and too young to understand, so they gave me the easy answer. No one taught her how important it was for her to find a way to share this reality with me a little piece at a time. She didn't know how to do it, and she didn't know how essential it was to do it. She also feared that if I didn't understand how terrible it was, I would go around telling people or asking about it. As far as I can remember, it had not come up since I asked the first time. No one ever talked about it. They rarely talked about my grandfather, but if they did, it was in glowing terms. Like most family secrets that stay buried a long time, it had been hidden almost perfectly. Mother said she was sorry, but she hoped I would understand that in those days suicide was something a family was deeply ashamed of. She told me of times after that when she would sit in church and listen to a preacher talk of suicide as the unforgivable sin. She would cry to herself as she envisioned her loving father burning in the flames of hell. It is little wonder that no one wanted to talk of something so horrible.

I didn't forget that my parents had hidden truth from me, but I didn't obsess over it, either. My mother had two very distinct sides to her. One was a woman with a clever sense of humor who had many friends to laugh with her. The other was a woman who had a deep sense of sadness about her, a secondhand sadness, passed down from her father and handed down to me. Because she never resolved it, she reproduced it in me. She didn't talk about the pain or seek counseling for it. It was something that I could sense was there. Until then, I didn't fully understand the source of that pain; I understood only how deep was her wound of a dad lost to self-destruction.

TWENTY YEARS ALONG THE JOURNEY

It was exactly twenty years later that I came to understand just how much my mother's wound had affected my life. My twenty-year journey for truth reasserted itself after Madeline, my daughter, came into my life. My bachelor's degree is in elementary education, so what you have here is an author who adores children. For about twenty years I had wanted to be a father. It was an honor that I thought might elude me forever. Shortly after Sandy and I were married, she became pregnant, but it didn't last long. The embryo settled on one of her ovaries, and it required surgery to be removed. Before Sandy went to the hospital, she almost bled to death internally. The doctor saved the ovary, but she has never gotten pregnant since.

In July of 1990 Sandy and I were in Atlanta, Georgia. I was to speak at a conference, and since it was the July 4 weekend, Sandy decided to come along. She rarely travels with me, but God needed her with me on that trip. I met with my publisher, Victor Oliver, on July 3. He ordered me a bowl of chili that almost left me gasping for air. In the course of our discussion about publishing, Victor asked me what Sandy and I were going to do about children. I told him she had just completed a procedure that had once again failed to produce a pregnancy. We had been working with an infertility specialist for about three years, and both of us were ready to discontinue the agony. If you have never been through the "infertility rites" of the medical profession, you cannot come close to understanding how embarrassing, humiliating, painful, and depressing the process is.

About two weeks prior to the trip, Sandy mentioned that perhaps we would consider adoption someday. Neither of us was ready for that grueling process, either. Infertile couples feel enough rejection from not having children. With so many people looking for babies, the private adoption process means repeated rejection for most who enter it. We had already had a small taste of that rejection a few months earlier.

A few months before my meeting with Victor, I had spoken at a meeting, and afterward an unmarried pregnant woman approached me and asked me to consider raising her child. Sandy was there, and we talked with the woman and gave her our phone number if she wanted to talk further. She did, and she called to set up a meeting between us and her adoption counselor. From the very first second we talked with the counselor, it was a disaster. She didn't like us, and we didn't like her. Although her client wanted us to have the baby, the counselor would not allow it and persuaded the woman to choose someone else. The feelings of rejection were very sharp. We did not ever want to experience them in that way again. So adoption was not an attractive alternative. Not because of the baby it would bring us, but because we were so burned out from the infertility rites, we were not ready for another troubling ordeal.

That was why it was so ironic that Sandy mentioned she might consider the adoption route. It was only one of many ironies that would come our way. When I explained all that to Victor, he had a quizzical but optimistic look in his eye. Then he revealed the news that would bless our lives more than we ever dreamed. He told me that the daughter of one of his friends had become pregnant. The couple were not going to abort the baby, nor were they going to marry and keep it. They had considered all the options, and since they were so young, not out of high school, with no means to support each other or a baby, they decided on adoption. They wanted to find a couple they knew would love their child. When Victor asked me if I wanted to meet them, I told him I thought Sandy would want to. I left the lunch to tell Sandy, and Victor left to ask the brave sixteen-year-old and seventeen-year-old if they wanted to meet us. Everyone agreed to the meeting, including the young woman's parents. On July 4, 1990, Sandy and I met the wonderful couple.

He looked like he could have been my brother, and she had many of Sandy's features and personality traits. Not that any of that really matters, but it was a nice coincidence. We loved them and left the meeting with Sandy saying, "If they will allow us to raise their baby, I want to do it." That statement was a major jump for both of us. I was in total agreement, and as amazing as it was, they decided we were the ones to have their baby. My life made a 180-degree turn from that moment on. I couldn't wait to be a father. I was already in love with whoever was going to live with us, boy or girl.

Then on Christmas Eve, December 24, 1990, Madeline Victoria Arterburn was born. Victor saw her before Sandy and I did, and he told us she was the most beautiful baby he had ever seen. When we flew to Atlanta and she was handed to me, I realized he had not been exaggerating. The beautiful gift from God could not have been more perfect. It was a gift that I was able to have because the mother decided not to abort her baby. That I would be given a baby saved from abortion was another stunning irony. You see, I had paid to have another woman abort a baby I was responsible for. It caused me tremendous guilt, shame, and remorse. I felt I had destroyed a child. Now, a gracious God and a courageous young woman had given back to me an opportunity I had earlier destroyed. I was a proud father and ready to change as many diapers as I needed to change. I knew her infancy wouldn't last long, and I wasn't going to miss it. It has been better than I ever imagined.

Although the entire experience has been wonderful, one part has been far more painful than I ever imagined. It is the pain I feel when I hear her cry. From the beginning, her cries have ripped through me like a jagged saw cutting at my heart. I know a baby's cries hurt most parents, but I also knew, and Sandy knew, that my reaction wasn't normal. There was something more to it than a caring father who didn't want his little girl to experience pain. It became such an issue for me that Sandy finally asked me to get some counseling and find out what was going on. I agreed because I knew I needed the help.

Most men shy away from counseling because they fear someone might think there is a problem or a weakness that no one else has ever experienced. It's as if they think everyone is overlooking the wounds and scars and believing they are wonderful. I believe a lot of people are just one counselor away from happiness. They need an objective third party to help them sort through painful issues of their lives. Until they are willing to do so, they will only be able to find a way to cope, to exist.

Counseling could free them from some of their secrets that make them sicker the longer they keep them. Men use a lot of lame excuses to avoid looking at themselves.

I'm glad I went. The counselor appeared to sincerely want to help me, so I could search for answers without worrying about being rejected by the person who was supposed to help me. I also felt good about being there because his values were so closely aligned with mine. The journey for the truth about my troubled soul began. I told my counselor what was going on with me, and we discussed my relationships with friends, family, and Sandy. Together we dug and probed for insight into why the tears of a baby were so painful to a grown man.

One day I told him of a sad memory from childhood that continued to come back to me. I was standing outside the bathroom door inside our small house in Ranger, Texas. I was about one year old, and I had my pajamas on. As I stood there, I listened to my mother inside the bathroom, crying uncontrollably. I am sure she went in there to prevent me from seeing or hearing her, but I could not help hearing her. Her sobs turned into deep moans, producing tears on my face. I wanted to go in, but I didn't dare. I just stood outside, waiting for her to come out and pick me up and tell me everything would be all right. I never felt like everything was going to be all right.

I remember that moment as if it were yesterday. And I certainly remember that bathroom. It was the location of more terrible memories from my first three years. Another tragedy of the Ranger, Texas, bathroom occurred a short time after that. I was placed in the bathtub in a couple of inches of water, and the faucet was running. Something happened that demanded my mother go outside or next door to my grandmother's house. While she was gone, I guess I thought there was enough water, so I reached over and tried to turn off the water. I turned the cold handle and shut off the cold water all the way. I screamed in terror as the scalding hot water literally burned the flesh off my feet and ankles.

The other bathroom disaster was also a burn. Our family went to church every Sunday morning, Sunday night, and Wednesday night. One afternoon we were preparing to go to an evening service. That required my having a bath. When the bath was over, I was lifted onto the toilet seat so I could be dried off. The second I was placed up there, I slipped, and my hand went palm down onto the small gas heater next to the toilet. The top of the heater was as hot as a stove, and it instantly cooked my hand. I screamed and screamed in agony. I can still remember my brothers and mother going off to church while my dad rocked me to sleep. For days my hand was one big blister. I can almost feel the pain today.

As physically painful as the burns were, those memories did not affect me like the one of my mother crying inside the bathroom and me crying outside the bathroom. The burn memories were a result of accidents, but I had no idea why my mother was crying and why that memory was so important to me. I considered all of the emotions around it, and I asked my father what was going on in our lives about that time. He was able to fit many pieces of the puzzle together for me. He explained that when I was about a year old, the suicide of my grandfather had occurred. He reminded me of my confronting Mother about that being kept secret. He told me I had no idea how hard that had been for her to accept and get over. He said it took her at least five years to resolve the anger around her father's death.

With this new information I went back and talked with my counselor about my baby's tears and how they hurt me so badly. He questioned and guided until I was able to see the source of my current pain. While I needed my mother, she was struggling with her own pain. When I needed her to dry my tears, she had tears of her own. Her own crying drowned out mine. At a critical time in my development she needed time for her own healing, time to shed her own tears. My baby's cries tap into those painful first years of my own life that set me up to overreact, overprotect, and overnurture out of a lack in my own life. Those years also left me unable to fully trust authority to protect me, care for me, or tell me the total truth. After thirty-nine years it was about time I had some insight into who I was and why I did things the way I did, why I hurt so much and what I did to medicate the pain.

BLAME, SHAME, OR CHANGE?

Now that I am aware of some early childhood deficiencies, the question arises as to what to do with them. Do I blame my parents for my problems? Not in a million years! I have no need to blame anyone for my difficulties. I have them because I have chosen not to deal with certain painful realities about myself and because I have made some quick decisions that have had long-lasting consequences. They were my decisions and no one else's. I am grateful for what my mother has done for me. She taught me something and implanted within me something that has kept me going through very difficult times. She taught me how to survive. When I needed her to nurture me, it was hard because she was struggling for her own survival. And unlike her father, she figured out a way to survive. How sad it would have been if my demands had been too much for her and put her over the edge. She made it, and I am glad she did.

My insight does not lead me to blame. It motivates me to continue to search for areas where I might be passing along some of the second-hand emotions of my past to my child. It motivates me to look at what I do from choice and what I do from some predisposing problem that has skewed my decision making. If insight leads me to blame and shame another, the process and motivation, which bring me into a greater awareness of who I am and what I do, are faulty. True insight should motivate us to make sure that today is better than yesterday and worse than tomorrow. We cannot improve tomorrow if we continue to point fingers at the past. We can make a decision today to blame someone else, shame someone else, or go through the more difficult, yet re-warding, process of changing ourselves.

PERSONAL PREDISPOSITION

What does insight into these events, and the memories I still hold, say about the person I am today? What has been handed down to me genet-ically and environmentally? What of my life is a result of nature, and what is a result of nurture? Some answers to these questions are quite obvious from the importance of these events and memories in my life. It is also obvious that just as I was protected from the reality of a family tragedy, I have started out with my daughter having to fight my urge to be overly protective of her. I do not want her to experience pain, yet I must relinquish that desire because I know that some pain is a natural part of life. Alleviating all the pain will only spoil her and turn her into an irresponsible adolescent and adult. By knowing my tendency, I can de-feat the urge to overprotect my child rather than blindly fall into an unhealthy pattern.

This is but a small example of the significance of resolving our prob-lems as adults before we hand them down. If we do not resolve them, we reproduce them in some other form in our children. In not wanting my baby to cry, my heart was in the right place, my intentions were good, but the result would have been a disaster. Babies need to cry. It is healthy for them to cry. Stopping her tears would not meet her needs; it would meet only mine. The great challenge of raising a child is to stop and ask, "What am I doing that appears to be for the child but in reality meets my own unresolved needs?" When we answer this question, we free our children to be all that God intended them to be rather than trap them with our own difficulties. It stops the cycle of the parent who was raised with rigidity from being so liberal that the child has no values. It prevents the mother who was sexually molested as a child from raising a daughter who is so prudish that once married, she can never enjoy sex with her husband. It also allows us to enjoy our children without living out their lives through our scars.

I know other things about myself. Somehow in my family the wiring did not get hooked up exactly right. I'm talking about the emotional wiring. The intellectual part worked fine; we have some brilliant people in the family. The emotional part did not come out so well. I believe my grandfather's depression was not just a situational type of depression that lifts when circumstances change and time provides natural healing. His was more inbred than that. It was chronic and severe enough that doctors recommended the most drastic treatment.

I believe the sad side of my mother that was always there came as a result of the loss of her father but also as a result of the biological predisposition passed down to her by her father. She has been depressed off and on, and if she had not found a way to deal with it, her life might have been as disastrous as her father's. Her predisposition to depression has to have had an impact on me. I have never been one of those people who just bounded out of bed ready to tackle the day with a smile. I have said that I was grounded in reality or that I was too much of a problem solver to know minute-by-minute joy. But what I have been is depressed many years of my life. And I don't believe it is due to some self-inflicted spiritual weakness because even at the spiritual pinnacles of my life, a recurring sadness would not go away. The reality for me is that I have a personal predisposition to depression I have been fighting all my life.

I have done many things to medicate my pain and depression. In the early years there was sexual promiscuity that I would undo if I could. It has caused me and others needless pain and grief. I have used alcohol and drugs and food to smooth the rough edges of despair. As a speaker I have used the laughter and applause of people I did not know to compensate for the pain I experienced with the people I did know. Like a metal ball in a pinball machine, I have bounced from home remedy to home remedy, trying to ease what I could not. The self-medications of choice only caused greater and greater problems for me. Only now, after many wasted years, have I started to deal with the reality of my family tree and the impact it has had on my past and the way I feel today.

I will never know the complete impact of my heritage, but I can come closer to knowing if I look rather than turn away. When Jeremiah wrote that wounds cannot be healed when ignored, he was saying something else, also. He was cautioning us not to treat lightly wounds that are serious. Many people would encourage us to treat lightly the deep wounds of the heart that need healing. Some tell us not to look back. Others tell us to turn to some simplistic philosophy full of quick fixes and instant solutions. Thousands of distracters refuse to look at their own pain and want to prevent us from looking at ours. It is not easy, but we must break free from what feels good in order to resolve what would be detrimental to reproduce. It is a difficult but extremely worthwhile journey.

I hope you have begun a journey to discover some of the truth about the foundation upon which you have developed. Perhaps my memories and my journey have sparked some questions in your mind about who you are and why you do the things you do. I hope a part of my journey motivates you to look at your wounds and find a way to treat them so they will heal rather than fester. I hope that this is the beginning of a time in your life that you will look back upon and say, "That was a time I gave up my comfortable, overly protective womb of denial and began to dig for the truth of who I am and why I do some of the things I do."

To begin the journey, you must undertake self-examination. The following questions should lead you to discover whether or not you are predisposed to certain problems and have wounds that need healing. These questions could lead you to discover whether or not you are predisposed to problems due to their biological, emotional, or spiritual foundation. (Some of the questions are adapted from material in Janet Woititz's book *Adult Children of Alcoholics*.)

ARE THERE SOME HIDDEN WOUNDS THAT NEED HEALING?

1. Are there major chunks of your childhood that you cannot remember, that perhaps are blocked out because of some unpleasant and painful event?

     ☐ Yes   ☐ No

2. Was your family so extreme or dysfunctional that you have no idea what normal means and you often guess at what is normal?

     ☐ Yes   ☐ No

3. Do you feel different from others, as if they were given a set of instructions that were never available to you?

     ☐ Yes   ☐ No

4. Do you judge yourself without mercy and always second-guess how you could have done something better?

   ☐ Yes ☐ No

5. Is it hard for you to loosen up and have fun? Has enjoying yourself become a rare event?

   ☐ Yes ☐ No

6. Are you constantly exhausted, wanting to get more sleep, yet when you try to sleep, it is very difficult to fall asleep or stay asleep?

   ☐ Yes ☐ No

7. Do people tell you that you try too hard, and you feel that your whole life has been spent ignoring yourself while trying to please others?

   ☐ Yes ☐ No

8. Has your life been full of the "overs"—overachieving, overearning, overeating, overdrinking, overspending, overchurching, over-working?

   ☐ Yes ☐ No

9. Do you have a history of constantly being involved in relationships that are self-defeating, unhealthy, and destructive?

   ☐ Yes ☐ No

10. Do you remain extremely loyal to someone, even though you have definite proof that your loyalty is undeserved?

    ☐ Yes ☐ No

11. Do you take yourself too seriously and have difficulty laughing off some of the minor problems you face?

    ☐ Yes ☐ No

12. Would you be at either end of the responsibility spectrum by being classified as superresponsible or as superirresponsible?

    ☐ Yes ☐ No

13. Do you constantly seek affirmation and approval from others?

    ☐ Yes ☐ No

14. Do you have a hard time being completely truthful and find yourself telling a lie when you could have just as easily told the truth?

    ☐ Yes ☐ No

15. Do you have a short attention span and find it difficult to concentrate on one thing for very long?
    ☐ Yes   ☐ No

16. Do you frequently feel so sad that it is hard to get out of bed?
    ☐ Yes   ☐ No

17. Do you have a string of short-term relationships and avoid people who have been around a long time?
    ☐ Yes   ☐ No

18. Do you often become so uptight and anxious around other people that you excuse yourself so you can be alone and catch your breath?
    ☐ Yes   ☐ No

19. Do you continue to harbor deep resentment toward your parents?
    ☐ Yes   ☐ No

20. Are you constantly obsessing over things from your past, starting many thoughts with *if only,* such as, *If only I hadn't been so stupid?*
    ☐ Yes   ☐ No

If you answered yes to at least three questions, there is a strong likelihood that some events or relationships from your past are adversely affecting the present. Predispositions may be affecting your life. You may be wounded in one of the areas of body, mind, or soul. As you read further, you will be able to more clearly identify the areas and begin to work through them. Remember, we reproduce what we do not resolve.

Chapter 1

◆

COULD IT BE PREDISPOSITION?

BIOLOGICAL AND GENETIC PREDISPOSITION

Just as I believe the wiring in my family was not exactly put together normally, I believe others experience the same predisposition to emotional problems. Ruth shares a similar background of emotional problems running through the family. I believe Ruth's problems were predictable. I also believe if she had accepted the reality of her heritage earlier, she could have avoided much of what she faced.

It was probably nothing to worry about . . . but Ruth was worried. It was just the normal stress of college life . . . that's what she kept trying to tell herself. The other girls in her dorm had talked about feeling depressed, too . . . but they didn't have her family history.

There was probably nothing to be afraid of . . . but the fear Ruth had first felt as a child had returned. That was when her father was in the mental hospital . . . before he died. The symptoms were coming back, too. Nothing seemed to matter anymore. Classes she once looked forward to became a drudgery. She hadn't slept well for weeks now . . . at least not all the way through the night. She tried to concentrate, but her mind wasn't cooperating with her. As the feelings of guilt and worthlessness began to get the upper hand, her roommate asked if everything was okay. "Sure," Ruth said (trying to convince herself as much as her friend), "I'm just worried about my final in Western history." Oh, how she wished that were true!

Ruth tried to fight it off. She tried to look on the bright side of things, to count her blessings. She even picked up a book on positive thinking at the library. Of course, she prayed, the same desperate prayers she had prayed the last time this happened. No matter what she did, she was unable to halt the darkening gloom of depression enveloping her mind. She fought off the thoughts of death, but they were calling to her once again. Was this the same curse that had finally defeated her father? Was this the same kind of depression that repeatedly laid hold of her mother, aunt, and older brother? She couldn't help wondering.

Ruth was the third child in a family of five. Despite having been hospitalized early in life for treatment of an infectious disease, she proved to be an active and even-tempered little girl, making friends easily. In grade school, she did satisfactory work, but she was not motivated to progress. She had a sensitive and outgoing nature. She had a particular love of reading fairy tales and making things with her hands.

Ruth's mother was religious and insisted that she go to Mass every morning. The child did not resist but was adaptable and seemed to be religious.

The mother's family were hardy people of French descent. Ruth's father, an immigrant Yugoslavian artisan, had spent years in state hospitals, diagnosed as schizophrenic. The family lived in terror of his release. He died when Ruth was seven. Three years before his death, her mother was treated for neurotic depression as an outpatient. Her father's sister, Ruth's Aunt Clara, had experienced severe depression after the birth of one of her children, just as her own mother had been depressed after Ruth's birth. Peter, the oldest child in the family, had also been treated for depression. The family tree was rooted in mental illness and depression.

As an adolescent schoolgirl, Ruth was admitted to a psychiatric ward after a long period of depression and apprehension. She was placed in foster care when her mother was unable to support her financially. Close to her mother, she grieved deeply over the separation and complained that she was lonely. After several months, she grew quiet, complaining to her mother during a visit that she always had someone watching her. Soon afterward she asked to go to confession since she had stolen some strawberries and was very upset about it. However, when in the company of the priest, she could not bring herself to say anything, and the "confessions" had no effect on her sense of guilt.

A month or so later, Ruth was released to go home. On the night she arrived she slept for a time, then woke and seemed to be musing on something. She told her mother that she was afraid God disapproved of her because she had stolen something. The following morning, she did not want to get out of bed. Her mother then decided to take her to the hospital, but the girl pretended sickness, acting drunk, and she was very frightened.

An examination showed that Ruth was in fine physical condition, and tests of her blood and urine were negative. However, she acted anxious and depressed. She was teary but refused to answer the doctors' questions. There were times when she appeared to be in a stupor. When the subject of the stolen strawberries was raised, Ruth appeared deeply disturbed.

After a few days in the hospital, she began to grow more cheerful and joined in prepared activities, but a week later, she was committed to a state hospital with complaints of headaches, weakness, and auditory hallucinations. However, she began to cooperate with her doctors quite quickly, improving to the point of release just a few months later.

After leaving the hospital, Ruth was sent to a convent school for orphans since her mother could not care for her at home. Within a year she was again at home and in public schools. She did well in school but was somewhat withdrawn and uncooperative at home. Her mother maintained strict control over her.

In the two years following her release from the hospital, Ruth continued to be reclusive and uncooperative at home. She grew interested in boys and began to experiment sexually. She was increasingly concerned about her appearance. Three years after her return home, she was arrested for shoplifting. A court-appointed psychologist found her normal in every way—physically well-developed, aware of her surroundings, and with appropriate emotional responses. There was no evidence of disorganized thinking or hallucinations.

Ruth was placed on probation and is now in her third year at the state college. She tells her mother and friends that she has begun to experience disturbing depressions, which interfere with her schoolwork. Life has otherwise been quite normal for her, with the usual social activities, romantic attachments, and academic stresses playing a central role in her life. Her family relationships are distant but not negative, and she has been successful in her studies. Her mother assumes that the depressions are what they seem to be—the result of natural changes and pressures usual in the experience of young men and women of Ruth's age—but there is a lingering question in the back of her mind.

The lingering question is whether or not Ruth is going to spend the rest of her life in and out of depressive episodes and in and out of hospitals. Because Ruth experienced so many problems so young and came from a family so riddled with mental and emotional problems, one would think that someone would have helped her deal with the reality that she would have to live her life differently if she were going to reverse the trend in her family. If she could accept that it is something that has been with her from the beginning of her life, perhaps she could finally accept that it is not going to magically go away. Then she would have a greater chance of being motivated to do whatever it takes not to become a victim of depression. If she continues to wonder, there is little chance she will take appropriate action.

In a recent article entitled "It's All in the Genes," the author writes about the growing research surrounding genetic predisposition. He says, "Some scientists think genes will be discovered that indicate whether a person will be tall, intelligent, shy, physically coordinated, musically talented, outgoing, sexually aggressive or, perhaps, naturally disposed to criminal behavior."[1] He cites incidences of people being denied jobs because of what is being called genetic discrimination. One woman in Chicago was turned down for a job when the employer found out her mother was schizophrenic. Others are turned down for insurance because the family profile indicates trouble ahead.[2] When I was given a physical for a life insurance policy, I was asked a set of questions relating to the emotional status of my parents and brothers. The clinician giving me the physical said that those were the areas that had a genetic predisposition.

Although we can be predisposed to problems from many sources, none are as controversial as the belief that certain emotional problems are a result of physiology. There is so much evidence of biological predisposition that it is hard to see why someone would doubt that certain emotional problems might stem from inborn physiology and not just as a result of spiritual depravity or poor life decisions. We are all predisposed to one degree or another from a variety of sources.

The young boy who is sexually molested by his father at age five is now predisposed to grow up as a victim and become a victimizer. It is something that he did not bring upon himself, and he can reverse the trend. If he does not know what he is up against, he is less likely to work on the problem. The predisposition goes beyond the fact that those who are abused model the behavior that hurt them and often grow up to abuse. If he was molested by his father, he is probably emotionally predisposed and physiologically predisposed to problems. There was a reason his father molested him. There was something about the father's makeup that led him to seek pleasure in that way. Did he pass that predisposition down to his son as well as the emotional yoke of abuse? There is a good chance the boy is emotionally and physically predisposed.

The predisposition goes even deeper than that. What of the spiritual life of the father? These sins of abuse are not just criminal acts; they are acts that violate God's plan. In violating the plan, the father establishes a negative spiritual heritage. The third and fourth generations often suffer because this rebellion against God is not easily put aside. A boy growing up under those circumstances will have to work hard and trust God more than most if he is to counter the forces that would lead him into a destructive life. The best hope for him is to learn as much as possible about himself and his father so he can work from the beginning on avoiding the trap of abuse.

If we learn about ourselves and our predispositions, we help in two different ways. We learn the truth about ourselves so we can better deal with the reality of who we are. We also are better able to educate our children and give them the greatest chance to survive. Consider the area of drinking. Some families have virtually no alcoholism, while others are full of people labeled heavy drinkers or alcoholics. If a parent has had a drinking problem and hides it from a child, the child might blindly walk into a drinking problem of his own. If the parent warns the child by revealing the family history, there is a greater chance that child might make a positive decision to abstain. Or when problems start to arise with drinking, the early discussions might come to mind, and the child might decide to stop drinking before destruction through alcoholism progresses. Knowing about the predisposing factors will help us only if we are courageous enough to face the truth and act on it.

Many problems have been proven to be genetic or have a genetic influence. More are added to the list every day. The March of Dimes lists medical problems that are now believed to either be genetic or have genetic components (see Figure 1.1).[3] I have italicized the ones most pertinent to the content of this book.

Because of continuing research efforts, one day more problems will be placed on the list than will be left off. It is helpful to know about any of these physical illnesses in our family heritage. We should look back at least two generations and learn about our parents and their brothers and sisters, then both sets of grandparents and their brothers and sisters. We should determine the ages that people died and some of their illnesses. We should be sure to ask about emotional problems, heavy drinking, and criminal records. If we start the search looking for physical and medical problems, most likely we will find some emotional problems that will surprise us. A tape recorder and Grandmother's time can be the keys to unlocking some of the hidden past.

From looking back at my tree, I have found two very glaring predispositions, one negative and the other positive. The negative I have already mentioned. There are quite a few emotional problems, especially de-

Figure 1.1

- *Alcoholism*
- Allergies
- Arthritis
- Asthma
- Atherosclerosis
- Bacterial pneumonia
- Birth defects
- Cancer
- Cystic fibrosis
- Diabetes
- Down's syndrome
- Dwarfism
- Emphysema
- Epilepsy
- Hearing disorders
- Heart attack
- Hemophilia
- Huntington's disease
- High blood pressure
- Liver diseases, like hepatitis

- *Mental illness*
- Migraine headaches
- Miscarriages
- Multiple sclerosis
- Muscular dystrophy
- Myasthenia gravis
- *Obesity*
- Phenylketonuria
- Rh disease
- Sickle-cell anemia
- Skin disorders
- Stroke
- Sudden infant death syndrome
- *Suicide*
- Systemic lupus erythematosus
- Tay-Sachs disease
- Thyroid disorders
- Tuberculosis
- Visual disorders

pression and issues surrounding depression. The positive is in the area of heart disease. We don't seem to have any. People in my family usually live to be quite old, often into their nineties, and when they do die, their hearts are in fine shape. I figured if I was going to live such a long time, I had better work on the depression so I won't spend all those later years in misery.

Emotional problems have been passed along to us just as our positive emotions that can help us. We are born with certain things that protect us from harm. From the early days of man we all inherit the quick reaction to loud sounds versus a calm reaction to soothing sounds. There are probably other fears that have been passed down from our earliest generations. Our irrational fear of snakes (as opposed to telephone poles) is probably a result of inherited, inborn safety mechanisms of the brain. If we can live today with inborn emotional responses from the early days of man, surely the genetic makeup of the past two or three generations must have a significant bearing on the behavior we exhibit and the emotions we feel.

THE BODY AS CHEMICAL REACTOR

Although our ancient ancestors reacted to mountain lions and snakes, our reactions have shifted to more modern objects. Last year on my wife's birthday we were driving home from Los Angeles on the 405 freeway. It had been a disastrous day with much of what we wanted to do being rained out. As traffic on the freeway slowed, we did, also, but the woman behind us did not until she plowed into the rear of the car. What I experienced is something most people can relate to. At first there were fear and peak alertness. Then my legs felt very strange. It was as if chemicals were surging through my body, down to my legs. That was exactly what was happening. My body is one big chemical reactor, and adrenaline was pumping as fast as it could through my system. I felt the chemical reaction that I had inherited from my ancestors. And my ancestors pumped chemicals at times other than just high stress or fear.

The emotions of love produce a chemical reaction in the brain. Recent studies have shown that the hormone oxytocin promotes the social bonding involved in choosing a mate and reproducing in animals. Researchers believe the same hormone, found in humans, may influence fostering friendship, love, and nurturance.

This same chemical brings on childbirth and lactation, but it does not seem to be limited to those areas. The levels of this hormone rise dramatically during sex, and many scientists believe it promotes the accompanying feelings of love or infatuation. Some researchers believe that this hormone, or the lack of it, plays a part in social behavior. "Human relations are influenced by the model of the parent-child relationship in that they include the notions of nurturing, care, help," says Cort Pedersen of the University of North Carolina. "The deficiency of a hormone tied to that parenting instinct may account for some of the anti-social behavior we think of as psychopathic."[4] We are, at our most basic level, chemical reactors. Some are born with chemical deficiencies, but others create them for themselves through poor choices. Not everyone starts out with the same emotional or chemical foundation. Not everyone is able to make healthy choices for the future.

BEHAVIOR AND EMOTION BEYOND CHOICE

One of the most troubling aspects of looking at predisposition is the issue of choice. Some want to believe that everyone has an equal opportunity, that the choice is completely in the individual's hands. That is a very simplistic view of people. Certain things that happen beyond our control influence the way we are. Some studies point to events in the womb that might predispose a person to problems later in life. One British study notes that brain cell development can be altered by the flu virus. Mothers who have the flu in their fifth month of pregnancy are more likely to have schizophrenic babies.[5] A UCLA researcher does not indicate cause but has learned to identify children who will grow up with the problem. This clear-cut pattern can be observed as early as one year of age. The symptoms include a distinct pattern of spurts and lags in weight gain, bone growth, and mental development. Children who did not fit into the pattern of characteristics did not develop schizophrenia later. The purpose of the study was to provide a way to screen for the children early and provide them with the help they need at the earliest possible age. The write-up on the study asserted, "The study provides the strongest evidence yet that the severe mental disorder, which affects one in 100 people, has a biological basis."[6] The article went on to say that the evidence continues to grow for a biological basis for the disorder. When one parent is schizophrenic, the child has a 15 percent chance of developing it. When both parents have the problem, the child has a 40 to 50 percent chance of developing schizophrenia.[7] One of the worst injustices is done when a person sees a severely mentally ill person and sums it all up as a result of poor choices. As in the case of these babies and young children, their dysfunction was not a matter of choice.

Other studies place a direct link from childhood abuse to adult social dysfunction. Childhood neglect was tied to lower IQs and misuse of drugs and alcohol. Abused children also will experience greater amounts of clinical depression along with suicide attempts.[8] The notion that those experiencing personal distress as adults are lazy, irresponsible, or more sinful than the rest is not always true. Some may come into the world with an equal chance at being normal, but shortly thereafter they enter a horrible world of abuse. These children, if not helped, are predisposed to a lifetime of adulthood problems. With help each of them will have an opportunity to choose to overcome their problems because their problems were a result of much more than just poor choices.

MALE AND FEMALE WIRING

Observation informs us that men and women are different in the way they perceive and react to the same situation or distress. The answers to the reason why may literally be all in the mind. A controversial article declared, "The newest scientific research shows men's and women's brains are 'wired' differently. Each sex has a mind of its own. Men are different from women. To maintain that they are the same in aptitude, skill or behavior is to build a society based on a biological and scientific lie."[9] The article cited research that shows men shed fewer tears than women because their brains are wired differently and "they are just biologically less disposed to cry."[10]

There are many other differences between men and women, the anatomical ones being the most obvious. This research and other findings reveal that not all the differences are so easily seen. Biological and emotional differences do not make either one better; they just point out that in the hidden cavern of the brain, very basic differences exist that influence emotion and behavior. I am sure that when I mentioned I felt my family's wiring was different from others in regard to depression, it was greeted with some skepticism. This study lends some credibility to my assertion. The brain wiring concept is a valid one. Since brain wiring differs from male to female, it is possible that it differs from individual to individual and family to family. Faulty wiring can form the foundation of problems unrelated to our behavior or choices.

SPIRITUAL PREDISPOSITION

The minds and emotions we live with today must be a combination of several types of predispositions. Perhaps the one most difficult to quantify, yet easiest to explain, is spiritual predisposition. When Cain slew Abel, one must wonder if the action was a result of Cain's receiving, from his rebellious father, destructive emotions of anger and rage that Adam had not resolved as a result of being thrown out of the Garden. Whatever its source, it was the beginning of a pattern whereby parents make mistakes with tremendous spiritual consequences for generations to come.

King David participated in adultery and then murder to cover up the adulterous act. As if his children inherited or were reenacting his sins, they were guilty of rape and murder. The passions of the father were passed along, and spiritual consequences were severe. Each of our decisions has a consequence. One consequence we rarely think of is the impact of what we do today on our children. As a result, some children come into the world through parents who are spiritually dead and out of touch with God. If the children of spiritually dead parents are going to find fulfillment in their faith, they will have to work to establish who God really is, since much of our concept of God comes from what we believe about the nature of our parents. A father who leads a son to reject him provides the son with a spiritual predisposition to reject God.

CONCLUSION

There are many sources of help for people in trouble, such as pastors, counselors, psychiatrists, caring friends, and the God who created us. No matter how much any of these sources want to help, they cannot do so if we live in the deadly place called denial. The sooner we come to accept the full depth of our problems and stop hoping they will magically go away, the sooner we will start to work on them and refuse to become their victim.

If I wake up one morning in a hospital bed to find that I have a leg missing, I am going to be in both physical and emotional pain. I will grieve the loss of my limb. I will want to know what happened to me and how I lost the leg. As I lie there in my bed and deal with the reality of the problem, I eventually will reach a point where I will have to make a decision. The decision will be whether or not I am going to lie in a bed for the rest of my life or I am going to get up and learn to get around on one leg.

Emotional problems are not as easy to see as the obvious missing leg. That is why we have to search for the truth about our past and our heritage. Once we discover that we are made or bent in a certain direction, we have to decide whether to go with the bend until we break or to do everything in our power not to succumb to the predisposition. I believe we all are called to do the best with what we have. There is never a good excuse to fail, no matter how much more difficult life is for us than someone else. The challenge is to accept our hardships and move beyond them. We need to conquer them rather than be victimized by them. In so doing we make an impact on our world for years to come. Our courage can reverse a family trend and affect the future positively.

If we have sensed that maybe some things have set us up to experience certain emotions more severely than others, we are making great progress toward breaking through the deadly denial. The decision to continue in the search for the truth about who we are and why we do certain things is a decision not to be victims. It is a decision that needs to be made every day.

Dr. Thomas R. Reardon, a family practitioner in Portland, Oregon, states well the caution we should all heed: "The time to research your family history and do something about it is in your 20s and 30s—not in your 50s. . . . In other words, those who never learn about their family health history may be condemned to repeat it."[11] For those of us brave enough to look into the past for wounds and predisposing factors, there is freedom rather than condemnation.

Notes

1. Jim Detjen, "It's All in the Genes," *Orange County Register,* Jan. 1, 1992, section E, pp. 1–2.

2. Detjen, "Genes," pp. 1–2.

3. See listing of resources at the back of the book on how to contact the March of Dimes for more information.

4. Joannie M. Schrof, "The Chemistry of Romance and Nurturance," *U.S. News & World Report,* June 24, 1991, p. 62.

5. Randi Hutter Epstein, "Study Links Pregnant Women Who Get Flu to Schizophrenia in Babies," *Orange County Register,* May 31, 1992, section A, p. 10.

6. Thomas H. Maugh II, "Growth Patterns of Infants May Warn of Schizophrenia," *Los Angeles Times, Orange County Edition,* March 15, 1992, section A, pp. 3, 37.

7. Maugh, "Growth Patterns," p. 37.

8. Thomas H. Maugh II, "Studies Link Childhood Abuse to Adult Social Dysfunction," *Los Angeles Times, Orange County Edition,* Feb. 17, 1991, section A, p. 5.

9. Karen S. Peterson, "Debate: Does 'Wiring' Rule Emotion, Skill?" *USA Today,* July 8, 1991, section A, pp. 1–2.

10. Peterson, "Debate," p. 2.

11. Melinda Beck with Farai Chideya, "Hand Me Down Genes," *Newsweek,* Jan. 27, 1992, p. 53.

Section 1

◆

DEPRESSION

Yet I am standing here depressed and gloomy, but I will meditate upon your kindness to this lovely land where the Jordan River flows and where Mount Hermon and Mount Mizar stand. All your waves and billows have gone over me, and floods of sorrow pour upon me like a thundering cataract. Yet day by day the Lord also pours out his steadfast love upon me, and through the night I sing his songs and pray to God who gives me life.

—**Psalm 42:6–8** TLB

Chapter 2

◆

THE VALLEY OF
THE SHADOW OF DEATH

Few people escape going through life without having to experience the depths of depression. Those dark, lonely days of emptiness are hard to avoid. Almost everyone goes through them after a great loss of a spouse, a child, a friend, a job, or a major expectation that did not work out. Short periods of depression are a normal part of life. Some people spend more of their days in depression than out of it. It costs them their jobs, their futures, and often the relationships with others who refuse to stay while they continue to suffer. There are not a lot of things worse than living in the misery of a life beset by depression.

I happen to be someone who has spent many days in depression. I believe the predisposition to it was there when I was a small child. It raised its head in the form of my faking some illnesses, just to get additional attention and nurturing, and actually experiencing headaches so severe that I thought I was going to die from my head exploding. I believe I saw depression modeled in my family when disappointments in life set in. I also think the depression was more than just a reaction to events. I think my family wasn't wired up normally. Depression took its toll on my body. Sometimes I lost twenty or thirty pounds in my despair. Other times I put on sixty pounds. Dissatisfaction was a way of life.

I once told my wife that I never had a job I didn't hate. She couldn't believe it because I have been blessed with success in many things I have done. There has been about a 50 percent dissatisfaction factor in almost everything I have done. That dissatisfaction has driven me to do more, hoping that the next promotion or rung on the ladder would provide me with the satisfaction and fulfillment I was looking for. Until I reached the job I have now, nothing satisfied me. Few people have ever known what a battle it was for me to get out of bed and go to work and face the problems I found there. I have fought the constant battle with depression with many weapons. Humor, work, and exercise have helped me continue to fight it when I was often tempted to give in to it.

The ongoing depression I have felt has always been punctuated with times when life seemed almost unbearable. After the breakup of a very important relationship, I was so low that I put a knife to my chest, wondering if that was the only way I could cope with the pain. I lost over thirty pounds very quickly and didn't know when my weight loss would stop. If I had not had a rewarding job then with people who cared about me, I probably would have given in to the depression and moved into a self-destruction mode.

Today I am glad that I experienced it and came through those times. I have greater insight into the struggles of many of the clients at the New Life Treatment Centers where I work. And I am motivated to stay as healthy as possible so that my body can help my mind fight off its greatest enemy. Each day is a new challenge for me to work through the feelings I have rather than deny they are there or stuff them down inside where they would be temporarily silenced and buried only to rise again someday in a more destructive force than ever.

People who have struggled with depression know how hard it is to deal with all the negative feelings and how deadly it can be not to address what is happening. They also know of the fear that the depression will never get better; the fear that life will always be one sorrowful day after another.

Having been around people in the church all of my life, I have heard a lot of different messages about depression. One such message is that a person cannot be right with God and be depressed. I have also been told that depression is the result of demon possession and that it is God's way of trying to tell me something. Folks that told me those things said they wanted to help. I'm sure most of them meant it. But in reality, probably because they didn't know better, they were trying to shame me into emotional shape. It didn't work, of course. My depression may be a result of any or all of the spiritual causes they told me about, but I have not found the fluctuation of moods to be based on moments of spiritual depth or rapture. I have found that depression does not have to be debilitating. It can be managed and minimized so that its power is not so all-consuming. I believe that no matter the form or the severity, people can do something to lessen the impact of the problem on their own lives and the lives of their loved ones.

My life today is a radical contrast to the days when depression had me in its grips. Picture a 220-pound fat lug sitting in front of a television set eating potato chips out of a can at night and cinnamon rolls and soft drinks in the morning. That was my life as an isolated, depressed human being who punished myself for the way I felt by making myself look uglier, more unacceptable, and more miserably depressed with each pound I gained. And worst of all, I had no energy to do the things I wanted to do or the things that would have been good for me. Today I have a lot of energy and get more done than most people. I weigh around 160 pounds and exercise at least five days a week. I have run my first marathon and am looking forward to my next. I am living proof that there is a way to move beyond depression.

Since depression is the most common of all emotional problems, we must understand it. Each of us has a greater chance for depression, or the opportunity to help someone with depression, than for any other problem. By following the story of Nathan and Elizabeth, perhaps we will develop insight into our depression or the depression of someone we care about. Here is their story.

NATHAN AND ELIZABETH

Elizabeth lurched for the phone on the first ring. "Hello," she said in a studied voice, trying to sound normal in case it wasn't Nathan (although she silently prayed to hear his voice).

"Hello, is Nathan there?"

"No, I'm sorry. He's out. Can I take a message?"

"Oh, hi, Elizabeth. It's Joseph. Nathan was supposed to be here at 8:15 for a modeling shoot. There's too much money on the line for him to be flaking out on me."

Elizabeth glanced at the clock, 8:50. She hadn't seen Nathan since the previous night when he stormed out of the house, taking his camping gear and photography equipment with him. She didn't even know what had prompted his latest "mood" since he hadn't been speaking to her for days . . . or to anyone else for that matter. Now he was late for an important job. "Joseph, I don't know what to say. Nathan has been ill. I thought his secretary had called you." She lied, not wanting to say too much in case Nathan was able to pull himself together to arrive for the photo session. The call-waiting beep got her off the hook. "I need to get this other line, Joseph. Can I call you right back?"

"No need. Look, if Nathan doesn't show up in the next ten minutes, there's no reason to talk."

She tried to say she was sorry, but he had already hung up. She took the other line with trepidation and growing anger at having to cover for her husband one more time.

It was Chris, Nathan's closest friend (although Nathan hadn't really let anyone get close for months). Chris sounded concerned. "What's up with Nathan? He dropped by this morning, barely said two words, and gave me all his equipment. Said he was through with the rat race, that I could have it. Said he wouldn't be needing it anymore. Then he took off before I had a chance to wake up enough to argue with him."

"Oh, Chris," she managed to say.

"Elizabeth . . . ELIZABETH!"

She didn't respond. She was lost in her fears.

"Elizabeth, I'll be right over. Stay there."

Of course she would stay there. She was keeping a vigil that had become familiar—waiting to see if Nathan was going to be okay, waiting for him to break the silence, waiting for the phone to ring, for him to call and tell her he was all right . . . or for someone to call and tell her he was dead. She was lost in waiting, immobilized by indecision, not sure what it all meant or what she could do. Her times of waiting were filled with questions: Was there something wrong with her? If she were a better wife, would he be so miserable? Why couldn't she make him happy? She tried to keep the kids out of his way. She tried to create a buffer from the stress that he no longer seemed able to bear. Maybe it wasn't her. Maybe there was something wrong with him. Once she had ventured to mention Nathan's depression to her mother-in-law. Nathan's mother was consoling, in a way. She said that she had spent thirty-six years married to Nathan's father, who acted the same way. She empathized but offered only a pessimistic view, "That's what a wife is for, to help him keep up a good front, to cushion him from life . . . and to pray."

Depression definitely ran in Nathan's family. His father had been in and out of psychiatric hospitals throughout Nathan's childhood. Some days his father was up, but most of the time he was so depressed that he did not want to be with the family. He would run away for days at a time, no one knowing if he would ever come back. Now Nathan was playing out the same role as his father. The unresolved problems of the parents were perfectly reproduced in Nathan.

Nathan already despaired that there was something wrong with him. He knew it wasn't normal to live with the inner rage he felt, rage so intense that it would shut him down completely. The anger seemed to drain him of all his resources. Try as he might, some small irritation would lead him to lash out in anger, then retreat in isolation with tremendous guilt, shame, and remorse. Life with Nathan was never easy and always unpredictable. It was an emotional roller coaster, and it was no fun for anyone who came along for the ride.

It was twelve minutes after ten. No one had seen Nathan for hours, since his cryptic conversation with Chris. Elizabeth's troubled thoughts tumbled into prayer, "Dear God, please protect him from himself. Help me know what to do. God, please . . ." Please what? What did she want from God? Maybe their spiritual failure was at the root of what was happening. Maybe it was the result of their sins. Sure, they weren't perfect, but what were they supposed to do? What if it was their fault, their lack of faith? Nathan's resistance to God ebbed and flowed. Sometimes he was almost tolerant of her faith, at other times antagonistic. His own relationship with God was distant at best. Often he blamed their troubles on God. Wasn't it God's fault that he was subjected to this miserable existence? Nothing was clear.

Chris's arrival brought a welcome escape from the circle of questions without answers. He looked worried, entering forcefully into the room without knocking. Years of friendship had earned him entrance into their home and their problems. "I'm worried, Elizabeth. He's been acting strange for weeks now . . . like he's off somewhere. Any idea where he is now?"

She shook her head aimlessly. "He left here last night with his sleeping bag. He hasn't spoken to me in days. I hoped that he had stayed at your place."

"No, he didn't show up till this morning, about six I guess. I was still sound asleep."

Elizabeth was glad to have someone to direct her questions to for a change. "Chris, do you think I should call someone, I mean the police or . . . ?"

Chris replied, "Well, nothing has really happened. I don't know. Maybe I'll call around and see if anyone else has seen him." He reached for the phone, then stopped. "Has anything happened, I mean between you two?"

Elizabeth hesitated, then went on. "No. I mean . . . nothing that would warrant this kind of reaction. You know how he gets."

"Yeah, but this is worse than before, Elizabeth." Chris didn't want to intrude, but he felt that if he didn't and anything happened to his friend, he would never forgive himself. "Don't you think it's time to face this thing, whatever it is, and get some real help?"

She looked at him and shrugged her shoulders. "I guess. I just don't know where to turn. We both know he's always been like this. His mom says his dad was the same way."

"Well, whatever the case," Chris said, "I'm worried. I'm worried about him." He hesitated for a moment, then added, "Frankly, I'm worried about you and the kids. He's not tracking with us, and he's obviously miserable."

The mention of the kids brought Elizabeth back to full attention. She had worried about them, too. Not only that they would suffer from living lives that had to constantly accommodate their father's shifting moods, but also that the malady might be hereditary and the eerie shadow of depression would fall across their lives in time. Her own father had been hospitalized with clinical depression. If Nathan's condition was hereditary, where did that leave her two small children in terms of risk? Even if they did not succumb to it, would they do exactly what she had done, marry a man with similar problems to those of her own father? It had taken her a few years to realize it, but she had been more attracted to the unhealthy things about Nathan than the healthy things.

Chris's next question coincided with her own thoughts: "For their sakes, don't you think you need to face this thing?"

She was grateful to have someone else confirm that her fears weren't unfounded. She said, "You're right. I can't go on living like this . . . and Nathan can't, either."

He seemed to be able to read her mind. "Hey, Elizabeth, I know this will be hard for you alone. Why don't we take this on together? We don't even have to say anything to him about what we're doing until we know what we're dealing with and what kind of help is available. But he's out there somewhere, and he needs our help, even if he can't admit it." She nodded, half afraid at what Nathan's reaction might be, half relieved to have the motivation she needed to finally address the problem. "Look, even if he drives up right now, we can't just go back to pretending that things are okay until the next crisis. We need to see this thing through."

"You're right, Chris. I'm glad to have the help."

That was a major turning point for Elizabeth. She would no longer settle for that terrible place called emotional limbo. She was determined to face her own fears so she could confront Nathan and encourage him to find the help he needed. Although she felt tremendous despair, she was beginning to feel that there was hope for Nathan, her, and the kids. And with new insight, there really was hope.

THE GOAL OF FREEDOM

The above narrative is a re-creation of a true story. Every day there are countless untold stories like this one as families alternately try to ignore and then try to deal with the impact of depression. There are no villains in this story, except perhaps the disease of depression itself. All the characters are doing the best they can with the knowledge they have. And yet, they are captives, despairing of the loss of their freedom to enjoy life. The chains of depression might have been forged out of a genetic link with the past or perhaps their upbringing and patterns of thought. The chains might have been forged out of some experience that happened to upset their physiological, psychological, or spiritual lives. There are various causes, various types of depression, and various approaches to dealing with the problem, all of which need to be considered.

Our goal is freedom from depression. The means to the goal is understanding and action. The information presented in the remainder of this section is to help us understand depression enough to deal with the problem and persist in our action until we find the way to freedom. Knowing the truth brings this freedom. Coming to a true understanding of depression—its causes and influences and, most important, what can be done about it—can unlock the chains of depression, releasing us to experience fresh new lives.

The following material summarizes what both Elizabeth and Chris needed to know to help Nathan. It enabled them to understand the different types of depression, various causes, and appropriate treatments. Their desire to learn and take action was the key to Nathan's eventually finding freedom from depression.

If you have a "Nathan" in your life, someone you worry about, someone whose emotional ups and downs set the course for your family life, someone your family consistently tiptoes around for fear of driving the individual over the edge, you may have a personal interest in the information that follows. It helped Elizabeth and Chris plot a course that would lead Nathan out of depression.

From the onset you need to know that if you are living with someone who suffers from untreated depression, you may need to find a person to encourage you as you address this problem in your family. Like Nathan, a depressed person is not in a frame of mind to see things clearly or to make the best life decisions. Like Elizabeth, you may find that your perspective has become distorted, also. You may need a caring friend, like Chris, who has enough distance from the problem to see clearly and to offer continued support.

One very important caution needs to be sounded. Elizabeth and Chris worked on the problem together. That was a very bad idea. More affairs get started due to helping someone of the opposite sex through a difficult time than from any other source. You should find your support from someone of the same sex. If you want to help someone of the opposite sex, call on your wife or girlfriend, or refuse to get involved. The best intentions have frequently been overcome by feelings of passion. Don't make a foolish mistake that could affect you the rest of your life.

With that caution out of the way, our first order of business is to clear away some of the confusion regarding exactly what qualifies as depression, what the symptoms are, and what the causes may be.

PICTURES OF DEPRESSION

Sometimes, trying to identify a problem is like looking at a bunch of old snapshots. Recently I went back to Ranger, Texas, to help my grandmother celebrate her ninetieth birthday. While I was there, I went through about a thousand old pictures that had been lying in a drawer. Several pictures had some things in common, the same people wearing the same clothes and doing various things around the same table that had a loaf of Wonder Bread on it. I kept all those pictures with common characters in them and put them in a pile. When I had gone through all the photos, I looked at them as a group. When I was finished, I had a pretty good idea of what went on at a picnic fifty years ago. No single snapshot could have revealed what the whole group revealed.

That is the way it is with depression. One snapshot into a person's life will not reveal whether depression is an ongoing problem. When a single friend's dog died, he was depressed for a month. If you judged his mental health based on that month, you would judge him clinically depressed. In reality, he is one of the happiest and most productive people I know. One slice of a person's life will not tell the story or accurately reveal the nature of the problem. It takes many "snapshots" over time to produce an accurate portrayal of emotional health or mental problems such as depression.

In looking at depression we see similar symptoms that we would recognize as depression or define in those terms, whether we view it from a psychological, physiological, spiritual, or hereditary perspective. Although we may have a sense of what depression is and may be able to recognize certain symptoms, we may not realize that different kinds of depression can appear alike but respond *very* differently to standard treatments because their origins are different.

Even though someone's behavior fits with the terms of what we know to be depression, important distinctions must be made. We cannot assume that another's depression is like what we have experienced just because it has common elements, nor can we automatically assume that what made us feel better will help the person. If the depression has different origins, it may stubbornly remain, even though the person tries to apply someone else's home remedy.

DEPRESSION IS NOTHING NEW

The condition we call depression has a long history of being recognized by certain characteristic groups of symptoms. Ever since the earliest medical observations were recorded, twenty-five hundred years ago, descriptions of what came to be called melancholia, and later depression, have changed very little, despite great differences in the languages and cultures of the observers. Listen to the way Hippocrates, a Greek physician from the fifth century B.C., described it: "Fear or a depressive mood which last for a long time render [patients] melancholic."[1] Galen, who lived in the second century A.D. and was the most famous of the Roman Empire's physicians, observed, "Although each melancholic patient acts quite differently than the others, all of them exhibit fear or despondency."[2] A contemporary description declares, "The essential feature of a Major Depressive Episode is either depressed mood or loss of interest or pleasure in all, or almost all, activities, and associated symptoms, for a period of at least two weeks."[3] After more than two thousand years, the core of the description remains the same. We usually recognize a person who may be seriously depressed by prolonged and often extreme dejection or lowering of mood.

No one better describes the condition of depression than David did in the Psalms. Listen to the despair in his words:

My God, My God, why have You forsaken Me?
Why are You so far from helping Me,
And from the words of My groaning?
O My God, I cry in the daytime, but You do not hear (Ps. 22:1–2).

King David knew the depths of depression, and he expressed the pain of hopelessness and isolation from God better than any contemporary writer. No one reading David's work could doubt that he had been through terrible times of depression. Fortunately, the Psalms don't record just his despair. They record his powerful praises of God, which are healing words for a depressed soul. In David's depression, God was there for him as He is there for us in our despair.

WHAT'S IN A NAME?

Depression by any other name is still as sad, but it helps to understand the various names and how their meanings have been derived. The words most commonly used to describe this condition of prolonged despondency continue to be *depression* and *melancholia* (or *melancholy*). The Greek words *melan cholē,* from which the Latin word *melancholia* is derived, literally meant "black bile." They were probably first used by Pythagoras and his followers in the sixth century B.C. to describe a bodily fluid, or "humor," thought to be the cause of a whole group of diseases.[4] Versions of *melancholia* have been used throughout most of the twenty-six centuries since then to refer to various groups of symptoms to which a condition of severely lowered mood is central.[5] By Renaissance times, and continuing through the seventeenth and eighteenth centuries, the word had acquired a broad range of meanings, running the gamut from postured seriousness to special giftedness to states of sorrow or despair to diseases involving despondency. Having briefly faded from medical usage during parts of the late nineteenth and early twentieth centuries, *melancholia* has again been revived as a subtype of major depressive episode in current professional diagnostic literature.[6]

The use of the word *melancholy* today has produced some confusion and often unnecessary suffering. Melancholy carries with it a romantic flavor and is often associated with a person who is lovesick over the loss of a romance. There is nothing romantic about the word *depression.* Some people are described as having a melancholic personality, and they take that to mean a combination of moody and romantic. Being moody and romantic almost seems normal and even desirable. They learn to live with the moods and the label. They come to believe the label is so much a part of them that they don't do anything to treat their depression. People who have been told they have a melancholic personality need to ask if a more appropriate term might be *chronically depressed.*

FEELING BLUE?

Did you ever wonder why depression has been associated with feeling blue? Since the origin of the word *melancholia* came from black bile, you might easily conclude that being depressed would be called *feeling black.* Popular terms for depression have a long and varied history. *Feeling blue* or *having the blues* is related to centuries-old folk beliefs. In the eighteenth century, the devil was said to be present whenever candles burned with blue smoke, resulting in dejection for those exposed. Today, we still *sing the blues.* Some metaphorical descriptions, like *being in a state of darkness,* have been used since ancient times. Others, such as feeling *down* or *under it* or *weighed down,* are clearly related to the meaning of depression but reach back into ancient times as well.[7]

The word *depression* is derived from the Latin *de* (down from) and *premere* (to press), and from *deprimere* (to press down). Those of us who have been through depression know how accurately that fits the mood. It seems as if there is a constant heaviness, pressing down everything in life, including mood, relationships, and the ability to think clearly. First used metaphorically in English in the seventeenth century, it meant "dejected or lowered spirits" in the sense of normally lowered mood. Sometime in the eighteenth century, it began to be used in relation to *melancholia.* Nineteenth-century literature continued to use the term *depression* and related terms to mean "dejection" or "melancholia." However, clinically, *melancholia* continued to be the term most often used until 1899, when Daniel Tuke used *depression* to diagnose "manic-depressive insanity."[8]

Daniel Tuke is an important character in understanding the treatment of depression. Before he came along, most people were interested in how to cure it. They came up with some very strange ways to go about doing that. They tried scaring patients by sneaking up on them and firing a gun. They used tonics to purge the demons out of them, and sometimes they even tried to beat them back to mental health. Daniel Tuke was more interested in the care of patients than in the cure. He tried to help them feel appreciated and loved; he hired a staff of people who served the patients as if they were special and significant. His results were phenomenal, far more successful than anything that came before him. He treated his patients morally and kindly, and they responded by showing improvement.

If we have been depressed for some time, we may feel we have been treated as brutally as some of the earliest patients. If we love someone who is depressed, we must be aware that those who are depressed have an ongoing feeling of being abused. The tendency is to take the one thing we do not experience in our lives and make others who do experience it feel inferior. That is why people who don't drink often make alcoholics feel worse about themselves than anyone else, even though they say they want to help. Their railings against the alcoholic are acts of superiority that are quite damaging. People do the same with those who are depressed, often unconsciously trying to shame them back into shape. It never works. People with emotional problems respond to love, respect, and guidance from a heart that really cares.

SYMPTOMS

The easiest way to determine if someone is experiencing depression is to look at the symptoms that surround the problem. A person may not experience all of them. If several (five or more) of these symptoms are present for more than two weeks, the person probably needs to get an evaluation or at least sit down and talk with a counselor. These symptoms include the following:

1. Depressed or "down" mood, often described as feeling low
2. Loss of interest or pleasure in people, things, or activities that used to be pleasurable
3. Depressed mood lasting most of the day for prolonged periods of time, regardless of whether the circumstances of life are good or bad
4. Noticeable shift in behavior from the way a person usually functions when not depressed
5. Sad expression; crying easily; blank or hollow facial expression
6. Lack of motivation to do anything
7. Sleep disturbances (either trouble sleeping or sleeping excessively)
8. Appetite disturbances (loss of appetite, bulimia, insatiable cravings, etc.), sometimes accompanied by constipation or bowel irregularity
9. Loss or reduction of sex drive
10. Constant fatigue, sluggishness, or reduction in energy level, unrelated to overexertion
11. Slowed and monotonous speech; hesitation to speak; speaking ceased altogether
12. Increased signs of agitation, such as handwringing or pacing
13. General thoughts of death and/or suicide
14. Inability to concentrate; slow thought processes
15. Inability to make otherwise simple decisions
16. Thoughts consistently negative or pessimistic, regardless of circumstances
17. Intensified feelings of guilt (both legitimate and unfounded)
18. Lowered self-esteem; feelings of worthlessness, feeling unwanted, unloved, dirty, or sinful
19. Inability to function well with others socially and at work

20. Loss of ability or motivation to care for personal needs (i.e., feeding, grooming, personal hygiene, etc.)
21. Irritability; overreacting to little problems that otherwise would not be upsetting
22. Mild headache, which is present much of the time, feeling like a dull ache or band around the head and radiating down the neck
23. Chronic pain, which may be quite severe, sometimes in back, abdominal area, or almost anywhere

Experiencing or exhibiting these characteristics doesn't mean the person has a mental disorder. Very few depressed people are out of control or unable to improve the way they function and feel. These symptoms identify depression in general, so we can determine if it is actually what we are dealing with. But they do not distinguish the various kinds of depression. The following information clarifies that one person's depression may be totally different in cause and need a completely different type of treatment from that of someone else.

MODERN PERSPECTIVE ON THE VARIETIES OF DEPRESSION

Mistaken impressions and the resulting lack of appropriate response can leave the person suffering with depression, as well as the family, in a life of unnecessary misery. Clarifying our definition of depression and becoming familiar with the meaning of terms associated with depression provide greater comfort in dealing with the problem. Knowing the varieties of depression also leads to a greater likelihood of obtaining the most appropriate help.

Joseph Talley, M.D., and Beverly Mead, M.D., explain the comprehensive impact of the illness we know as depression. They say that depression "is a somewhat mysterious illness which can affect both our bodies and our minds. Depression can thus be responsible for many kinds of miserable feelings. It is a common illness, one of the most common in all of medicine."[9]

In response to the question, "What causes depression?" they explain,

We used to think that unusual Depression was due to some hidden unhappiness or conflict in a person's life. We now know that many otherwise healthy people who have no reason to be unhappy become depressed, too.

We now understand that most Depression is caused by a deficiency of one of two special chemicals that carry messages from one nerve ending to the next, across the little gap between them, like little messengers. They deliver the message to the next nerve, then jump back to the nerve they came from. When there are enough messengers to do the job, there's no trouble. But when there are not, whatever that nerve transmission is supposed to do doesn't happen.

When this deficiency occurs in a person's arms or legs or trunk of the body, various kinds of loss of motion or limitation of function can occur. *When the deficiency of messengers occurs in the brain, the result is Depression.* We don't always know why these messengers, those special chemicals that carry nerve impulses, become deficient. However, we do have medicines that correct the deficiency; either by keeping the little messengers from being further destroyed or by preventing them from being removed from the gap between nerves where they're supposed to do their work.[10]

They are saying that depression is a chemical imbalance in the brain. Let me clarify this chemical issue. If a perfectly healthy individual took a new job that permitted only six hours of sleep a night, when normally there would be eight, that alone could be enough to cause the imbalance. Sleep allows us to restore certain chemicals, and if we don't have enough sleep, the restoration will not occur. Similarly, if a person is worried over a failing business, resulting in lack of sleep, the situation could be further complicated with depression compounding the effects of worry. Other things could lead to this imbalance, including lack of sunlight or a physical injury. If depression is going to be overcome, the normal chemical balance must be restored to the brain.

With someone like Nathan, who has a family history of depression, there is good reason to seriously consider the possibility of a genetic predisposition to this kind of depression caused by a deficiency of certain neurotransmitters. This chemical problem may be corrected in several ways. A change in diet may completely solve the problem. Change in sleep environment, producing deeper sleep, may also produce the desired change. For me, it was exercise. When I started walking every day, then running long distances, my mood lifted as the exercise increased. Often there is a simple solution to the problem, such as giving up alcohol or changing some other life-style factor.

Antidepressant medication should be used only when all other sources of treatment have been tried and failed. At New Life Treatment Centers we like to see the effect of spiritual renewal on a person before prescribing medication. Sometimes nothing else will work, and we have to recommend medication. We must be careful not to shame those who need to take it. For some, it may be the only hope for a normal life. Any reliable physician who deals with clinical depression would be able to make an evaluation and recommend whether antidepressant medication should be tried. Caution is advised because some prescribe it as the first course of treatment without considering other alternatives that may be contributing to depression.

This is a very tough area for some Christians to handle. They do not fully understand the way the mind works. They would think nothing of taking penicillin for the body, but taking something for the mind is completely unacceptable to them. They might have been taught that having true faith will clear up all emotional problems. We have seen some of our ex-patients, who were doing well, go back into churches where a pastor—with good intentions but in ignorance—told them to stop taking their medication. It did not take long before they returned to a depressed life-style. I hope that some of these ministers will free their people to obtain the best help possible, even if as a last resort, it must come in the form of antidepressant medication.

I think there is reason for optimism in this area. Just a few days ago a minister and his wife came to see me in my office. He told me of the times he preached against people's taking medication to be normal. He honestly believed that greater dedication to God would fix the problem. Then he found himself going further and further down into depression. He began to overeat, and he could not sleep. His anger increased until no one could tolerate him. He was far from being Spirit-filled in his encounters with others. His wife had finally gotten up enough nerve to ask him to get some help. He did, and the doctor prescribed medication. He told me that since he was an adolescent, his mind had been spinning with destructive thoughts and obsessions. He said that the medication turned all of that off, and he has never felt more freedom. He believes God is using the medication just as He uses a brain surgeon on someone else. What a shame it would have been if the minister had reached the point of suicide before discovering that his problem was easily solved by medication that altered his physiology. Trying harder spiritually would have produced only more despair.

FIVE TYPES OF DEPRESSION

Depression can be identified by or classified into five basic categories. The five general categories we will discuss are (1) melancholic type personality, (2) normal depression, (3) major depression, (4) manic-depression, and (5) organic depression.

1. Melancholic Type Personality

This term accurately describes Nathan's depression. He felt sad very early in his life. Some times were tougher than others, but he always felt a bit sad and withdrawn. Even his face had an aspect of sadness as if gravity affected it more than other faces. He always saw the downside of everything and never figured that life would work out very well at all. His depression didn't just crop up one day. It had been with him ever since he could remember. Nathan was chronically depressed.

Someone suffering with a melancholic type personality or *dysthymia,* the clinical term for chronic depression, has probably felt depressed for most of life. This chronic or persistent depression (lasting two years or more) may seem like part of an individual's personality. The symptoms are usually less severe than a pronounced bout with another form of depression. Those who have been diagnosed as the melancholic type will often wake in the early morning, usually around 4:00 A.M., and be unable to fall asleep again.[11]

The persistent nature of less severe symptoms may lead the persons and their loved ones to accept the depression as being "just the way they are." When that is the case, melancholic types probably won't seek professional help. They also rarely experience anything that makes them feel better without treatment. They often get into a self-destructive, inactive, and isolative rut that compounds their depression. Sometimes a complete life-style change will produce positive results. If not, medication may be the only source of hope. Melancholic type personalities usually respond readily to antidepressant medication. Once they are using the medication with competent supervision, they are amazed to find that they feel "like a whole new person." Life is suddenly worth living . . . maybe for the first time. This type of depression is thought to be linked to a genetic predisposition.

Having a toddler around the house has acquainted me with some new characters that exhibit various personality traits. The melancholic type personality might well be symbolized by Eeyore the donkey in the Winnie-the-Pooh series. Eeyore moves slowly. Nothing ever gets him excited. If there's a dark side to any situation, Eeyore can be counted on to bring it to everyone's attention. Eeyore obviously has low self-esteem. Even when a visit by Pooh and Piglet brings troubling results, Eeyore responds, "Oh, well . . . thanks for noticing me." Eeyore tries to find the bright side, but it always comes from a depressed mood.

It doesn't seem fair that some people start out with the cards stacked against them. Because of their makeup, they are going to experience more sadness than others. Fortunately, tremendous research has resulted in treatments that provide relief or at least allow them to function on an even plane with others. Melancholic or chronically depressed persons have a greater tendency to believe they will be that way forever and feel that misery is their only option. It is not. People with this type of depression need to be encouraged to make the best of what they have. They should search themselves to clear up any spiritual problem that might compound the depression. They should change diet and exercise to provide the healthiest life-style possible. They should seek out a strong counselor who can provide encouragement and confrontation when needed. And they may have to consider medication. Life can be wonderful for a melancholic personality. It is just more difficult to find the wonder.

2. Normal Depression

Before starting New Life Treatment Centers, I was in charge of another company that provided alcohol and drug treatment centers as well as pain treatment centers in rural hospitals. I was so optimistic about what might happen as a result of my hard work. It was an exciting time. The excitement soon turned to panic when I was informed that all the money supposedly available to run the company was not there. It was just a receivable that would never be collected. Shortly after discovering the reality of the company I had taken over, I put the company in Chapter 11 and set off to find another job.

I had tremendous faith in God, that He had something very special for me to do as He does everyone who puts trust in Him. I was anxious to find out what it would be. The anticipation quickly turned to depression. With each day that I had less and less money in cash reserve, the depression grew worse and worse. I was sad over my lost opportunity, and I was concerned about my next move. But more than anything, I was depressed because of the lost expectations that would not come true.

During that time, it was hard for me to concentrate and easy for me to eat. There were days I didn't want to get up and shave. I guess I wanted the outside to look as bad as the inside felt. I didn't want to be around people. They drained me of what energy I had left. It was a struggle to make it through the day. At the height of my misery I wondered if I would ever be happy again. Fortunately, the feelings did not last. Within three months things began to get better. I could think again, and my energy returned. Life felt good again. What I went through would be considered by most as a time of normal depression. Perhaps with a different history or a different set of genes I would not have experienced it. But I did, and the depression I felt was like that experienced by most people at least once during their lifetime.

Most people are probably familiar with and understand what is called normal depression. Normal depression is the normal response of the human body to overwhelming personal loss or stress. This type of depression is always directly related to clearly identifiable stresses in a person's life. It can vary in length and severity but is tied into the normal human grieving process in response to overwhelming circumstances. The symptoms can be every bit as debilitating as clinical depression. The individual would most likely benefit from counseling, and some even need inpatient treatment. However, as the grief process goes along without interruption, the person will naturally come out of the depression and resume a normal life. Normal depression can happen to anyone who suffers severe emotional trauma. It is precipitated by identifiable stressful situations or events and is not thought to be brought on by genetic predisposition.

The term *normal depression* is frequently used to distinguish the normal lowering of mood, which all of us experience at one time or another, from more serious clinical depressions. A normal depression is characterized by "a transient period of sadness and fatigue, generally responding to clearly identifiable stressors."[12] Normal depression is the body's way of taking us out of circulation, making us withdraw from the usual activities of life so that the body will rest and recover from excess stress.

Another case of normal depression was much more severe than the one I experienced. Michelle and her husband, Gregory, were committed Christians working together in full-time Christian ministry, Gregory as youth pastor and Michelle as a paid youth minister on the church staff. They were well-respected in the community, often pointed to as being a good example of a happy marriage and good role models for the 150 teens to whom they ministered. Michelle was often asked to speak to various women's groups and solicited to be on the boards of community and Christian associations.

Michelle had worked hard in youth ministry for ten years to be able to expertly perform the ministry with the kids she loved. Her four-year-old daughter, and the scores of kids in the youth group who needed her and appreciated her, gave her a sense of value and a great deal of satisfaction. She loved teaching the Bible studies and having a platform for sharing her faith in God. The ministry, her faith, and her family life were woven together in such a way that she felt she had everything she had ever hoped for.

The couple's social life was centered on the church and the ministry, but that was a happy necessity. The other members of the church staff were vibrant, talented people whose company they enjoyed. Their volunteer youth workers made up most of the rest of their circle of friends. The blending of work and play, social and spiritual, was a happy life, which promised only to continue to grow and improve.

Life was as happy as Michelle had ever known it to be. She finally felt safe. Growing up in a dysfunctional family, she thought she was breaking the cycle of abuse and had purposely picked a wonderful Christian guy who would be committed to the Lord and not fall into the drugs and alcohol that had devastated much of her childhood. Gregory was the guy. She saw, in him, her Prince Charming. After nine years of marriage, she was more in love with him than ever. Life as she knew it was great . . . but she didn't know everything.

Her whole life was about to come crashing down in one revelation. In August of that year her husband confessed to her that he had been sexually unfaithful; he had been involved in an illicit sexual affair with another member of the church staff (who also happened to be one of their closest friends). In the following months, everything Michelle had trusted in, including her ability to perceive life accurately, crumbled and became suspect. When they found New Life Treatment Center's sex addiction program, they wanted to seek treatment, so they went to their senior pastor to ask for help. The couple sat down with the man and openly and honestly told him what had happened.

Michelle expected the pastor to be supportive, a comforter and a protector for her. Instead, the church leader publicly exposed the sexual misconduct, fired her husband, and forced her resignation.

Michelle felt utterly devalued and abandoned. Every shred of her life was stripped away. Her husband became suicidal and was admitted to one of our centers. He was experiencing a major depressive episode, to which he was probably genetically predisposed. In the next section, we'll look at Gregory's experience, but for now let's turn back to Michelle. She was left home alone, afraid for her husband's life and deeply confused about their marriage. Their friendship with the other couple was a thing of the past; their income was gone; their reputation was ruined; their daughter was removed from the church school because tuition was part of their benefit package. Michelle's ministry and career seemed lost; she was no longer involved with the teens she dearly loved; she felt she was misunderstood and convicted without a hearing. Under such extreme circumstances, it was a normal human emotional reaction to become depressed, and that's exactly what happened.

Once her husband was released from the hospital, Michelle displayed severe emotional and physical symptoms of depression. She could not sleep, would not eat, cried unceasingly, and became obsessed with righting the wrongs the church had done to her. Her health was a major concern, especially because she was five months pregnant at the time. She wisely chose to be admitted to an inpatient counseling program where she spent two weeks. The supervised medical, spiritual, and psychological therapy program helped her understand the severity of her depression and allowed her to accept the validity of her feelings and to develop an emotional road map for recovery from her very real bout of depression. Today she says, "I don't think I could have pulled out of the depression and rebuilt my life in a healthy way without the understanding I gained in the program." Spiritual and emotional support from friends in the church and the community helped immensely after her release from the hospital during the seasons of grieving her losses. She also listened to inspirational tapes and read several good books that supported her desire to feel better.

It's been three years now since the traumatic unraveling of Michelle's world sent her hurtling down into a deep depression. Life is much different from before . . . but in many ways much better. Their marriage doesn't seem like a fairy tale anymore, but it's growing in honesty and real love. Gregory is no longer involved in ministry, but he is also free from the bondage he lived with and is in recovery from sex addiction. They relocated to a larger city where they could continue in counseling and deal with some of the underlying issues that affected their lives deeply. Their faith in God is intact and growing. The symptoms of depression are gone, replaced by normal ups and downs of life.

Michelle's part in this story illustrates that even normal depression can become so severe that if adequate help is not obtained, the person may decompensate (fall apart emotionally) and lose total control or, worse yet, go through with plans for suicide. If a professional has told us the one we love is going through normal depression, we can't assume all is safe. We must keep a careful watch so that the person is not allowed to reach a point of no return. Having a few sessions with a qualified counselor is a small price to pay to keep the person we love or get our own lives back in shape.

Grieving

People who have experienced a serious loss (e.g., loss of a spouse, child, job, etc.) may exhibit many of the same symptoms associated with normal depression during the time of grieving. Grief, under such a circumstance, is not only to be expected but is necessary for the ongoing health and well-being of a bereaved person. The depressive symptoms usually seen in the company of grief are to be considered a normal part of human experience. In fact, if they are absent, there may be greater cause for concern. Even such normal experiences, though, may often be facilitated and eased by treatment, especially if there is a lack or absence of relational support, if others deny the persons the right to grieve, or if they are in an environment of greater-than-ordinary stress.

3. Major Depression

Major depression can be characterized by a single bout of a *major depressive episode* or recurrent bouts with depression. A major depressive episode is a season of time when the symptoms of depression are present without clearly identifiable emotional stressors (which would indicate normal depression). Major depression is sometimes called a *unipolar disorder,* which refers to one singular pole or point of depression without swinging to the other extreme pole of mania (an emotional high).

The first incidence (onset) of a major depressive episode can happen anytime from birth to old age, but the average age is twenty-nine.[13] An adolescent may appear angry or antisocial or irritable, the symptoms of an older person may ape the "dementia" of Alzheimer's disease, or a child may appear passive and withdrawn. But usually, for the person experiencing a major depressive episode, there is a dependable pattern in the way symptoms are expressed.

As mentioned earlier, the most prominent feature of a major depressive episode is depressed mood or loss of interest and pleasure in persons, things, or activities that used to be pleasing. In normal depression, these symptoms will be fleeting, but in a major depressive episode, they will last most of the day, every day, for two weeks or longer. Depressed persons will usually describe their condition by saying that they feel discouraged, sad, depressed, or "down."

Of the many physical symptoms that may be associated with a major depressive episode, one of the most prominent is disturbance of sleep. People may have great difficulty falling asleep or remaining asleep (*insomnia*). Alternatively, they may sleep excessively or feel sleepy frequently during the daytime (*hypersomnia*). In clinical studies, many of those suffering from major depression have been found to have problems with the length and frequency of the rapid eye movement (REM) stage of sleep. Since they cannot get enough deep sleep, they cannot restore the chemicals needed to function normally. Problems with sleep will often be the primary reason that depressed persons seek help.[14]

Persons experiencing a major depressive episode will also behave differently. Usually, there is an appearance of sluggishness with slowed body movement, slow and monotonous speech, hesitation before spoken responses, and sometimes no speech at all. But in some, there is increased agitation—maybe pacing, pulling at clothing or skin, or handwringing. It may be associated with anxiety, which frequently accompanies depression, or may only be an alternative form of expression for deep depression. Agitation, irritability, and behavior problems are characteristic of some childhood and, especially, adolescent depressions.[15] Suicidal thoughts or attempts are also a symptom of a major depressive episode, as might be expected. It is a growing problem among adolescents. One study indicates that rates of major depression among older teens have risen by 500 percent since the end of World War II, and rates of suicide among boys fifteen to nineteen years old have risen by 136 percent.[16]

A major depressive episode also affects the thinking of those who suffer from it. Thinking is slowed, and there is marked and consistent inability to concentrate or make decisions. Sometimes a disturbance of memory occurs. Thoughts are consistently negative and pessimistic, self-accusing and self-denigrating. They are sometimes suicidal. Generalized thoughts of death are also common. Feelings of guilt (legitimate and illegitimate) as well as extremely low self-concept are associated with the negative thought patterns of depression.

Along with the most prominent symptoms of a major depressive episode just described, features of the syndrome are sometimes present as "satellites" to it. They include crying (frequent), anxiety, panic, excessive fears about physical health, and obsessive thinking. In some instances, hallucinations or delusions associated with the disturbance of mood are present as well. Less frequently, other psychotic symptoms may be present and may be either primary or secondary in nature. In a major depressive episode there is always at least some impairment of ability to function in social and vocational settings. Impairment may be so severe that affected persons cannot feed or care for themselves hygienically. Hospitalization is sometimes required, although antidepressant drugs, first used in the 1950s, have dramatically decreased the rate of hospitalization for severe depressive disorders.[17]

A publisher of one of my first books displayed an unusual form of depression. During the spring and summer, she was full of life and enjoyed herself greatly. But as soon as fall came and moved into winter, when the days grew shorter, she became more and more depressed. She lived in New York where it is cold and winters are long. She felt hopeless as she succumbed to that pattern year after year. Her profession caused her to make a dramatic change of location all the way from New York to San Diego, California. She could not believe that just changing addresses helped her so much. After she moved to a milder climate, her depression never came back.

Sometimes recurrent major depression is described as having a seasonal pattern. For certain people, the onset of these mood disorders coincides with a particular sixty-day period of the year, typically during seasons with reduced light, which is not associated with other sources of seasonal stress, such as the seasonal loss of work. Remission also occurs seasonally. These depressions often respond to a special light therapy. It is called seasonal affective disorder—SAD for short. Trying to run from problems by moving is called the attempt at a geographic cure. This problem often can be legitimately resolved with a change in location. Even though it comes and goes in a predictable pattern, it is considered major depression.

Gregory's story

Gregory, Michelle's husband from the story related earlier, is a good example of someone who suffered with major depression recurrently throughout his life. He never thought much about it since he came from a family where those feelings and symptoms were accepted as being the way life was. Beginning during adolescence, Gregory struggled with many of the symptoms of major depression. He was suicidal throughout much of high school but says he lacked the motivation to actually kill himself. He sought relief through his relationship with God, and that did help some. However, he could never tell when the depression would reappear for no apparent reason. He also battled with obsessive thoughts that seemed to be beyond control. He tried every technique he could find, including praying, meditating on Scripture, fasting, casting out spirits, breaking generational bondage, positive thinking, pastoral counseling, and so on, but nothing seemed to stop the episodes.

When he became a Christian, the shame of having the negative moods (since Christians are supposed to be happy) and the accompanying obsessions caused him to live in emotional hiding. He learned to pretend to be what his church members expected of him when he was in public. Privately, he was like a different person. He still thought about death and occasionally suicide, but that almost seemed a normal fact of life. When he became involved in sexual sin, he was horrified at his own behavior, which violated the values he held most dear. He wanted to do whatever it took to find freedom from his bondage and to save his marriage.

After going into New Life Treatment Center's sex addiction program, he was diagnosed with major depression. He has benefited from Christian psychological counseling, but that is in conjunction with antidepressant medication. The results have been surprising in that the medication cleared up problems he had always just accepted as being part of his makeup. The obsessions have become manageable, although they are still there. He has brought his sexual behavior under control and has remained sexually faithful to Michelle for almost three years now. He is able to focus and concentrate as never before. He is able to handle the emotional ups and downs of life and has not had a major depressive episode since beginning medical treatment.

He deeply regrets the pain and humiliation he put himself and his family through. However, he says the results of what he learned in the hospital, and the real help he's received by being on the medication, almost make it all worthwhile. For the first time in his adult life, he doesn't want to die anymore. He sees this as God's answer to his life-long prayer for freedom from his miserable existence. He had been living in the middle of a "happy" life, which he was *physiologically* unable to enjoy. Dealing with his sin and his emotional ills also revealed real physiological components of his problem. The discovery reduced the shame and encouraged him to pursue complete healing of his whole life and his marriage.

This type of depression is thought to be genetically inherited. Gregory has good reason to believe that holds true for him. His maternal great-grandfather was seriously depressed. His mother's father was depressed throughout life and ultimately committed suicide. His mother has had recurrent bouts of depression for which she has been hospitalized on numerous occasions; she has attempted suicide several times. His younger sister is permanently hospitalized in a state mental health facility, and his older brother has been seriously depressed off and on for much of his adult life. Although it seems that Gregory will always live with a genetic sensitivity to depression, he has found hope and significant help through dealing with the root of depression along with all the other problems that may or may not be directly related.

Gregory obtained more than his fair share of hand-me-down genes and secondhand emotions. His predisposition was very strong biologically, emotionally, and spiritually. He is a great example that predisposition does not have to become a predictor of the future. People with all the cards stacked against them can reshuffle the deck and find a meaningful life.

4. Manic-Depression

Manic-depression is a rare and particularly serious form of mood disorder that involves extreme mood swings from a state of profound depression (a major depressive episode) to a state of abnormally heightened mood called manic episode. It is sometimes referred to as a *bipolar disorder* because the person swings wildly between the two opposing poles of a major depressive episode and a manic episode. The essential feature of a manic episode is "a distinct period during which the predominant mood is either elevated, expansive, or irritable, and there are associated symptoms of the manic syndrome."[18]

A similar disorder called *cyclothymia* differs from bipolar disorder only in duration and severity of symptoms, with many rapidly alternating but milder mood swings experienced consistently for two years or more. Persons diagnosed with cyclothymia are predisposed to experience the more severe disorder.

Dr. Frank Reid is a good example of someone predisposed to manic-depression. For years, Dr. Reid's wife, Helen, noticed wide mood swings in her husband's temperament. They caused a higher level of stress than Helen would have invited, but she was able to handle his mood swings with the patience and grace she was known for. Dr. Reid and his wife were upstanding members of their church and community. The stress of a busy medical practice always provided enough explanation for the seasons of depression and exhaustion. The wonderful family, solid marriage, strong Christian faith, and their secure financial situation were always explanation enough for the emotional highs. For years, Helen tried to swing along with the good doctor's moods and compensate in whatever way she could. After Frank turned fifty, there was a marked change in the severity of the seasons of depression. There was also a marked irrationality during the high manic moods.

When he was down, Frank was unable to get out of bed or even to uncover his head to face the day. If he did make it out of bed and go to the office, chances were, he would be unreasonably stern with his patients. He would berate mothers for not caring properly for their children, leaving them in tears as they hurried away in confusion. Was he the good Christian doctor they trusted, or Dr. Jekyll and Mr. Hyde? His practice began to suffer noticeably, which took its toll on the family's financial stability.

When he was up, Frank exhibited bizarre and irrational behavior. He would offer to send any couple in their church on a vacation to Hawaii. The amazed recipients had nothing but appreciation and happiness as they jetted off for the islands. They didn't know how the illogical generosity deeply troubled Helen. Frank would donate large sums of money to any worthy cause that happened to come to his attention. Life was wonderful. Nothing could get him down. He couldn't sleep, but he didn't seem to care. Although Helen enjoyed the fact that her husband was happy again, she realized there was a problem. Even though Frank was a medical doctor, he could not see through the haze of his own manic-depression to recognize that he needed help.

The more severe the mood swings became, the more Helen tried to keep them under wraps. Finally, she realized there might be a physiological cause to the problem. She recalled that Frank had mentioned another relative who had suffered from depression. She began to suspect a biological predisposition. It took her some time to get Frank to agree to humor her and seek help. Then it took almost another year to find the right doctor to diagnose and treat him correctly. However, she says that it was worth the trouble it took to isolate the right medication to alleviate Frank's depression. The medication stabilized his mood swings and allowed them to resume their social life and begin to rebuild his faltering medical practice. Frank was free of manic-depression for the next five years, which happened to be the last five years of his life. Now, Helen shares their story in the women's Bible study she teaches. She hopes that anyone who loves a person suffering with manic-depression will do whatever it takes to have it medically diagnosed and treated.

The most common drug prescribed for manic-depressive persons is lithium. It seems to help them level out and avoid the extreme highs and lows. One of the problems with this form of treatment is that when people start feeling better, they frequently stop taking the medication. They last a few days, and then the destructive patterns of extreme highs and lows return.

5. Organic Depression

Depression that is a secondary symptom of an organic disease or injury may be referred to as *organic depression.* The common organic causes include hypothyroidism, infectious disease, high blood pressure treatment with hydrochlorothiazide, drug and alcohol use, or damage to a significant part of the brain. The resulting depression is classified as *organic mood syndrome, with depression,* rather than a major depressive episode.

Much of the research surrounding these organic problems is significant when considering the causes of depression since it clearly shows that there are predictable physiological causes for what we often interpret as merely a change in mood or emotional response to life.

Usually, the person will feel depressed and complain of the symptoms, as anyone might do. Occasionally, there will be no acknowledgment of suffering on the part of the organically depressed person. That is especially true of some types of organic brain-damaged patients, whose brain can no longer "know" that they are feeling depressed. In these cases diagnosis will depend on the observations of those who are in close contact with them.

These types of depression are physical responses and are not usually recognized as brought on by a genetic predisposition. However, our genetic sensitivities may play a part in the severity of our reaction to these external depressors.

Sandra and Rick suffer with different types of organic mood syndrome, with depression. Sandra was a happy and relatively healthy mother of four. She and her husband had a warm and loving relationship. Finances were tight, and they had their share of problems, but they were always able to work them out together. That was before Sandra was thrown from a horse. Her head struck a sharp rock, resulting in severe brain damage. Since the fall, Sandra has been depressed. She seems unable to cope with the least of life's normal pressures. She can't get along with her husband and is barely able to tolerate her children's company. Sandra is suffering from organic depression. In addition, some type of predisposition may be intensifying her reaction. However, when I last had contact with her, she insisted that she was going to get better, and that the real problem was a spiritual one. Her denial was so strong because she did not want to believe she had a permanent condition. She was seeking counseling from their church's pastoral staff. I hope the pastor will guide her to competent medical help as well as provide spiritual guidance for a family living with such trying circumstances.

Rick has been prone to depression for most of his life. However, when he began to take medication for a heart murmur, he noticed a dramatic change. One of the side effects of the medication is depression. He and his doctor are working together to try to find the right balance of medication to control the heart problem while also keeping the depression down to manageable levels. Imagine the possible consequences if Rick hadn't realized that the significant changes in mood were related to his medication. He is a great example of the fact that it is not "all in your head." He also is evidence that spiritual weakness is not the source of all emotional problems. It can be something as simple as heart medication. Knowing about his predisposition to depression and being sensitive to the effects of his new medication prompted Rick to seek help at the first sign of trouble and perhaps avoid a lifetime of unnecessary suffering.

TERMS OF SEVERITY

Some terms are useful in figuring out the severity of a problem. If we or someone we love struggles with a problem, knowing these words will help us communicate with those in charge of therapy. The terms *neurotic* and *psychotic* generally refer to degrees of severity in all kinds of depression. *Neurotic depression* indicates a milder form of depression, usually with a good track record for successful treatment. *Psychotic depression* indicates a more disabling form of disorder, which is severe to the point of serious inability to discern the realities of life, often including one's own disabled condition. It may be characterized by such symptoms as delusions (persistent false beliefs) and hallucinations.

One of the first psychotic people I worked with was suffering from this form of depression. His wife left him and took the kids. He became so depressed that he could not function normally at work. His inability to think clearly cost him his job, which thrust him further into depression. Finally, he was in a car accident that killed another person. He walked away with a broken arm. The wreck caused him to experience a psychotic break. By the time he arrived at the hospital, he was trying to communicate with the world through the cast on his arm. He thought it was a specially designed CB radio that only he could talk on. One of the most dramatic changes occurred only two days after he was given medication. As I said earlier, medication is not the treatment of choice, but sometimes it is the only choice.

Two more terms clarify the kind of depression a person is experiencing. These terms refer to the supposed source of the depressive disorder. The first is *exogenous depression,* which is clearly associated with external (environmental) factors (e.g., stressful circumstances, meaningful life events, conditions in the physical or social environment). The other term used in relation to the source of depression is *endogenous depression,* which describes depression associated with internal (i.e., genetic or biochemical) factors. Exogenous depressions are generally considered less severe (neurotic), but they are often serious enough to merit clinical evaluation and treatment—a fact that much recent research tends to support. Serious depressive disorders may originate with external as well as internal factors. However, both terms remain valuable for differentiation when discussing causes of depression.

WHO IS AT RISK?

Anyone can get depressed. No race, gender, socioeconomic class, religious group, or age group is immune from depression, even serious depression. We all have *potential* for depression because we are human. But some people—people with certain physical, psychological, or social characteristics, people from certain families, in certain environments, or perhaps even people from certain cultures—seem to be *predisposed* to developing states of depression. That is, they are somehow more vulnerable or at risk or susceptible to the condition. Whether people have a family history of depressive disorders and consider themselves "predisposed," or if they have had no previous indicators of possible depression, those who find themselves dealing with depression deserve help to get out of depression and get on with life.

EARLY DIAGNOSIS AND TREATMENT

In Nathan's case, described at the beginning of the chapter, his depression was allowed to continue unimpeded for many years as it gradually worsened. It was only when the depression led him to show signs of becoming suicidal that Elizabeth was ready to deal with the problem honestly. Depression can be deadly. Without early diagnosis and treatment, a depressed person may never have a chance. Someone who appears normally depressed may be careening toward a much more serious state or, in fact, may really be marginally clinically depressed or have masked symptoms.

The sufferer's ability to mask the depression often prevents it from being accurately identified. For example, often children who are diagnosed as hyperactive or labeled troublemakers are struggling with a deficiency of neurotransmitters in their brain chemistry. If the parents focus only on the presenting symptoms and miss the depression, the children are going to suffer needlessly. In adolescents, seasons of depression may be written off as normal teenage moodiness. These symptoms need to be evaluated thoroughly. Some research indicates that early treatment, with appropriate medication or other therapy, of persons with a budding clinical form of depression (especially children) may prevent recurrence of the symptoms altogether.

Depression is often hidden by the one experiencing it. Some people dive into their work. Others dive into a bottle of alcohol. Still others just isolate themselves so no one can see the severity of the problem. They believe they are acting in a way that will save them, but they only prolong their agony. When we experience or see out-of-the-ordinary behavior or symptoms, we must consider whether or not it might be the result of depression in hiding.

IS THERE HOPE?

Most likely each of us knows someone who is going through a very tough bout of depression. We may know someone who approaches life like an Eeyore. We may wonder at times if life really has to be so bad. Good question! The answer may be a resounding *No!* Maybe life can become a whole new experience of happiness. Elizabeth and Chris have made a decision to continue in the pursuit of answers and to help Nathan until his depression is understood and treated. We owe it to ourselves and to those we know who may be suffering depression to question the assumptions that have been made about the condition. We owe it to ourselves and to them to find out for sure whether life can be a great deal brighter.

SPIRITUAL, MENTAL, OR PHYSIOLOGICAL?

Depression is a mysterious adversary, blurring the lines between body, mind, and spirit. Approaching the problem by isolating any one of these dimensions of life as the root of the problem may limit access to appropriate help to deal with the reality of the depression. No human being is ever solely spirit, mind, or body at any given moment. We are all three, in one person, although we may be dealing with something that originates primarily in one part of our being (body, mind, or spirit), which affects the whole person.

In eighteenth-century England, a poet and hymn writer named William Cowper chronicled his life experiences of melancholy madness in forty-five years of letters and a memoir. Cowper's life is a tragic example of the futility of viewing depression solely as a spiritual (or mental or physiological) problem.

Born in 1731, Cowper first experienced severe "dejection of spirits" at the age of twenty-two. The experience was described as one of "lying down in horror and rising up in despair."[19] Ten years later, Cowper experienced a still more horrible depression. He believed it began with moral transgression. Having wished for the death of the incumbent in a government position he coveted, and having been offered the position when the man did indeed die, Cowper was overcome by guilt. When he learned that his nomination to the position had been questioned, and that he would need to endure an interview, he grew melancholy and attempted suicide.

Mr. Cowper did not die but lived to despise himself for what he had done. That, he claimed, was due to conviction of sin. A sense of God's wrath overcame him, which he despaired of escaping. Satan tortured him with dreadful delusions, tormenting him with sounds and visions of the damned. His hands and feet grew numb, rigid, and cold, and his heart pounded as though it would leave his body. He was seized with fear of death.[20]

A seeming "heavy blow" to the brain marked a transition to madness, evidenced by wild and incoherent thoughts: "All that remained clear was the sense of sin, and the expectation of punishment. These kept undisturbed possession all through my illness, without interruption or abatement."[21]

William Cowper's brother and friends sent him to spend the remaining period of his depression in the private asylum of Dr. Nathaniel Cotton, a Puritan doctor at St. Alban's. Of the doctor, he said, "Not only his skill, as a physician, recommended him to their choice, but his well-known humanity, and sweetness of temper." The sense of God's judgment, of conviction of sin, and of Satan's accusations never left him during the eight-month period of affliction. A converted Mr. Cowper, writing two years later, attributed all of that to the skillful pressure of God, urging him toward repentance.

By the time his brother came to check on his progress in July of 1764, Cowper had grown numb to despair and able at imitating recovery, fooling even his devoted doctor. All that he did "carrying a sentence of irrevocable doom in my heart." Confessing to his brother, he received an unexpected protest that his thoughts of hopeless damnation were a delusion—a protest so strong that it broke through his anguish: "Something like a ray of hope was shot into my heart; but still I was afraid to indulge it."[22] Slowly, he became aware of the possibility of mercy. A vision of delight prompted him to begin reading the gospel of John, which encouraged and softened his heart: "The cloud of horror, which had so long hung over me, was every moment passing away; and every moment came fraught with hope. I was continually more and more persuaded, that I was not utterly doomed to destruction."[23] Reading Romans 3:25 (which speaks of God's atonement for the sins of those who put their faith in Christ), he said, "Immediately I received strength to believe, and I saw the sufficiency of the atonement he had made, my pardon sealed in his blood."[24]

Cowper spent another joyful year in Dr. Cotton's company, after which time he moved to a new town. Following a short period of mild depression, which was dispelled as he began to make new friends, Cowper was able to say, "No trial has befallen me since, but what might be expected in a state of welfare." He then reported being tempted to anger: "But Jesus being my strength, I fight against it; and if I am not conqueror, yet I am not overcome."[25]

Sadly, William Cowper's experience did not remain one of prevailing joy. Not long after his recovery he wrote, "I have known many a lifeless and unhallowed hour since; long intervals of darkness, interrupted by short returns of peace and joy in believing."[26] In 1773, he "plunged into a melancholy that made me almost an infant."[27] It was deeper and longer than any previous experience. He had a dream that he was permanently forsaken by God and lived in chronic despair, with only three days' respite, for the rest of his life. In his many letters, he continued to describe his experiences, simultaneously writing poetry, which eventually made him famous in his own lifetime. He credited dejection with having made a writer of him.[28]

In 1787, Cowper had yet another period of derangement. Beginning in 1791 and coinciding with a friend's paralytic stroke, he entered a period of serious depression that was to last most of the decade, that is, most of the rest of his life.[29] He died in 1800. The brave soul used all the spiritual and emotional resources at his disposal to battle a baffling enemy: depression. He never lost his faith throughout the suffering. However, he was never really free from the depression, either.

Some people say that it's just a matter of negative thinking that gets individuals trapped in depression. Their solution is to learn to look on the bright side and develop an attitude of hope. Mr. Cowper exhibited a great deal of courageous hope, which he expressed in his poetry and hymns. Unfortunately, in the end Mr. Cowper's relief wasn't found this side of heaven. His hope sustained him, but it didn't cure his debilitating depression. He was an intensely spiritual man, but something beyond the spiritual realm held him captive.

Many today say that if a person just understands and applies biblical principles to the issues surrounding the episode of depression, it will go away. If the depression hangs on, they assume that the person suffering is morally or spiritually unwilling to do what it takes to solve the problem. A quotation from a Christian magazine illustrates this point of view: "Depression is not something you catch like a cold. It's something you bring upon yourself by free choice."[30] But Mr. Cowper spent most of his adult life diligently applying the Scripture to his problem, with the support of a minister and his family. He wrote hymns and poems showing that he understood the Scripture. It helped him cope with the pain, but it didn't make the pain go away.

There are probably as many suggested remedies for depression as there are people who have ever felt depressed and bounced back. We tend to apply the solutions that have worked for us as a model we suppose should work for others. However, several different kinds of depression have very similar symptoms. Although the symptoms are alike, the causes are different and require different types of treatment. Many times the symptoms of depression are a normal human reaction to overwhelming stress. In these cases, resorting to spiritual and emotional help, linked with a new attitude, is often all that's needed to alleviate the problem. But if the cause is physical, and the person is physiologically predisposed to depression, these remedies won't bring relief, only frustration and self-condemnation.

People today, like Nathan in our opening story, suffer in much the same way Mr. Cowper did two hundred years ago. In fact, medical records going back over twenty-five hundred years chronicle bouts of depression that would not respond to treatment as they knew it. They had vague theories that something physical was involved; they called it black bile. They were never able to pinpoint the physical cause and, therefore, never able to develop effective treatment. For those who suffer today, there is a new understanding of depression based on clinical evidence, and there are new options for getting help that makes a difference in their lives. Although depression may have a spiritual source we now know for sure that many types of depression have their roots in physiological, biochemical, and genetic causes. This new research offers new hope for hurting people who have tried everything within their power to cope with depression . . . to no avail. Perhaps the greatest hope for them is that they no longer have to accept the shame that others would heap on them. Free from the indictment that they have brought it upon themselves, they can seek the solution rather than withdraw in pain.

Spiritual and emotional counseling alone does not always adequately address these types of clinical depression. By understanding the real causes of depression and addressing the real causes with appropriate solutions, people can bring the misery of depression to an end. Some people may think this comment suggests that spiritual help is somehow deficient. That is not the point. Spiritual help is beneficial to anyone who is suffering. But to seek only spiritual help for a problem that may be physical in nature usually leaves the person with the illness intact (barring a supernatural miracle). It may also leave the person feeling like a spiritual failure in addition to being clinically depressed.

We need to ask ourselves if we would suggest only spiritual help for someone suffering from any other inherited illness, physical injury, or biochemical imbalance. Even most people who have a strong faith in God would allow medical treatment for medically identifiable conditions while not excluding spiritual and emotional support. Perhaps the reason we feel differently about depression is that we don't truly believe it can have real physical, genetic, and biochemical causes.

In the next chapter we will try to do away with this misconception so that those who are dealing with a physiological form of depression will not be condemned to suffer because of the misunderstanding. I would hope that this understanding will help those who need it obtain the medical, spiritual, and emotional care necessary to break free from depression.

DEPRESSION QUESTIONNAIRE

If you wonder whether or not you suffer from ongoing bouts of depression, the following questionnaire may provide insight:

1. Did either of your parents show extreme mood swings, going from times of high energy to times of isolation, sadness, and despair?

   ☐ Yes   ☐ No

2. Do you weigh more than thirty pounds over the normal weight for your height?

   ☐ Yes   ☐ No

3. Do you often call in sick because you feel so "low" you cannot get out of bed?

   ☐ Yes   ☐ No

4. Do you find ways to isolate yourself from others by spending hours reading romance novels, watching soap operas, or working on projects late into the night?

   ☐ Yes   ☐ No

5. Has a friend or family member ever confronted you about drinking too much or taking too many prescription drugs?

   ☐ Yes   ☐ No

6. Do you frequently try to cheer yourself up by going out and spending money you don't have for things you don't really need?

   ☐ Yes   ☐ No

7. Have you lost interest in people you used to enjoy or activities that were once very pleasurable to you?

   ☐ Yes   ☐ No

8. Do you often find yourself in miserable circumstances, as if your life was plagued with bad luck or many negative consequences?

   ☐ Yes   ☐ No

9. Do you often become choked up or cry over things that most others do not react to?

   ☐ Yes   ☐ No

10. Do you frequently miss out on opportunities that would be good for you because many of the decisions you make seem to be self-defeating and self-destructive?

    ☐ Yes ☐ No

11. Are you frequently angry about your situation, the way others treat you, and the easier lives that others seem to have?

    ☐ Yes ☐ No

12. Do you have a hard time falling asleep, and then once you do, do you wake up frequently during the night?

    ☐ Yes ☐ No

13. Do you spend many hours in bed, perhaps twelve or fourteen hours a day and more when possible, but you still are left without energy and feel exhausted?

    ☐ Yes ☐ No

14. Are you below your normal weight by twenty pounds or more because you have lost your appetite and food just isn't appealing anymore?

    ☐ Yes ☐ No

15. Do you wonder why everyone makes such a fuss over sex when you hardly have any sex drive at all?

    ☐ Yes ☐ No

16. Do you think about death a lot or perhaps what it would be like to commit suicide and how you might do it?

    ☐ Yes ☐ No

17. Have you been going to a doctor for some time in an effort to treat a pain that is hard to explain and appears impossible for a doctor to cure?

    ☐ Yes ☐ No

18. Is it more and more difficult for you to concentrate, and your brain just seems to work slower than it used to?

    ☐ Yes ☐ No

19. Are you frequently irritable, and do you overreact to things that are very insignificant to others?

    ☐ Yes ☐ No

20. Do you often feel worthless, like a second-class person with little reason or purpose to live?

☐ Yes ☐ No

If you answered yes to three or more and the symptoms you experience happen over an extended period of time, there is strong reason to believe you are suffering from some form of depression. Sitting down and talking with a counselor would be a good first step to solving the problem and easing this negative emotion.

Notes

1. Stanley W. Jackson, *Melancholia and Depression: From Hippocratic Times to Modern Times* (New Haven: Yale Univ. Press, 1986), p. 41.

2. Jackson, *Melancholia and Depression,* p. 42.

3. Diagnostic criteria from *Diagnostic and Statistical Manual III-R* (Washington, D.C.: American Psychiatric Association, 1987), p. 218; hereafter referred to as *DSM III-R.*

4. *DSM III-R,* p. 218, and Jackson, *Melancholia and Depression,* pp. 4–6.

5. *DSM III-R,* p. 218.

6. *DSM III-R,* p. 218.

7. Jackson, *Melancholia and Depression,* pp. 396–97.

8. Jackson, *Melancholia and Depression,* pp. 4–6.

9. Joseph Talley, M.D., and Beverly Mead, M.D., "What You Should Know About Depression," prepared by Merrell Dow Pharmaceuticals, Cincinnati, Ohio, Oct. 1985.

10. Talley and Mead, "What You Should Know About Depression."

11. Lee Willerman and David B. Cohen, *Psychopathology* (New York: McGraw-Hill, 1990), p. 351.

12. *The Concise Encyclopedia of Psychology* (New York: John Wiley & Sons, 1987), p. 302.

13. *DSM III-R,* p. 219.

14. Willerman and Cohen, *Psychopathology,* p. 351.

15. Joseph Alper, "Depression at an Early Age," *Science-86,* May 1986, p. 46.

16. Alper, "Depression at an Early Age," pp. 49–50.

17. Archibald D. Hart, *Counseling the Depressed* (Dallas: Word, 1987), p. 40.

18. *DSM III-R,* p. 214.

19. William Cowper, *Memoir of the Early Life,* in Karen S. Peterson, "Debate: Does 'Wiring' Rule Emotion, Skill?" *USA Today,* July 8, 1991, section A, p. 68.

20. Peterson, "Debate," p. 68.

21. Peterson, "Debate," p. 69.

22. Peterson, "Debate," p. 70.

23. Peterson, "Debate," p. 71.

24. Peterson, "Debate," p. 72.

25. Peterson, "Debate," p. 73.

26. Jackson, *Melancholia and Depression,* p. 138.

27. Thomas Wright, ed., *The Correspondence of William Cowper,* 4 vols. (New York: AMS Press, 1968), letter 3:9, in Jackson, *Melancholia and Depression,* p. 138.

28. Peterson, "Debate," p. 64, and Jackson, *Melancholia and Depression,* p. 138.

29. Jackson, *Melancholia and Depression,* p. 138.

30. Hart, *Counseling the Depressed,* p. 23.

Chapter 3

◆

THE CAUSES OF DEPRESSION

Karen felt that she had married the wrong person about two hours after she said, "I do." It was at the reception that she believed Paul began to change. She just mentioned that she was sad to be leaving so many great friends behind, and he snapped back, "Well, you'll just have to get over it." He had never been that insensitive to her before; he would continue to be again and again. That response established a theme for the rest of their marriage. She would get depressed or bothered, and he would demand that she "get over it."

The longer they were married, the harder it became for her to "get over" anything—especially a few days before her period. In those times nothing made her happy, and everything seemed to make her more miserable. She found herself doing what she had seen her mother do. She created a womb from which she did not want to come out.

During those terrible times of depression, she almost followed a ritual. She began to stock up on junk food that didn't have to be cooked. She preferred things with a lot of sugar and chocolate when possible. She would load the stuff in the drawers of her bedroom and under the bed and on the shelves in the closet. Then with three or four romance novels by her side and soap operas on the tube, she would close the blinds, shut the doors to the bedroom, and not come out for about ten days. When she started doing that, her husband would come in and give her the get-over-it line, but soon he stopped trying to help her. Once she was entrenched in her self-made womb, he slept in another room and carried on his life separate from her. Karen copied her mother, but her mother never went to such an extreme. Karen's mother got better on her own. Karen could not.

Karen started locking herself away when she was about thirty-seven, and by the time she was forty-three, she was spending more time in the bedroom than out of it. Paul had adapted. He had taken a mistress to meet his needs, someone who wanted nothing more than a companion. Karen and Paul lived under the same roof, but they had totally separate lives. The sicker Karen became, the freer Paul felt and the more justified in doing what he wanted to do. They probably would have continued that way until the day Karen died if she had not developed a major bowel obstruction. The pain forced her out of her seclusion and into the hospital. There a social worker uncovered the life she was living and determined to help her.

The social worker thought something could be done. She had seen the pattern of other depressed women moving into seclusion a short time before their period. She had seen others helped with medication and hormones. She conferred with her doctor, and they made a referral. It took Karen six weeks to fully recover from the surgery, but while that recovery was going on, she was recovering emotionally, also. The medication and hormones had a dramatic effect on her. She saw life from an entirely different perspective. She laughed for the first time in years. Her weight started dropping, and she was ready to have a husband and a marriage again. The only problem was that her husband was not so quick to change.

The better she looked, the more threatened he felt. He had learned to live with a sick wife and had learned to enjoy being completely irresponsible. As her recovery intensified, he became more angry and distant. Rather than be challenged by her anymore, he moved out and filed for divorce. A healthy wife was just too much for him. The divorce was sad for Karen, but she didn't let it destroy her emotional strength. Through all of the pain of separation and divorce, she never once went back into the bedroom to hide from the world.

Karen discovered that there is a world beyond depression. It's too bad she wasted so many years before she discovered it. If someone had intervened, Karen could have seen some of the symptoms and learned how to get over them the best way possible. She had some symptoms in common with her mother and others who suffer from depression. Even the age at which the problem got worse fits the profile of depressed women. That her depression came as a part of her menstrual cycle was further proof she had inherited something her mother experienced, something that could be treated.

SOME EVIDENCE FOR PREDISPOSITION

People who experience major depression usually do so between the ages of thirty-five and forty. People with a manic-depressive disorder first experience symptoms between the ages of fifteen and thirty-five, with the average age being late twenties and early thirties.[1] By the age of sixty-five, seven out of ten women and four out of ten men will experience major depression. As you can see, approximately twice as many women will experience depression as men.[2] Although cultural factors must be taken into account, the scientific studies done so far indicate that women are clearly more prone to depression than men due to a genetic predisposition.[3] Karen had a built-in likelihood of depression at some point just because she was a woman.

Scientific studies also reveal that someone with depressed relatives is much more likely to experience it than someone without depressed relatives.[4] When the person is a primary next of kin, such as brother, sister, mother, or father, the incidence is highest. A female like Karen who had a depressed mother had two strikes against her from the outset.

Further evidence of a genetic predisposition is found in a study of identical twins. Since identical twins have the same genetic makeup, the study of them leads to knowledge of genetic foundation of problems. The development of the same problems in identical twins raised in different environments indicates a genetic link to the problems. When one identical twin has depression, the rate of depression is almost twice as high for the other identical twin compared to the rate for fraternal or nonidentical twins or the general population. That holds true even when twins were separated at birth and raised in completely different homes.[5]

A tremendous amount of research is going on today to further identify the genes responsible for causing a higher predisposition to depression. Researchers are also looking at other disorders that coincide with depression, such as migraine headaches. Almost every study points to a physiological basis that makes one person more susceptible to depression than another. The evidence is overwhelming in this area, but it is not the only way some people have higher odds of being depressed than others.

PREDISPOSING PHYSICAL INJURY TO THE BRAIN

If I take a brick and throw it down and smash my foot with it, my foot is not going to do a very good job of getting me where I want to go. It may swell, hurt, bleed, and do all sorts of obvious things that will lead me to conclude that it is a sick foot and I should not expect too much normal walking out of it. When the brain has received a physical injury, it is not that easy to detect. Even people who have a memorable accident, where the head suffered significant damage, will often deny the lasting consequences of the injury. Consequences of emotional problems can come from more than accidents that cause physical injury to the brain. Both disease and medication can produce the same effect as a physical injury to the head, resulting in a secondary condition such as depression.

The most common form of this physically based, chemically induced, secondary depression involves alcohol. Alcohol is a depressant drug. A person who drinks enough of it will be depressed and feel depressed. It has very predictable effects on the nervous system. Ask an alcoholic why he drinks, and the answer might be, "Because I am so depressed." If a person started drinking because she was depressed, she could not have picked a more harmful self-medication for it. After prolonged drinking, the chemically induced depression will far surpass that of the original mild depression.

The abuse of alcohol, the abuse of prescription drugs, and the abuse of nonprescription or illegal narcotics can trigger depression. Research has confirmed that alcoholics and substance abusers have a high incidence of symptoms connected with major depression, indicating that the *physiological* changes induced by these substances may cause secondary depression.[6]

Once a person is addicted to a depressive chemical, it doesn't really matter which one came first, the addiction or the depression. If a person is an addict and depressed, both problems need to be treated in an appropriate treatment center in most cases. Treating the addiction without treating the depression is foolish. But the drug problem should be treated first. Most addicts who get off drugs do not need any medication. They need time because the nervous system takes a lot of time to restore itself to normal. Without appropriate treatment, addicts will often turn back to drugs before the healing process of the nervous system is complete.

The head can be damaged physically with a blunt object or chemically with a drink or a pill. Both injuries will cause emotional distress and often lead to depression. The conclusion to be drawn here is that body, mind, and spirit are intricately interwoven, one affecting the other in ways we may not be aware of. If it is a physical injury beyond the control of the person who is depressed, the person must find ways to minimize the symptoms. If the problem is caused by ingesting chemicals, the person must find a way to stop complicating the problem with irresponsible behavior.

BIOLOGICALLY BASED DEPRESSION FROM THE ENDOCRINE SYSTEM

Karen's depressions, as were her mother's, were brought on by premenstrual syndrome, or PMS. Many women experience mild to serious depressive symptoms related to hormonal fluctuation associated with the menstrual cycle. These imbalances are typically experienced during the time preceding the onset of menstruation, at menarche (when a girl first begins menstruating), at the onset of menopause, after a miscarriage, after the birth of a child, after an abortion, or after tubal ligation.

Up to 30 percent of women report being seriously depressed for several days to a week before and/or just after the start of menstruation. This physiologically induced depression, which was ignored or disregarded for ages as imaginary, has recently been accepted by the medical community. These symptoms of depression are affected by the changes in hormonal balance between the ovarian hormones, estrogen and progesterone. Drugs that block the release of these hormones sometimes relieve the depression and other symptoms commonly associated with PMS. One research study, conducted by McClure, Reigh, and Wetzel in 1970, reports that women who are predisposed to depression are also predisposed to PMS and postpartum depression. The use of contraceptive pills, which affect hormonal levels in women, is also recognized to cause depressive symptoms in some women.[7]

For years the argument has raged about whether the depressive symptoms suffered by many women were real or imaginary, whether they were physiological or just a female excuse to whine and complain. Those who would argue in general that identifying physiological causes for predisposition to depression results in people relying on an excuse to wallow in their negative emotions need to consider the widespread reaction to the availability of PMS medication.

Women who have suffered from depression due to hormonal imbalances have responded enthusiastically to the medication and progesterone therapies available to relieve the depression and other symptoms associated with this physical condition. In the midst of PMS the woman may blame herself for being so moody; she may experience self-pity, introspection, and self-condemnation. However, when the medical community finally began to openly acknowledge that there was a physical cause for the moodiness, women were anxious to be relieved of the depression. Being depressed is painful! Although the person may become dependent on the attention received while depressed, it is not generally chosen over freedom from the depression when that is available.

I would broaden this observation a bit. I believe that when people are miserably depressed, they want help. They want freedom from the misery and a way out of the pain more than they want an excuse to stay miserable. People who struggle with depression are willing to take the blame, willing to try various self-help approaches to overcoming the depression. However, when the depression has a genetic or physiological component and that is identified, I believe the result is *not* that the sufferer says, "Oh, good! Now I have an excuse to stay miserable, and no one can blame me." Instead, I believe the response in most cases is, "Oh, thank God! Now I understand why all my other attempts failed. Now I can take steps to get free from this depression and get on with my life." That is what we have seen in the female population enthusiastically working through the PMS program of Holly Anderson.

I had a secretary who struggled terribly with PMS, and one day I suggested that she seek some help. She went to Holly Anderson's PMS Treatment Clinic, and the results were amazing. She had a miraculous change. Her moods were much more stable throughout the month. There were no more emotional crises that would interfere with her work. She and the women who went to that clinic did not change their attitude or grow instantly stronger. They just corrected a physiological chemistry problem. Once they did, their depressions were eased, and all of their emotions were more manageable.

Conditions other than PMS commonly produce depression as a side effect. Hypoglycemia (commonly known as low blood sugar), hypothyroidism, and influenza are conditions associated with the abnormal functioning of the endocrine system that can also produce depression. Depressive symptoms are often present in those who suffer from Cushing's syndrome, an illness characterized by a dysfunctional pituitary gland. These conditions can be treated by diet and/or appropriate medication. In the case of hypothyroidism, antidepressant medication is sometimes less than effective. Through medical testing the thyroid condition can be identified and medication prescribed to balance the level of thyroxin. Oftentimes this hormonal balance will allow the antidepressant to have full effect.[8] The point is that mood is affected by physiological conditions people may not even realize they have. The most noticeable symptoms may be the symptoms of depression. If people don't want to appear as if they are looking for an excuse, they may try to brave the depression with emotional and spiritual gymnastics, and at times neglecting the basic cause of their darkened moods.

THE IMPACT OF AGING

In addition to the obvious psychological explanations for why more and more elderly people are suffering from depression, we should not ignore physical changes that may play a part in making one's autumn years darken under the cloud of depression. The prevalence of serious depression in the elderly is partially affected by the fact that their biological functions are reduced below normal levels. And the rate of this biological deterioration often has more to do with the genes people were born with than the environment they lived in. Some physiological abnormalities that partially account for the prevalence of serious depression in the elderly are a lowered physical threshold for manifesting major depression, lowered endocrine levels, changes in metabolic and other brain functions that inhibit the experience of pleasure, and side effects from medications being used to treat other physical conditions developed in their later years.

One key factor in depression due to aging is the lack of physical activity. Since the body is a chemical reactor, once the reactor stops moving, fewer chemicals are going to be produced. If we can keep aging people moving and exercising, we can keep the healthy chemicals pumping through their bodies, which will allow them to stay free of depression for as long as possible. Too often the elderly are overmedicated for the convenience of the professional staff in a facility. Walking and doing other forms of light exercise can produce far more wonderful results than medication that merely sedates them into compliance. Anyone with an aging parent who is depressed should first look at the amount of exercise the person is getting and try to increase it.

BIOLOGICAL PREDISPOSITION VERSUS PREDICTOR

Some people are confused by what the word *predisposition* means. It does not mean that we can predict who will or who will not have problems. It does mean that we can determine who has a greater likelihood than others. According to Demitri F. Papolos, M.D., and Janice Papolos in their book *Overcoming Depression,* current research indicates only that the vulnerability to these disorders (depression or manic-depression) is "passed down" (inherited) in families—the way a physical illness such as diabetes shows up in a family pedigree. "Family studies continue to show that the relatives of people who have manic-depression or depression have a significantly higher rate of these disorders, perhaps two to three times higher, than occurs in the general population."[9]

Persons from families with continuing emotional disorders have the option of speaking with a doctor who specializes in genetic counseling. The geneticist can help identify those who are at risk for the disorder by examining a family's history and explaining the risk estimates based on current genetic research findings. This practice is widely accepted for other inherited illnesses and conditions, such as inheritable birth defects and diabetes. As the general population begins to realize and accept that depressive disorders have a biological and genetic base, I believe the element of genetic counseling will also become more widely accepted. This approach can assist families in dealing with depressive illness that is already evident and will encourage them to watch for early symptoms of depression so that treatment can begin promptly. An unattended depressive illness can develop into a chronic condition that has the power to devastate family life needlessly for many years.

The Papoloses asked geneticist and psychiatrist Dr. Miron Baron, of the New York State Psychiatric Institute in New York City, how families react to the knowledge that a predisposed emotional problem (such as depression or manic-depression) seems to have a genetic basis and how they react specifically to genetic counseling. "Most people are relieved," he answered. "The information puts an end to self-blame and guilt. Often, in the fearful playground of the mind, people tend to exaggerate the risk factors, and counseling helps inject reality into the situation and puts things in perspective. As a matter of fact, sessions like this allow the families to vent a lot of concern and work through some of their anxieties. Genetic counseling shows a family how to retain a quiet attentiveness but go on with the business of living."[10] (If you are interested in this area, you can contact one of the resources listed in the back of the book.)

GENETICS AND PREDISPOSITION

The belief of inheritability of emotional problems is not a new idea. Throughout the ages, there have been observations that certain mood disorders seemed to be inherited. In medieval times it was believed that a mental disorder called insani was an inherited disease.[11] However, although ancient medical records and folklore tell of these observations, it wasn't until the last century that genetic theories gained scientific credibility. In 1865, Gregor Mendel observed certain patterns in his breeding of hybrid plants. He formed a theory that was helpful in explaining the patterns he noted. Mendel hypothesized that basic units of inheritance, which we know as genes, were either dominant or recessive.

In his experiments, Mendel observed that the parent characteristics of his hybrid plants were distributed in offspring according to a mathematically predictable pattern. Simply put, if Mendel crossed a tall plant (dominant genes) with a short plant (recessive genes), the result was always a tall plant. The offspring of one tall and one short parent was known as a hybrid, having one dominant and one recessive gene for height. When he then crossed two hybrid plants, he found a consistent pattern in the way traits or observable characteristics were distributed in the offspring: 25 percent were short (indicating two recessive genes), 25 percent were tall (indicating two dominant genes), and the remaining 50 percent were tall hybrids (having one dominant and one recessive gene). Mendel noted that whenever one dominant gene was bred with a recessive gene, the dominant trait was manifest as being observable. If one looked at two tall plants, there was the distinct possibility that one could have two tall genes and the other, one tall gene and one short gene.

Mendel concluded that the genetic description, which was arrived at by carefully tracing the genetic history, might be different from what the physical appearance indicated. Scientists call the genetic description a *genotype* and the physical expression of genetic makeup the *phenotype*. Mendel's research and theories were instrumental in helping researchers understand hereditary differences and similarities.[12]

Variations on Mendel's genetic theories have formed the primary basis for most genetic exploration and continue to be useful to genetic scientists studying patterns of inheritance. These principles also form the basis for the emerging theories relating to hereditary predisposition to various mood disorders. One such study looked at patterns of inheritance for manic-depression in a group of family samples. Researchers observed that the disorder appeared in most generations of the family, instead of skipping generations, and that both sexes were equally affected. Those observations led them to conclude that the disorder was most likely associated with a dominant gene.[13]

A REASON FOR SPIRITUAL RENEWAL

The evidence for predisposition should lead us to cling more to God and His Word than we would if we were not aware that predisposition could influence the way we feel and act. Those who think that depression is just a form of personal weakness try harder and harder to make themselves strong. The harder they try, the more hopeless they find it is to pull themselves out of depression. A much healthier attitude is to accept that they were born with a predisposition to depression and they will die with it. They will never get other predispositions to live with, no matter how hard they try. They have to do the best they can with what they've got. Under their own power, they can't do much. But with the help of God, they can live a life much more fulfilling than they ever dreamed.

When depressed people turn themselves over to God, they allow God to comfort the soul. They look for what God can do through them to help others. So many depressed people have lightened the intensity of the depression by developing a ministry to others experiencing the same problem. Rather than be members of the walking wounded crowd, they become part of the wounded healer group that affects thousands of lives.

A CAUTION ABOUT DEPRESSION

I have been trying to provide a message of hope for those who are depressed. I want to communicate that not all depression is a result of negative choices and spiritual problems. I don't want people to be shamed just because they suffer from a problem that few understand. However, I don't want to lean too far to one side and prevent them from doing what they need to do to heal their wounds of depression. The fact remains that some people are depressed because of things they have done and the guilt they feel over them. Some have gotten their lives into a big mess, and they sit on the emotional scrap pile of the consequences of that irresponsible and selfish behavior. There is only one hope for those who are feeling blue because of behavior that is open rebellion toward God.

The only hope is to come back into a relationship with God. It begins by admitting that the problems you confront are your own. No one caused them but you, and no one is going to fix them but you. Accept that you have created these problems, and then allow God to forgive you for them. God does not want you to continue to beat yourself up over mistakes you cannot undo, decisions you cannot remake. He sent His Son so you could be forgiven, and the sooner you accept forgiveness, the sooner you will be free from your emotional desperation.

The other thing you will have to do is to make amends to people you have hurt. Being irresponsible actually does produce guilt that must be resolved. Making restitution, and living life with the purpose to be responsible, will eventually help you overcome depression. But each time you slip back into your irresponsible ways, be ready for one of the consequences to be depression.

Whatever the source of your depression, I caution you not to blame anyone for it. I challenge you to make no excuses for your behavior. I ask you to do what I have had to do—make the most of it. You can rise above it. You can live free from constant feelings of despair. Your life may not be as rosy as it appears to be for the person who was born with optimistic lenses for life, but your life can be just as rewarding as you free yourself from being a victim and find new ways to win the emotional battle you face.

SUMMARY

When all the information is taken into account, we can conclude that not everyone starts with the same predisposition to depression. Some are more prone than others. Those of us with a higher predisposition will have to work harder to manage our lives so we do not become victims of depression. No one inherits the 100 percent certainty of becoming severely depressed. What is inherited is a greater liability or predisposition to depression.

The good news of the next chapter is that there is hope. We can take action to be free from depression.

Notes

1. Lee Willerman and David B. Cohen, *Psychopathology* (New York: McGraw-Hill, 1990), p. 360.
2. Bebbingon (1989), in Peter McGuffin and Randy Katz, "The Genetics of Depression and Manic-Depressive Disorder," *British Journal of Psychiatry* 155 (1989): 302.
3. Frank B. Minirth, M.D., and Paul D. Meier, *Happiness Is a Choice* (Grand Rapids, Mich.: Baker, 1989), p. 46.
4. Minirth and Meier, *Happiness Is a Choice,* p. 46.
5. Minirth and Meier, *Happiness Is a Choice,* p. 46.
6. William R. Yates et al., "Factors Associated with Depression Among Primary Alcoholics," *Comprehensive Psychiatry* 29 (Jan.–Feb. 1988): 29–33.
7. Archibald D. Hart, *Counseling the Depressed* (Dallas: Word, 1987), p. 99.
8. Al Masterson, M.D., Riverside Psychiatric Group, Riverside, Calif., interview with author, Aug. 1991.
9. Demitri F. Papolos, M.D., and Janice Papolos, *Overcoming Depression* (New York: Harper and Row, 1987), p. 44.
10. Papolos and Papolos, *Overcoming Depression,* p. 53.
11. Willerman and Cohen, *Psychopathology,* p. 30.
12. Willerman and Cohen, *Psychopathology,* p. 30.
13. Nancy Cox et al., "Segregation and Linkage Analyses of Bipolar and Major Depressive Illnesses in Multigenerational Pedigrees," *Journal of Psychiatric Research* 23 (1989): p. 109.

Chapter 4

◆

FREEING OURSELVES FROM DEPRESSION

THE TRUTH WILL SET US FREE

One of my good friends grew up in a very unhealthy home with a mother who was domineering and an unspiritual father who gave more attention to a bottle of alcohol than he did to her. The father was depressed, always had been, and he self-medicated with booze. She felt there was something missing in her life, and there was. In the emptiness she carried with her every day she began to crave fulfillment. Unwilling to find ways that would help her in the long term, she sought out the quick fixes of our society, the instant solutions of drugs and sex that never solve anything. There was no drug she would not take, from LSD to PCP. You name it, and she tried it as a means to fill the vacuum in her heart. Along with the drugs came men she tried to please so that they would accept her and love her as her father never had. She got by with doing things that way for some time. As she started her own family, however, she stopped the drugs, and her life seemed to level out.

In the second year of her second child's life, she hit the wall. The depression and lack of fulfillment began to paralyze her. She was turning out to be a terrible mother, neglecting the children she loved so deeply. As a wife, she demanded that her needs be met with no regard for the needs of her husband. In her eyes the world wasn't what it should have been, and she was just plain miserable about it. So she did what she had done so many times before: she turned back to drugs and alcohol and even flirted with an affair. Her emptiness was not fulfilled. It was only compounded by the guilt she experienced from her irresponsible decisions.

When the drugs and alcohol created only more misery for her, she lost it all. She fell apart. As she sank down by the fireplace in her living room, her face flooded with tears. She could not function. When her husband came home, he found her there in an almost catatonic state. Within a couple of hours she was admitted to a treatment center. There she confronted the truth about herself.

It was not an easy process, but she was able to complete treatment and start her life over, or start her real life for the first time. When asked about her struggles, she related the following: "For me, my life was just one big farce. I didn't know who I was, and neither did anyone else. I faked everything, including my relationship with my husband and kids. No one could fake it better than me, until I ran out of juice. Eventually, my resources were used up. I had nothing left to give. There was no way but up. The hardest part about getting up was facing the truth about my parents. I had tried to deny their neglect, and I had tried to believe they really loved me. Facing up to the fact that they cared much more about their own lives than me, that I was just an inconvenience, almost broke my heart in two. But once I accepted that fact, the fact they didn't love me like the parents on TV loved their kids, then I could be free. You see, once I was able to accept just how bad they were as parents, then I could forgive them for it. As long as I lied to myself about who they really were, I held deep resentment for them. I am the classic example of the truth setting someone free. It set me free, and I am a different human being because of it—a better human being."

This woman's story is no different from thousands of others by people who have sought professional help. Often in treatment centers we find that people are either living a lie or covering up a lie from the past. The lie becomes so important that the individuals start to believe that it is true. They become prisoners to what is not true. For them, hope for healing comes by facing the truth, accepting the truth, and taking responsibility for dealing with the reality that it presents for them. They are no longer bound by the lie. They become free indeed. The words of Christ ring true for their lives: "You shall know the truth, and the truth shall make you free" (John 8:32).

When we base our lives on a response to the truth, we move in the direction of freedom. When we act on incomplete information, or form our beliefs on the basis of erroneous information, we may apply ourselves diligently, yet find that we were left exhausted from the effort and still imprisoned. Freedom from depression will spring from responding appropriately to what is true about depression instead of acting on half-truths or false conclusions that we have drawn prematurely.

The truth about depression includes an understanding of the following:

1. Depression could be the result of a physical condition and could require medical attention. Especially if depression runs in the family, we need a physical examination from a medical professional well-versed in the causes and effects of depression.

2. Depression involves emotions and may inhibit the ability to judge what the best treatment would be. This emotional involvement has the effect of coloring our perspective on all of life. When we are depressed, we need the objective feedback of those who care about us, those who are not lost in the emotional fog of depression, to help us make positive life decisions. When suffering from depression, we need to respond to the other influences of life besides our emotions. If we are unable to do this, we need to allow someone who is not currently overwhelmed by emotional distress to get us the professional help we need.

3. The way we have learned to think and to cope affects our ability to deal with depression. Our patterns of thought may even lead to depression by letting negative thinking corner us into feelings of hopelessness that may not be realistic. Especially if we are found to be physiologically predisposed or genetically at risk for depression, we must evaluate thought patterns for evidence of negative thinking that can lead us back into hopelessness and depression.

4. Depression can also be related to spiritual life. There are times when neglecting spiritual disciplines or disobeying scriptural principles leaves us vulnerable to depression. The Bible says,

> The statutes of the LORD are right,
>   rejoicing the heart;
> The commandment of the LORD
>   is pure, enlightening the eyes. . . .
> Moreover by them Your servant is warned,
> And in keeping them there is great reward (Ps. 19:8, 11).

When we neglect understanding and observing the statutes God has laid out in Scripture, we disconnect ourselves from the source of joy, enter into danger, and lose the rewards of life God intended for those who would take His Word to heart.

There are other times when depression (even if it has its roots in a physical or genetic predisposition) will damage our spiritual life and our ability to maintain a positive relationship with God. If we are afflicted with some physical injury that shatters our dreams, we will naturally experience depression over the loss. But if we are not in a strong relationship with God, we will compound the problem. We will constantly thrust our emotions downward as we rail against God or continue to obsess over why God would allow something terrible to happen to us. The depression will make us feel alienated from God, and the alienation will make us feel further depressed.

One devout Christian man had suffered with depression for almost forty years. Several doctors told him he needed medication, but he refused. He believed it was a sign of weakness and refused anything other than purely spiritual help. Finally, after his wife threatened to leave him, he decided to get professional help that included medication. He explained his recovery this way: "When I was depressed, I wanted a close relationship with God. I desperately wanted to feel His presence and needed Him more than ever. I diligently applied all the self-help prescriptions my pastor suggested, as best I could in my condition, but my spiritual life remained bleak. I grew both discouraged and exhausted. My feeling of guilt accentuated my feelings of having failed spiritually to connect with God in order to receive His help. When I went for treatment and found that I needed some medical help to allow me to function, free of the debilitating depression, I was relieved.

"Now that I am able to face life again, I realize that my spiritual life did suffer significantly while I was out of circulation because of the depression. Now I am able once again to seek God with full strength. I am not exhausted daily by just battling the depression so that I can get through the day. Now I am able to address and deal with the real spiritual problems remaining in my life and to rejoice in the goodness of God on my behalf."

5. Depression is tied in to family relationships. Depression does run in families. Therefore, we may be born with a genetic vulnerability to depression. This is something that all members of the family should understand but not something the family should accept as an excuse to remain in depression. This awareness should give the family a degree of forewarning so that any symptoms of depression can be noticed early and steps can be taken to get help before the depression becomes debilitating.

Depression is also tied in to family relationships through what we have learned from the family. We might have grown up in families where anger was routinely repressed, where grudges were carried silently for years, where people responded to one another and gave attention to one another on the basis of how bad they felt. If we grew up in families prone to depression, and that created a family system that allowed rewards for depression, we need to reevaluate our assumptions about family roles, acceptable emotional expression, life, and how to cope or not to cope with stress. We need to consider every area that might have left us predisposed.

One young woman I'll call Lorna grew up with a mother who held the family hostage to her recurrent bouts of depression and suicide attempts. Whenever the children would make an attempt to lead their own lives or take steps toward healthy independence, the mother would lapse into severe depression and threaten suicide. When Lorna decided to move away to college, her mother tried unsuccessfully to persuade the young woman to live at home instead of on campus forty miles away. She tried the familiar guilt, then the bribery of offering a new car for the commute. Something inside told Lorna that her emotional health required her to move away to college.

During the first week of the semester, her father called to tell her that her mother was extremely depressed. Could she come home just for the evening? It was a familiar pattern Lorna had learned growing up. Mother's depression was the central force that kept the family together. She was expected to assume her role as comforter to her depressed mother, and a support to her abandoned and overburdened father, until Mother "got feeling better." This time she abandoned the role and explained that she was in the middle of classes and could no longer run to the bedside whenever Mother wasn't feeling well. She felt extremely guilty and angry at the weight of the expectations they placed on her. She had no vent for the anger. It simply wasn't allowed to be expressed, especially when Mother was depressed. Mother's depression exempted her from having any responsibility for the effect her emotional demands made on the other members of the family. Lorna felt herself slipping into the familiar pattern of depression.

As the depression took its toll on her over the next few weeks, she spiraled down emotionally, cutting herself off from the fun of her new environment. After all, why should she be enjoying life when her mother wasn't able to . . . and that was partially her fault? She began going home on the weekends. She felt so bad that she took comfort in the familiar role she played in the family. She was able to help her dad with the burden of extra responsibilities forced upon him without her mother's contribution to the household duties. She was a comfort to her mother, and she enjoyed the sense of importance she felt by being needed in such dramatic terms.

A few years later when Lorna became close to a man she loved deeply, her mother became desperately depressed and attempted suicide three times. Each time she let it be known that she couldn't bear the thought that her little girl might leave her and not be a part of the family anymore. Lorna resisted the temptation to put off the engagement and run home to the bedside of her depressed mother. She also found herself battling darkly powerful feelings of depression.

Several years later Lorna went through a stressful period in her marriage and sank into a deep, dark depression, which heightened her tendency toward suicide. She was hospitalized when her husband realized the depth of her pain and the risk she posed to herself. In the hospital the psychiatrist and her therapist agreed that Lorna was duplicating the pattern in her family set up two or three generations ago. The family history they took from her brought out the fact that depression had run in her family for generations; her maternal grandfather and great-grandfather were afflicted with depression, and both died by suicide. However, she readily admitted and accepted that the family ties were more than just genetic. Her mother had learned to use the bouts of depression as powerful bargaining chips in the economy of familial affections. Lorna had to learn to deal with her physiological predisposition to depression, and she also had to reevaluate the ways she had learned to behave in relationships duplicating family patterns that used depression as a means of control.

6. Depression takes its toll on our ability to relate well with others. We hurt people by our behavior when we were depressed. After the depression is under control, we need to go back and repair the emotional damage we did to others, even if we were so engrossed in our pain that we scarcely noticed the pain we inflicted on them. Even in a darkened state of mind, we were responsible for the way we treated others. Just because we were depressed did not mean that our behavior had less an effect on those whose lives interacted with ours. Especially if we have small children who do not understand a depressed state of mind, we need to help them understand that our treatment of them or our neglect of them was not their fault. If we have encountered marital or work-related difficulties, we need to mend the relationships that have been damaged.

People who have hurt others while under the influence of alcohol or drugs may not even remember what happened or may have a distorted perception of what really took place. Once they are in recovery for their disease, they need to go back to those they have hurt and make amends. In the same way, those who are in recovery for depression need to re-create the time they were debilitated and try to help persons who love them recover from the effects of their depression.

7. Depression is a complex illness. Anyone who sees depression as a simple problem characterized from one narrow perspective is mistaken.

The mistaken notion can also prove dangerous if adopted by persons suffering from depression. We need to realize that many contributing factors influence depression and involve body, mind, and spirit. Just as there is no one simple cause, there is no one simple cure. Although we may be physically or genetically predisposed to depression, it does not mean that we can take a magic pill and make life become wonderful. This illness with a variety of causes must be addressed on various levels: body, mind, and spirit.

8. Depression can be treated and cured, even if we believe ourselves to be predisposed to it. "70% of those with a major depressive episode have significant recovery."[1] Even though we may be more vulnerable to depression because of the body's ability or inability to deal with stress, there are ways to compensate and to make life changes that can free us from depression.

DON'T ABANDON THE BIBLE

When we fully understand what it is like to be depressed, we come to understand how so many negative decisions can be made, even sins committed. If we understand, we can develop compassion for those who are depressed; as we understand the condition, we come to understand how God uses the problems to bring us closer to Him. The worse the situation becomes, the more we realize we need the help of the God who created us. The more we understand God's Word through study, the more we understand our futility in attempting to fix our problems without God's help. When depression becomes so debilitating that we can no longer follow even the most basic scriptural admonitions (to pray, to be angry and sin not, to be anxious for nothing, to be kind to one another, etc.), we can use these infractions as markers that tell us something is out of balance and needs attention.

The biblical concept of sin is not erased by accepting that depression is a physical condition with emotional, relational, and even moral implications, or that one can be predisposed to depression. Rather, we can readily integrate the concept of sin with the experience of being genetically predisposed to depression, having this debilitating and destructive tendency woven into the fiber of our being. In Romans 7:18–25 Paul wrote,

> For I know that in me (that is, in my flesh) nothing good dwells; for to will is present with me, but how to perform what is good I do not find. For the good that I will to do, I do not do; but the evil I will not to do, that I practice. Now if I do what I will not to do, it is no longer I who do

it, but sin that dwells in me. I find then a law, that evil is present with me, the one who wills to do good. For I delight in the law of God according to the inward man. But I see another law in my members, warring against the law of my mind, and bringing me into captivity to the law of sin which is in my members. O wretched man that I am! Who will deliver me from this body of death? I thank God—through Jesus Christ our Lord! So then, with the mind I myself serve the law of God, but with the flesh the law of sin.

The word translated "sin" in this passage is the Greek word *hamartia,* which literally meant to "miss the mark" (as one would do when aiming at a target and failing to hit it). In the moral sense it described a principle or source of action, or an inward element producing acts. To accept that we may be predisposed to depression *physiologically, in our flesh,* is to see depression as a real example of "missing the mark" of what God intended for us. Depression can be a genetic deficiency and chemical abnormality; physiologically, there's something missing, missing the norm that God set up when He created the human brain as it should ideally function. This genetic brokenness is an example of an inborn condition we have no control over, which affects our ability to enjoy life as God intended, and at times contributes to behavior that misses the mark morally as well.

If a qualified professional diagnoses depression as the manifestation of a physiological predisposition or biochemical imbalance, getting medical treatment for such a medical condition does not go against any principle of Scripture. Although a few Christian sects' interpretation of the Scripture does not allow for medical care of physical ailments, the majority of Christian churches and denominations accept that there is nothing immoral about obtaining medical treatment for medical conditions. Even Christ Himself mentioned the accepted understanding that those who are sick recognize their need for a doctor. To illustrate a spiritual point, He said, "Those who are well have no need of a physician, but those who are sick. But go and learn what this means: 'I desire mercy and not sacrifice.' For I did not come to call the righteous, but sinners, to repentance" (Matt. 9:12–13).

Some people look down on individuals who need medication to restore their mental health. One such minister took a sixteen-year-old boy into the church. The boy had just been released from a psychiatric hospital, and he was on medication. He became a Christian, and the minister told the boy that since he was a Christian, he would no longer need the medication. The boy trusted the minister, so he stopped taking the medication. A few days later while baby-sitting a young child, he stabbed and killed her. The pastor, when interviewed later, said he would never recommend someone stop taking medication again. He had learned a very expensive lesson. Medication is not evil. In some cases it is a treatment that is a gift from God.

Complete treatment includes taking ourselves as whole persons to Christ for our spiritual needs, recognizing that we miss the mark, assuming responsibility for our reactions or responses to life's difficulties, and realizing our need for repentance (a change of mind that leads to a change of behavior). It also includes taking our medical needs to a doctor. Christ did not imply that all needs were only spiritual; He acknowledged the role of physicians for medical ailments while pointing us to Himself for our spiritual needs. We are not violating God's commands by accepting what is physical and recognizing what needs medical attention. The role of the counselor is to monitor the medical treatment and at the same time help us change our minds and our behavior. God can heal our minds and bodies. He often does so through gifted counselors and physicians.

WHAT CAN BE DONE?

If we or someone we love experiences depression, there are some things we can do to make the least of the problem and the most of life. The first step is to get a complete medical evaluation, which includes physical examination, complete family history to evaluate genetic contributing factors, and evaluation by a competent psychiatrist who understands the physiological components and treatments associated with depression.

We must get the whole family involved in being educated to understand the condition known as depression. As we expand our understanding of what caused our depression and what it will take to recover, the family also needs to set aside any misconceptions about depression.

We require supportive and qualified monitoring of necessary life changes to complement our recovery and maintenance. We need objective help to reassess our approach to life once the medical condition is balanced. That is best done by a health care professional who understands depression, its causes, effects, and treatments (and who also supports and understands our Christian commitment). This person can help in the following ways:

- Unraveling the delusional beliefs developed while viewing life from under depression, and replacing them with true and healthy beliefs that fit with our convictions

- Watching for indicators of possible relapse, and monitoring our medical treatment until the proper prescription is found
- Assisting in the learning of new coping skills to deal with the stresses of life that remain, even though the depression might have lifted
- Standing by as we sort out the emotional, relational, psychological, and spiritual factors that also contributed to our depression and work through any unresolved grief or other issues that would leave us at greater risk for a recurrence of depression
- Helping us shake free and remain free from any addictive-compulsive behavior by integrating treatment of these behaviors into our overall recovery process
- Assisting us in healing relationships that have been damaged as a result of the experiences shared previously, particularly while under the influence of the debilitating depression
- Providing educated and objective input to help us understand the particular contributing factors that affected our depression and to help us construct an appropriate maintenance plan so that we can live free from the effects of depression, even though we will always live within our "flesh," which remains the same

CREATE A SYSTEM OF SUPPORT

Each of us is body, mind, and spirit, an integrated person with three distinct parts, which must be addressed simultaneously. Support that is *not* appropriate to recovery as a whole person is from anyone who excludes the reality of the need for care of body, mind, and spirit. We need an integrated system of support—people working together to help us in our recovery—not anyone who would place us in the middle of a philosophical tug-of-war. We shouldn't

- go to a psychiatrist or psychologist who dismisses our values, beliefs, and commitments.
- go to a psychiatrist or psychologist who discounts the role of God in our ultimate recovery.
- go to a therapist or counselor who believes that there is only one cause of depression and ignores all other possible contributing factors. (That's like going to a car dealer who represents only one model and tries to warp our legitimate needs to fit what he happens to offer.)
- go to a counselor or pastor who believes that all depression is the result of a spiritual lack of faith or disobedience on our part and can be cured without responsibly facing the medical realities known to cause depression.

- go to a counselor who condemns us as being unspiritual for accepting help from medical doctors and counselors who are experienced in dealing with depression.
- look to a counselor to help us reestablish a stable view of life if the person's therapeutic principles or worldview is opposed to our biblical position.

  For example, we shouldn't follow the counsel of someone who does not believe that there are clear-cut biblical guidelines for sin and accountability for wrong behavior. We will find ourselves in a philosophical struggle instead of together agreeing on the goal and working together to reach it. The person may try to get us to accept behavior we know to be wrong and may try to erase true moral guilt instead of assisting us to acknowledge the wrong and find God's power to overcome the sin. The counselor's version of forgiveness may be to excuse the wrong as not being wrong because we were depressed instead of helping us accept accountability for our behavior, admit true guilt, and accept forgiveness on the basis of the shed blood of Christ as the atonement for our true moral guilt.
- confide in someone who will break our confidence for the purpose of making an "example" of us, shaming us into submission, or magnifying our past and insisting that we magically "snap out of it" and give God glory.

HESITATIONS TO OBTAINING HELP

Even though symptoms of depression are evident, we may hesitate to obtain help for ourselves or for someone who is beyond the ability to seek aid. There are legitimate reasons as well as unconscious reasons that cause us to balk at taking action. The following are some of the most common ones.

1. "I'm not qualified to judge if this is serious enough to warrant professional attention."

Most people who suffer from depression don't announce it. They may be in such emotional darkness and hopelessness that they see no point in consulting anyone. From their depressed perspective, life isn't even worth living. They may blame themselves or circumstances for their emotional pain. They are usually incapable of recognizing or reaching out for professional help. Usually, those who live or work closely with them notice their inability to function. Our qualification is that we can offer objective and consistent observations of the changes in their behavior and affirm that they deserve to be able to enjoy life.

2. "I don't know how to identify the roots of the problem, so I'm unclear about what needs to be done."

Uncertainty and confusion can cause us to hesitate because we aren't sure where to turn. However, if we realize that we do need help, our uncertainty and confusion could just as well be a starting point. We don't need to make a diagnosis; that's what professionals are trained to do. Our role is to initiate an investigation to get in touch with the people who are prepared to diagnose and treat whatever the cause of the depression may be.

3. "I'm very much aware of the social stigma relating to any kind of mental illness. I'm afraid that if it were a mental problem and people found out, well . . . I'm afraid of what they might think."

Realistically, a social stigma is associated with any kind of mental imbalance or condition. It is more prevalent in lower- to middle-class socioeconomic groups than in upper-class groups where consulting psychiatrists may even be in vogue. There are several ways to deal with this unfortunate reality.

If it is a form of clinical depression that could be seen as a "mental illness," the condition can remain confidential. All medical and psychological treatment can be kept highly confidential. There is no reason for others to know.

The social stigma is changing as our society becomes more aware of the research being conducted on the physical influences contributing to depression. Some have likened the social awareness and acceptance of those suffering from depression to be improving much in the same way the social climate has changed over the last thirty years regarding those who suffer with alcoholism.

We may feel that the family is all alone with this type of problem, but that isn't the case. Depression is one of the most common illnesses. We may find that if family members choose to become more open about the effects of depression on them, many people we know would confide that this problem has touched someone related to them, also. Regardless of which perspective is most comforting to us in terms of grappling with the possible social ramifications, in the long run, getting treatment for the depression and seeing a loved one able to enjoy life will be much less damaging than keeping up a false front while the individual's life disintegrates.

4. "I'm afraid of how a diagnosis of some sort of mental disorder would affect the person's image."

Depression distorts a realistic self-concept. Remember, the truth will bring freedom. A person who is suffering may not be able to see the good in himself. He is fragile. Trying to bolster self-esteem, pretending that his behavior is not a problem, only enables the depression to continue to keep him trapped within a negative self-concept. If he is in the care of someone who understands the complex nature of depression, the health care provider will be able to get to the root of the self-depreciation and deal with it honestly instead of allowing him to continue in denial.

5. "If we seek some kind of treatment, it could have negative consequences in terms of future career opportunities."

What we must face and hold in the forefront of our thoughts is that untreated depression can be deadly. We need to be realistic about the possible social and financial fallout of being classified in the minds of others as "unstable" and plan to do whatever is necessary to minimize any negative reactions from people who don't understand. However, there is the distinct possibility that not getting treatment for serious depression will leave us more deeply and permanently hurt than getting treatment and risking the reaction of those who may find out.

6. "We don't have the kind of money it takes to get treatment."

A lack of finances or insurance does not have to stop us from getting help for someone who is seriously depressed. If we are truly in a financial bind, financial support is available. One nonprofit program is available by calling the National Suicide Prevention Hotline ([800] 333-4444). The foundation provides comprehensive and intensive care at residential treatment centers. If we qualify, we can receive up to 100 percent coverage for all professional services, including transportation, supplemental income, and insurance payments. The foundation can also provide local referrals.

If we have insurance and are not sure how much it would cover or if it would cover this particular health problem, we may be intimidated by trying to decipher the insurance manual. All we need to do is call the counselors at New Life Treatment Centers or another competent treatment program. It is their job to make sense of the insurance manual and find out exactly what will and will not be covered. All we need to do is make the call, explain the situation, and tell them the name and policy number of our insurance plan, and they will do the investigation to determine what kind of help will be covered. Some doctors and therapists are set up to accept just what the insurance will pay for a financially troubled family. If we have some resources, with or without insurance, some care plan can be made to work for us. Many plans work on a sliding fee scale, based on our ability to pay.

If we consult a treatment center first and counselors find that our insurance or lack of finances makes their program out of our range financially, they will have referrals to others who can supply the care we need that will fit within our budget.

Much of the hesitation to deal with the financial aspect of getting treatment is an element of shame. It can be very frustrating and embarrassing to know that someone we love needs help and we aren't in a financial position to cover the cost of the care. This situation is common, although that doesn't make it any less painful for the family. The point is that the counselors who help people get into treatment are careful *not* to make us feel like second-class citizens just because we have to deal with financial difficulties along with the depression. Once we reach out for help and confide in a trained counselor, we will find a measure of relief from the shame because the person will help us find appropriate care without having to repeatedly discuss our financial situation.

What can we do about a depressed person who doesn't value herself enough to invest in care? We need to have some objective input. A depressed person may not be able to trust that there is any help available. Therefore, she concludes it is a waste of money to seek treatment. She also sees herself as a burden or a worthless person. We know better on both counts. There is help available, and it is worth whatever it takes to bring her back to being able to enjoy life.

Depressed people may view life in black-and-white, either-or terms: it's either getting Christmas gifts for the kids or getting treatment for themselves. In reality there is usually an option to integrate a financial plan that includes medical treatment for depression with a plan that allows the rest of the family to enjoy life as well.

7. "The person won't go to a counselor."

There are many misconceptions about the causes and cures of depression. Often a person erroneously thinks that during therapy he will open up his troubled soul, and someone will point out where he is wrong and tell him how to change. It's no wonder there are resistance and defensiveness when one fears an attack.

The way we start to influence a depressed person toward getting help is to point out that it may be something physical over which he has no control. It may be not a moral failure on his part but a biochemical imbalance. This reduction in fear and shame is sometimes all it takes to open the door of communication. No one wants to be miserable. Sometimes the resistance is a defense against an imagined attacker. Perhaps we won't start with a commitment to go into a full-blown treatment program. Perhaps the first step is to encourage the depressed person to agree to join us in finding out the possible causes of the depression. We defuse some of the defensiveness and show him that we're not blaming him for the condition.

If a person is dangerously depressed and shows signs of suicidal tendencies, we may need to intervene without his initial agreement. That may mean planning and initiating an intervention to get him into treatment, much like an intervention that would be used to get an alcoholic or drug abuser into treatment. We can discuss this possibility by calling a competent treatment program.

8. "If this problem runs in the family, probably nothing can be done to reverse it or make it better."

On the contrary, if the predisposition to depression is due to genetic factors, something can be done. If we have spent our lives trying to deal with a medical problem without medical care, discovering that it really does run in the family can be the first step toward freedom. We will be more likely to abandon home remedies that do not work to find the ultimate resolution to the problem.

9. "I am a Christian. It seems to me that if I had enough faith, I could pray for someone and see the depression removed. Jesus said that if we had faith the size of a grain of mustard seed, we could say to this mountain, 'Be removed and cast into the sea,' and it would happen. Maybe what I really need to do is to develop my faith in God and pray more fervently that this depression will be cast away."

It is true that faith can remove mountains. We all have probably heard stories of individuals who struggled with depression, prayed fervently, and saw the depression miraculously cured. God does heal in miraculous ways, and it is always a beautiful thing when He does. We need to give God glory for His mighty miracles and not discount them just because they have not been our experience. However, most people who have an active faith in God and suffer with depression in the family have prayed and made many of the other spiritual appeals to God to intervene on their behalf. Yet for some reason, the depression remains to be dealt with.

One thing we need to keep in mind is that we usually hear only of the miraculous healings. It's not often that someone is asked to stand up and give testimony of a heroic struggle against depression that has not yet resulted in a cure. Just as we acknowledge that God does heal depression miraculously at times, we cannot deny that God also chooses to miraculously heal other physical illnesses. Yet God allows doctors to provide the means of healing for some people who pray every bit as fervently as the one who is healed miraculously. Just as we would probably not allow someone we love to suffer and possibly die of diabetes because we insisted that God heal her miraculously without the use of insulin, we need to acknowledge that God might choose not to heal depression miraculously but instead with medications that can balance irregular brain chemistry.

10. "I know that I should do something, but I'm afraid of the emotional toll it will take on our family."

This comment is typical of an enabler, who would rather go through a long and lingering horrible existence than do whatever it takes to resolve the problem now. This reaction is typical of our society—to just hope and pray and wish that the problem will magically go away. It won't until we are willing to experience pain today so we won't have to experience it tomorrow or the rest of our lives.

11. "What if I suggest treatment and it doesn't work?"

Treatment doesn't work. The person who is obtaining help has to work treatment. It is not our job to ensure the outcome of treatment for someone else. It is our responsibility to do whatever we can to assist the person to obtain the help needed. Once we have done that, even if the person does not succeed in treatment, we can rest assured that we have done everything possible to improve and address the problem.

Fear and confusion have tremendous power to hold people captive. When we fear that a loved one may be predisposed to depression, we usually contend with an element of confusion as well. Many hesitations are valid. Research confirms some of the concerns: depression runs in families and often has its roots in physiological, genetic, psychological, and environmental factors. For those of us in a situation where we may be able to help, there are lives at stake, attitudes to weigh, and possible consequences to consider in approaching the problem of depression. This is especially true if there is evidence of predisposition to depression in the family history. We may be the only link to a world of sanity and peace. Remember, we are not responsible for the outcome, only the need to do whatever we can to help.

When we are called upon to help someone, we need to trust God. God is in control. He can use doctors; He can remove the thorn in the flesh to teach us to depend on His grace; He can miraculously heal; He can bring relief through applying His precepts and understanding His truth. Our part is to do what we can and leave the rest to God. We live in a generation where there is an understanding of the various causes of depression. We need to take whatever steps we can to maintain balance in body, mind, and spirit. That requires a "one day at a time" approach to life, acknowledging our weaknesses, and reaching out to others for the help that we need medically, spiritually, physically, emotionally, and socially.

DEPRESSION ASSISTANCE AND SUPPORT CHECKLIST

Go over the following checklist to ensure everything possible has been done to help the individual who is showing signs of depression.

_____ I have consulted a medical professional who is knowledgeable in physiological factors that may influence depression.

_____ I have had a complete physical examination with the focus on identifying any physiological factors that could be contributing to my depression.

_____ I have given my physician a family history for the purpose of tracking possible familial factors (both genetic and environmental) that affect my tendency toward depression.

_____ I have cooperated by participating in whatever treatment and medical program determined necessary to balance my physiological imbalance (this includes consistency and proper dosages of medication, honest communication with doctors, and dealing with the other elements that contribute to the depression through therapy and spiritual development).

My medical support consists of: _____

_____

_____

_____ I have revealed the use of any other medications, mood-altering substances, drugs, and alcohol to my health care providers.

_____ I have put a stop to self-medicating addictive-compulsive behaviors, or I am willing to go into a recovery program for those addictions that could cloud the issues related to the depression.

I have educated myself on the facts known about depression in the following ways:

_____ Reading books

_____ Attending seminars

_____ Talking with health care providers

_____ Entering an inpatient treatment program

_____ Entering an outpatient treatment program

_____ Studying related Bible passages

_____ Participating in therapy

_____ Other: _____

My family members have educated themselves on the known facts about depression in the following ways:

_____ Reading books

_____ Attending seminars

_____ Talking with my health care providers

_____ Participating in an inpatient treatment program

_____ Participating in an outpatient treatment program

_____ Studying related Bible passages

_____ Participating in family therapy or counseling sessions

My emotional support consists of: _____

_____

_____

The following people will help me seek the truth and assistance I need without condemning me:

_____

_____

My psychological support consists of: _____

The support group that is available to help me deal with the issues troubling me is:

_____

Meeting place: _____ Day and time: _____

A therapist who specializes in dealing with persons with a family history of depression and agrees with my spiritual beliefs is:

_____

My spiritual support consists of: _____

_____

The church where I regularly meet together with other Christians is:

_____

Christian-based programs available to deal with some of the stresses and family issues related to my depression are:

_____

_____

A pastor I trust to help me integrate my spiritual life with my other struggles is:

_____

A church group that would offer prayer support for my depression is:

_____

I can confide in them by: _____

My confidant or spiritual mentor is: _____

When we come to believe that we may be predisposed to depression, one of the dangers is that we will use this belief as an excuse for not taking action to help ourselves. This checklist gives us plenty of opportunity to consider how much we have actually done to deal with our depression or that of a loved one. Even if we are predisposed to depression, there are many contributing factors to be addressed, and there is help available for every contributing factor. Depression, even depression that runs in families, can be cured. This list is a starting point. If we have not yet done the things listed above, that is where we need to begin. The professionals who are experts in healing body, mind, and spirit will be better able to advise us concerning what can be done to receive the kind of healing available for our unique condition.

Note

1. Lee Willerman and David B. Cohen, *Psychopathology* (New York: McGraw-Hill, 1990), p. 345.

Chapter 5

◆

FREEING OUR CHILDREN FROM DEPRESSION

Katie was the youngest of three children. She was bright and pretty and outgoing. She loved life, and it seemed that she loved everyone around her. There was something very special about her that attracted people to her. Her mother loved her dearly and was grateful she had decided to have one more child. She told several of her friends that Katie was the love of her life.

Katie's mother noticed a marked change in her at the age of twelve. Katie became isolative, and the sparkle was gone from her eye. She no longer enjoyed being around people, and it seemed she had lost her love for life. She seldom wanted to be with her friends. Her mother was worried.

Katie's mom talked to her friends about the problem and was assured it was just an adolescent adjustment reaction. But her mother had seen the adjustment into adolescence with her other two children, and this one seemed much more difficult with more marked struggles than she had observed before.

When Katie's appetite went away and she started to lose a considerable amount of weight, her mother sought professional help. She called a local child psychologist she had met through her church. She scheduled an appointment for herself, and she laid out her observations about Katie. The counselor confirmed that the behavior was probably not normal and arranged for Katie and her mother to come in together.

What the counselor saw in Katie was dramatically different from the way her mother had described her. Although her mother knew there was a problem, the visions of the old Katie were so prevalent that she was unable to see how severely the girl was suffering. As the counselor told her mother later, it was a brave thing to bring her in and a good thing for Katie.

After some weeks of therapy, Katie dropped the bombshell that explained the dramatic change in her behavior and mood. She finally told her therapist the source of her pain. Katie had been sexually molested by the father of one of her friends. A notification of the authorities followed, and the man was arrested.

Katie continued in counseling and was able to resolve many of the confusing thoughts and emotions she had experienced. Her depression lifted as her sessions freed her to discuss her pain with the counselor she trusted so much. Because the mother was observant and sharp enough to act, she saved her daughter from what could have been years of suffering. Katie's mother sets a good example for all of us to be aware of our children's pain and to avoid brushing off every problem as a phase or a stage. The facts are that more and more children are experiencing emotional trauma, and they desperately need our help.

The rate of depression and the accompanying rate of suicide are soaring in America. Since World War II the rate of suicide, usually preceded by depression, has risen over 500 percent.[1] Just because children in our culture are experiencing this devastation as a group does not mean that we should throw up our hands in despair. There are things we can do to prevent depression in our children before it develops, identify the early signs and symptoms when they occur, and get appropriate help that will free our children should they suffer from depression.

POSSIBLE CONTRIBUTING FACTORS

Physiological Factors

As with adults, some children are physiologically predisposed to depression. Physiological influences need to be diagnosed as such and treated promptly. We can begin early to help our children understand the relationship of the health of body, mind, and spirit. We can protect them from formulating a darkened self-image and worldview by having the depression treated immediately. Undiagnosed and untreated depression leaves them on their own to assign meaning to their troubled feelings. Their conclusions will tend to be egocentric. Since children view the world as revolving around them, they may decide that they are at fault for not being able to shake free of something that is a medical problem. The understanding of the physiological component can be a great relief to children, especially adolescents, who may condemn themselves for not being able to be happy like everyone else.

Here are some preventive measures we can take if children are in families with a history of depression that would indicate a predisposition to depression for the children:

- Get professional help for any adults in the family who suffer from depression, and follow through with advised family therapy.
- Work to build up a positive and realistic self-image in the children.
- Make sure they get a healthy, well-balanced diet, plenty of exercise, plenty of rest, and nourishment for the spiritual being.
- Help the children develop effective stress management and coping skills.
- Monitor what is going into their minds by way of television, music, books, and so on.

Children's responses to life will be determined in large part by how they view themselves, this world, their parents, and God. This view will be shaped in some way by everything that enters the mind.

Societal Factors

Since the rates of depression and suicide have escalated dramatically, we cannot attribute all depression in children to genetics or physiological imbalances; societal and environmental factors must also be considered seriously. Parents can be aware of these undermining influences and work to counteract them in their own home and family.

It is no mystery that children need their parents to care for their needs, to protect and nurture them as they develop. When the children are deprived of having their needs met by their parents, as God intended, they are left to cope in whatever way they can. The breakup of the family, the soaring divorce rate, the prevalence of single-parent homes, demanding financial realities, both parents working away from the children, and the proliferation of child abuse and neglect—all are indications of a society that is not adequately prepared to meet the developmental needs of our children.

These are social realities. Most parents who find themselves in one of the categories noted above did not choose to be there. The bottom line is that as we put our priorities in order, we need to do all we can to design a life-style to be available to our children, providing protection and nurture and attending to their needs as best we can. If we are unable to meet their needs, we must overcome whatever shame may be associated with that confession and reach out for help from others. Parenting help can be found through the extended family, government-sponsored programs, church programs, parenting support groups, the local chapter of the Parent Teacher Association, books, tapes, and other educational programs.

Depressing Social Messages

On a recent Sunday in church we had the pleasure of seeing the three- to five-year-olds perform. Of course, all the proud parents were straining their necks to see how their stars looked. They did a great job of entertaining us and a fair job of singing. It was the song they sang that got to me. The title was "I Am One Important Kid." To hear those great-looking kids sing about how important each one was to God was a tear-jerking experience, especially in light of how devalued so many of our children feel today.

Our society is sending strong negative messages about the value of human life, the relative worth of individuals, and the future of our world. These messages, which have permeated most facets of our society, influence our children's minds as they develop a view of life. These beliefs are often subtle, but they are being mixed in with the concepts we are trying to teach our children to help them build a strong foundation for life. Unless we counteract them before our children adopt them as truth, we will have much greater difficulty undoing the damage later.

Society's message #1: We are nothing special.

Some people take animal rights very seriously. They speak out against what they see as abuses of animals, and at times others fear the activists are saying that creatures are more important than the creation created in God's image. The message many of our children hear is that we're all just animals in the evolutionary process. These messages come from a variety of sources.

Animal rights groups oppose the use of animals in medical research in efforts to save human lives from deadly diseases. They oppose the timber industry for destroying land and endangering the spotted owl in the Pacific Northwest, and families are affected economically. In a family where Daddy has lost his job due to the economic downturn, what conclusion might the children come to about the value of human life compared to animal life?

In many ways, a troubling message is being proclaimed, one that some interpret as saying we are all animals of equal worth who must therefore share the planet equally. This message affects our children and how they think about the nature of being human. These ideas, added to much of the teaching of evolutionary theory as though it were fact, can lead some children to believe that they are really no more significant than any other animal. And that simply is not true!

Our counteracting message: As human beings we are special.

We need to teach our children their exceptional place in God's scheme of things. They need to learn early in life what God tells us in Genesis 1:26–31:

> God said, "Let Us make man in Our image, according to Our likeness; let them have dominion over the fish of the sea, over the birds of the air, and over the cattle, over all the earth and over every creeping thing that creeps on the earth." So God created man in His own image; in the image of God He created him; male and female He created them. Then God blessed them, and God said to them, "Be fruitful and multiply; fill the earth and subdue it; have dominion over the fish of the sea, over the birds of the air, and over every living thing that moves on the earth." And God said, "See, I have given you every herb that yields seed which is on the face of all the earth, and every tree whose fruit yields seed; to you it shall be for food"; . . . and it was so. Then God saw everything that He had made, and indeed it was very good.

We need to take every opportunity to reinforce this belief: we are made in the image of God. Animal life and plant life were created to be under our dominion and to be used to meet our needs. That does not mean we become cruel or irresponsible in our responsibility to care for the earth. However, it clearly does *not* mean that we are just like the other animals and that their lives are as valuable as human life. There is a crucial distinction.

Society's message #2: Our lives are worthwhile only if we can contribute "something of value" to this world.

With the proliferation of abortion and euthanasia, the justification for ending human lives becomes a discussion of usefulness, the ability to survive on their own without support, the burden they represent to others, and their prospective status in society. These attitudes permeate the beliefs of adults and affect our children's self-concept.

Our counteracting message: Our lives are worthwhile for who we are, not just for what we do.

As parents, we need to let the truth that our children are valuable because they're unique creations sink deeply into our hearts and minds. We may still be evaluating our children (and ourselves) on the basis of performance rather than giving acceptance and affirmation for their unique makeup and attributes.

We won't get very far trying to lecture a four-year-old about being valued for who we are as opposed to what we do, but we can begin teaching with simple examples. Here's one used by a family I know who just had a baby. They would talk to their older daughter and say, "Look at Haley. What can she do? Scream and cry and go to potty in her diaper . . . but do we love her? YES! Because she is precious and God made her special. Someday she will learn to do more things. Will we love her more then? NO! Your brother can do more things than Haley. Do we love Taylor more than Haley because now he can help carry things to the trash? NO! Why do we love him? Because he's special. Why do we love Haley? Because she's special and God gave her to us. Why do I love you?" The girl replies, "Because I'm special." Right. Over and over they play the game. Over and over they reinforce the understanding that we are valued because of our inherent worth as the unique masterpiece created by the master Creator.

Society's message #3: Life here is futile in the shadow of weapons that could end the world.

The underlying message here is that this life is all there is. If it's falling apart, what's the use of going on?

Our counteracting message: This world is only the prelude to eternity.

We can instill great hope and a sense of adventure in our children by teaching them that we will all take part in eternity. They need to be taught that the lessons we learn here and now will carry over into eternity. Their imaginations can be sparked by realistic hopes of receiving eternal rewards for how well we use the talents and opportunities we have during life on earth. They also need to be taught that we will be held accountable for how well we respond to the difficult circumstances faced during our lives. The main point to emphasize is that this life is not futile; it has eternal significance.

Society's message #4: The goal of life is to feel good and have fun; when we face too much pain, there's no reason to go on.

So many people believe that God's goal is to make everyone happy. They think His entire purpose is to give us what we want, including entertainment. If God is not delivering on His duty, as they would have us believe, there is nothing good to life. And if God is up there allowing us to have problems, perhaps there really isn't a God at all.

Our counteracting message: The goal of life is to please God, to develop into the people He created us to become, as we live lives that display our faith in action.

We need to prepare our children for real struggles and provide realistic explanations of the purpose of pain in our lives. They need to understand that life involves struggle because we live in a world that is broken and under evil influences. One of a child's first Bible memory verses should be, "Do not be overcome by evil, but overcome evil with good" (Rom. 12:21). By helping children understand the nature of evil versus good, they can see themselves in heroic terms instead of just giving up in the face of difficulty or pain. They need to know that God is always watching us with loving eyes. When we cry, He is sad. He sometimes allows the pain to help us learn and grow from our difficulties.

They also need to know that some pain comes from sin and brokenness in our world, and that God does not send all pain. Overcoming the pain and injustices of life is one reason to keep on living, not a reason to give up. Point out examples of people who face injustice and pain that they don't deserve, yet still find a way to bring something good out of the situation. One recent example was the case of the young woman Kim Bergalis, who contracted AIDS from her dentist. She did nothing wrong to deserve the pain inflicted upon her by this terrible disease, and yet she had to suffer through. At one point her family and her doctors felt that she was surely close to death. Every day was filled with agony, and her body was so weak she could barely talk, much less function in any other way. Every day represented additional pain leading only to certain death at the age of twenty-three. However, the young woman courageously faced the pain for the sake of being able to do something constructive to fight the spread of AIDS and to protect others from the same injustice. She faced the pain, clinging tenaciously to life so that she could testify before Congress, asking for legislation that she felt would protect others. Keep your eyes open for real-life examples of people who don't allow pain to make them give up on life.

As we consider the negative messages our children are being bombarded with daily, we need to look for ways to point them out, explain what the world says, and then counteract it with a true and healthy perspective. Lectures don't work very well. Instead, we can find interesting people who are living examples of what we are trying to teach and use their lives as role models. We can look at the newspaper with new eyes, obtain books that reinforce these values from our local library or bookstore, and watch for specific video selections. Please note that it's not just the content of these messages that will teach our children they are valued; it's the time we spend with them to convey the message. The way we spend our resources (time, attention, money, etc.) demonstrates what we really value. If we don't have the time to spend with our children to explain to them how valuable they are, they will feel worthless, even if the words on the video or in the books we buy them say otherwise.

Influences at School

Guy Doud, the 1986 Teacher of the Year and author of the book *Molder of Dreams,* said in a radio interview on "Real Talk," with Helen Fabian on KBRT in Costa Mesa, California, that parents need to be aware of and actively respond to the "hidden curriculum" children get at school. This hidden curriculum is the message they get from the social interaction at school that tells them who they are and where they fit (or don't fit) into the world as they know it. It has the power to negatively affect children's self-regard. Mr. Doud is a Christian who teaches high school, and he also has four young children of his own. He is well aware of the wide range of negative influences that children and teens face at school. From their interaction with peers, children form their opinions about how smart they are, how nice looking or how ugly, how popular or socially inept, whether they are "poor" or "rich," their value within their social circle, and so forth.

We should talk and listen to our children each day—not just ask what grade they got on the spelling test or book report but also ask about who they played with at recess, what happened, who their friends are, and how the day went on an emotional level. There is plenty of stress in going through a day interacting with other children. The teacher or playground supervisor is not always able to respond fairly or sensitively to the conflicts our children face. We need to be there for them daily to help them debrief about the comments and actions of other children. In this way we can protect them from coming to negative conclusions about themselves that may be a misconception based on the attacks and reactions of other children. We can also look out for accurate feedback that will let us know our children need help in developing certain social skills, manners, or coping skills. We will be there to help them adjust to their peers in a healthy way without accepting everything said about them as fact. As we do this with our children, we lay the groundwork for them to learn to base their self-estimation on God's view of them, His unfailing love, and their estimation of how they are measuring up to the timeless, unchanging standards God provides in His Word.

Grief-Related Factors

There is a very close relationship between grief and depression. When someone is grieving in a healthy way in response to a loss of significance, it may appear quite similar to depression. In distinguishing depression from grief, it is possible to identify a specific or recognizable loss causing the grief, but with depression, a specific loss is difficult to identify. What we may see in our children and presume to be depression may be related to unacknowledged or unresolved grief over losses of importance to *them*. When children are not allowed to grieve their losses or are even punished for acknowledging the pain of their losses, suppressed feelings may go underground. Like seeds, they hide in the inner recesses of the children's hearts and minds until they grow and appear again in the new form of depression.

Because of this possible contributing factor, parents of depressed children must take a fresh look at how they view grief and a fresh look at life from the perspective of their children.

Helping our children learn to grieve

1. Allow them to grieve openly without being reprimanded. When there has been a loss of significance to children, we are probably tempted to minimize its importance because we don't want them to hurt as much as they do. How many times have we heard or said, "Don't cry. There's nothing to cry about"? In essence, that tells them their loss is of no importance, and they have no right to their feelings of pain. Some parents go so far as to threaten punishment for the honest expression of sad feelings. When they are dealing with loss, children need supportive acceptance of who they are and what they are feeling.

2. Acknowledge the value of their feelings and their losses. What is important to us, and what would constitute a loss in our minds, is not what is of value to them. They feel grief on the grounds of the value they place on what has been lost. For example, if a teenager comes home despondent because of the breakup of a romantic relationship, we should not minimize it because it doesn't qualify as significant to our way of thinking. Parents may minimize the grief by saying things like, "Oh, well, you were only dating for two weeks," or "There are plenty of other nice guys." We must remember, puppy love is very serious to the puppy! The teen needs from us affirmation of feelings and acknowledgment that the feelings are valid. We should listen to the cry of the heart and make our support and love available as the teen works through grief.

Hillary, age five, found an injured butterfly and brought it home. In her eyes, she was performing a task of immense significance. She loved the beautiful creature and set about making it as comfortable as possible. She collected flowers, "so it can have a pretty place to live, and maybe it will feel well enough to eat." When Hillary came home from kindergarten, the flower that housed her butterfly was vacant. The butterfly had died. Hillary experienced a tremendous loss, which many parents might minimize or disregard. She needed someone to acknowledge that she was feeling sad and to help her process those feelings. Her parents didn't tell her that it was "just a butterfly." Instead, they allowed her to put the beloved creature in a tissue box casket and say good-bye with tears and fond words of affection. The "casket" was later thrown away, but the child had been able to grieve a loss that was important to her.

These are relatively routine or minor examples. How devastating it must be when major life losses, such as a divorce, are experienced, and we tell our children that it's not really a big deal!

3. Learn to recognize the stages of grieving, and teach children to accept them and move through them with every loss. According to John W. James, coauthor of *The Grief Recovery Handbook,* a step-by-step program for moving beyond loss, five phases are involved in resolving grief.[2] He suggests it is important for every parent to learn to counteract the influences in American culture that tell us *not* to grieve. He outlines five steps that we need to become familiar with and teach our children:

First, we are aware that a loss has occurred.

Second, we accept that we can recover from this loss and the pain of the loss.

Third, we identify the components necessary to recover. That is, we identify unresolved grief or undelivered emotional communications related to our losses that might not have been acknowledged.

Fourth, we take action; we do something to deliver the emotional communication that has been held inside. We talk it out, take a visit to a grave, write about the pain, cry, etc., but in some way we *do* something to express the grief.

Fifth, we move beyond the pain. We do that by establishing new behaviors to replace the habits ended by the loss.

Family-Related Factors

The loss of a healthy parent-child relationship, through neglect and overcommitment on the part of one or both parents, can cause a child grief and lead to depression. That is true even of infants and young children. They may not be able to put their sense of loss and insecurity into words, but they will experience the effects nonetheless. We as parents need to accept our responsibility to meet our children's basic needs and order our lives as best we can around their needs. These needs are especially great between birth and age three. If there is any way, while a child is younger than three, one parent should be available a significant amount of the time. If that is not possible, given other realities we must face, it is best to find one child-care provider who will stay with the child to provide a sense of stability, to love and nurture. This situation is preferable to a day-care center where children are cared for by a rotating staff, even if the staff is competent.

The loss of a parent through emotional unavailability can contribute to depression in children. Sometimes when there is a loss to the family, a parent may be so consumed with his own pain that he doesn't face the pain being experienced by the children. His guilty feelings over family losses should not cause him to distance himself from the children when they are feeling sadness over the situation. For example, in the case of divorce or separation, the parent experiences the loss of a marriage at the same time the children experience the loss of security and the loss of a parent. Some parents might feel such guilt or powerlessness in the face of their children's pain that they withdraw. The problem is compounded because the children are abandoned again; one parent abandoned them physically, and the remaining parent abandoned them emotionally. In such situations it is better to share the time of grief and make it clear to them that they are in no way at fault for what has happened.

The loss of a healthy parent-child relationship can also occur through role reversal. A parent with a history of depression especially needs to be careful not to let children take on the role of caretaker. The weight of her depression or unresolved grief can become a burden for children by relying on them to "cheer Mommy up." She should take her problems to competent adults who can help her deal with her needs. Then she as the parent is responsible to help the children cope. It should not be the other way around.

In this regard parental guidance is much like that given by airline attendants when they explain how to use the oxygen masks. They always tell adults flying with small children that in the case of a sudden loss of oxygen, the masks will drop from the overhead panels: "Place the mask firmly over your nose and mouth, then do the same for your child." I don't know any parent who doesn't flinch at the thought of taking care of himself or herself first. However, without a source of oxygen, the parent might become unconscious and leave the child with no one to help. And can you really imagine any parent asking a small child to place the mask on the adult's face, as though it were the child's responsibility? Of course not!

The same holds true for dealing with depression. During the crises of life, we should take responsibility for getting our sources of life in place to deal with whatever problems we are experiencing. Children should not be called on to do that for us. Neither should we neglect the problems and needs in our lives and relationships under the well-meaning guise of helping someone else first. If we do not attend to our own needs, we will be unconscious or otherwise unable to meet the needs of our children.

If we have poured our burdens onto our children, we must stop it immediately. We must make apologies to the children and get professional help. Then we must take steps to help our children or line up professional help for them simultaneously.

STRESSES THAT CAN PRODUCE DEPRESSION IN OUR CHILDREN

Many times depression in children can result from a combination of unresolved grief over losses and other stress-producing life events. These are changes children feel powerless to control or even to fully understand. By considering the following questions about each child's life, we can construct a helpful profile of possible contributing factors that *may* play a part in depression. For all of these questions, answer yes if it has taken place in the last year.

1. Has anyone in your immediate family, or another person in the child's extended family, died?

   ☐ Yes   ☐ No

2. Has anyone close to the child dropped out of the child's life unexpectedly or suddenly (teacher, baby-sitter, relatives, etc.)?

   ☐ Yes   ☐ No

3. Has a beloved pet died or been lost?

   ☐ Yes   ☐ No

4. Has a family member been added to or moved from your home, thus changing family roles and dynamics?

   ☐ Yes   ☐ No

5. Has a treasured possession been lost, stolen, or destroyed?

   ☐ Yes   ☐ No

6. Has your child lost a close friend through death or a move?

   ☐ Yes   ☐ No

7. Has your child been a witness to violent behavior or crime?

   ☐ Yes   ☐ No

8. Has your child viewed frightening events, violent behavior, crime, or explicit sexual behavior through some form of media?

   ☐ Yes   ☐ No

9. Have there been increased tensions between you and your spouse or an increase in the frequency and intensity of arguments between the two of you?

   ☐ Yes   ☐ No

10. Have the parents of one of your child's friends divorced, leaving the playmate dealing with separation from a parent?

    ☐ Yes   ☐ No

11. Have you and your spouse separated or divorced?

    ☐ Yes   ☐ No

12. If parents are no longer married to each other, has either parent entered into a serious new romantic relationship?

    ☐ Yes   ☐ No

13. Have schedule changes or changes in living arrangements caused your child to see less of you or your spouse?

    ☐ Yes   ☐ No

14. Has your child started school, changed schools through a move, graduated to a new school, or finished school?

    ☐ Yes   ☐ No

15. Has your child experienced marked rejection or the death of an important dream (for example, hoping to make a sports team or win some competition, only to lose)?

    ☐ Yes ☐ No

16. Have you or your spouse experienced serious illness, injury, or depression that had a noticeable effect on the family?

    ☐ Yes ☐ No

17. Is a family member abusing drugs or alcohol?

    ☐ Yes ☐ No

18. Has your child struggled with issues related to gender confusion?

    ☐ Yes ☐ No

19. Has physical, emotional, or sexual abuse taken place in your home or in a home where the child spends time?

    ☐ Yes ☐ No

20. Has your child had a serious or prolonged illness, or is the child adjusting to limitations of dealing with a chronic or progressive disease?

    ☐ Yes ☐ No

21. Has your child experienced the development of secondary sexual characteristics (growth spurt, breast development, voice change, onset of menstruation, etc.)?

    ☐ Yes ☐ No

22. Has your child not yet experienced the development of secondary sexual characteristics when most peers have?

    ☐ Yes ☐ No

23. Has your child been injured so severely that normal activities are no longer possible?

    ☐ Yes ☐ No

24. Do your child's biological parents come from families that have experienced depressive disorders or symptoms?

    ☐ Yes ☐ No

25. Has your child been compared to other siblings or peers who are excelling beyond the level of the child's achievement?

    ☐ Yes ☐ No

26. Does your child have a problematic relationship with a teacher or other significant adult authority figure?

    ☐ Yes ☐ No

27. Has your child been the target of scorn, teasing, or rejection from peers?

    ☐ Yes ☐ No

28. Is your child punished for or otherwise discouraged from openly expressing anger in appropriate ways (if your internal response is to wonder whether there are any appropriate ways to express anger, that's a good sign that the answer to this question is yes)?

    ☐ Yes ☐ No

29. Is discipline of the child arbitrary, based more on emotion or whim than on clearly defined expectations?

    ☐ Yes ☐ No

30. Is there a lack of discipline in your home, allowing siblings to harm one another without parental protection?

    ☐ Yes ☐ No

31. Has there been a sharp change in the life-style of the family due to circumstances beyond the child's control: job transfer for parent, loss of employment, financial bankruptcy, jail sentence for a parent, parent entering the job market after being at home full time, etc.?

    ☐ Yes ☐ No

32. Do you and/or your spouse have extremely high or perfectionist expectations of the child and display disappointment when your expectations are not met?

    ☐ Yes ☐ No

This list of questions is given to help us better understand each child's level of stress, pain, and grief. Perhaps we will become better able to acknowledge and affirm the validity of the feelings when we take time to consider life from the child's perspective. However, this list is not provided so we can diagnose our children and dismiss the depression just because we feel we now understand its origins. Our understanding is helpful, but it is not a solution. We should consult a professional who has the medical expertise and emotional objectivity to diagnose and treat our children for depression.

DEALING WITH DEPRESSION IN CHILDREN

A child of any age can become depressed. Dr. Grace Ketterman in her book *Depression Hits Every Family* gives examples of depression in infants, toddlers and preschoolers, young children, and adolescents and older teens.[3] We need to be aware that depression could be a factor in a child of *any age* and be alert to the signs. Included here is a summary of the signs and symptoms to look for in each age group. They are condensed from Dr. Ketterman's book, which I highly recommend.

Signs and Symptoms of Depression in Infants

1. *Facial expression.* They appear sad, somber, or expressionless.
2. *Activity level.* Initially they may display excessive crying or restlessness, but they eventually withdraw and sit or lie still for long periods of time.
3. *Responsiveness.* By three months of age, normal infants respond to a friendly adult with rapid motion of their arms and legs. Depressed infants lie passively, unsmiling, as if they do not see the onlooker.
4. *Failure to thrive.* Although they may eat well, they fail to gain weight, don't develop motor skills, and become emotionally passive. These symptoms may be mistaken for retardation or other conditions.

Signs and Symptoms of Depression in Toddlers and Preschoolers

1. *Stop, look, listen.* At first they are carefully observant of adults around them.
2. *Run for safety.* They run to an adult with whom they feel safe at the first sign of sadness or anxiety.
3. *Demand attention.* When they lack reassurance, they act up. They may kick, hit, bite, or destroy treasured toys.
4. *Yell for help.* Rather than cry, they are more likely to yell and act angry.
5. *Regress to security.* They may regress to earlier habits such as wetting the bed, soiling their pants, having temper fits, sucking the thumb, and acting babyish.
6. *Experience sleep disturbances.* They have nightmares, have difficulty getting to sleep due to anxiety over previous dreams, and often desire to crawl into bed with parents as a source of security.
7. *Cry and whine.* Those who have a habit of crying or whining will be more likely to do so when depressed.

Signs and Symptoms of Depression in Young Children (Ages Five through Twelve)

1. *They are noticeably sad.* They will not tend to cover their sadness with anger as younger children but will cry openly until they reach about age ten.
2. *Within limits they will discuss their depression.* Depending on the strength of their relationships, they will talk openly about their feelings with adults.
3. *They refuse to discuss the problems very much.* Trying to force answers doesn't work when they don't want to discuss the problems.
4. *Their academic work suffers.* They often lack the mental energy to learn.
5. *They become moody.* They may withdraw from usual activities and spend time in their rooms, watching TV or otherwise escaping. They may snap at their parents or act sullen.
6. *Their social lives suffer.* Depressed children may feel different from their peers, fear being hurt, or just lack the energy to socialize.
7. *They may change physical habits.* They may seek solace through eating or sleeping too much or too little.
8. *They may have suicidal thoughts or make a suicide attempt.* Children as young as six or seven may say, "I wish I was dead," or "Why do I have to live?" Few preadolescent children commit suicide, but the possibility is real. Parents must watch for signs and hints children drop.

Signs and Symptoms of Depression in Adolescents and Older Teens

1. *A subjective feeling of sadness and hopelessness.* A careful observer can pick up clues of this in their facial expression, posture, and tone of voice.
2. *Moodiness.* A clear demonstration of sadness and hopelessness, moodiness may well be masked by irritability or anger. Almost all youths have these feelings at some time, but those who are depressed have them for weeks at a time.
3. *A bleak outlook for the future.* They have no plans for the future and express no hope of anticipated happiness after their crisis is over.

4. *Disturbances of eating.* There is a prolonged change in eating patterns, either eating too much or too little. Eating disorders are often related to depression in some way.
5. *Sleep disturbances.* They may have frightening dreams, may have difficulty getting to sleep or staying asleep, or may sleep excessively.
6. *Changes in social life.* They may withdraw completely from social interactions, even by phone, or immerse themselves in feverish social interactions trying to lift themselves out of despair.
7. *Chemical abuse.* They may begin using drugs or alcohol to relieve the depression. For some this use develops into addiction.
8. *Suicidal ideas.* They may leave notes or drawings around that clearly allude to depression and death.

WHAT TO DO WHEN SIGNS AND SYMPTOMS ARE EVIDENT

We Must Not Ignore Them.

When we are aware of signs and symptoms of depression in our children, we must not ignore them. We may want to ignore them, especially if we fear they are related to some lack in ourselves as parents, or if they may be evidence of family problems that are being kept secret. If we are from a family where depression has been prevalent throughout the generations, we may not want to face the frightening thought that our children could be afflicted in this way. Denial in the face of childhood depression can be disastrous, if not deadly!

We Must Not Underestimate the Danger.

According to a report issued in June 1990 by a commission formed by the American Medical Association and the National Association of State Boards of Education, "About 10% of teenage boys and 18% of girls try to kill themselves at least once. Despite the urgency of the problems, only 1 in 5 children who need therapy receives it."[4] These statistics are evidence of the fact that far too many parents underestimate the deadly power of childhood depression or mistakenly pass off the symptoms as normal childhood phases. When young people are killing themselves at epidemic rates and in growing numbers, it is not enough to accept signs of depression as normal. The norm among today's generation of children is to have undiagnosed and untreated depression. We can choose to make a difference for our children.

We Must Keep Our Eyes Open for Clues of Something Traumatic We May Not Be Aware Has Happened in Our Children's Lives.

Sometimes childhood depression is the result of traumatic events that we may not even be aware of in their lives. Children who have been abused, molested, or injured by someone who has threatened them into silence may be afraid to tell parents what has happened to them. They may repress the memory of the painful events so that they are not conscious of them. When that happens, depression can be the result. For observant parents it can also be the clue that leads us to discover our children's worst nightmare so that they can receive the help they need to begin recovery.

We Must Come to Their Rescue.

When our children are depressed, they need us to come to the rescue and free them. To leave them undiagnosed and without appropriate help is to leave them feeling abandoned in the midst of their pain. We do not need to know the exact origins of the problem to get them help. We only need to be willing to acknowledge the symptoms and continue pursuing help until we understand the causes. Then we can lend support as they seek appropriate solutions.

We Must Get Them Professional Help.

The best thing we can do when our children show signs and symptoms of depression is to get a competent professional to make a diagnosis and suggest a plan of recovery. I suggest a physician who specializes in working with depression in children or health care providers who have previously helped others in the family.

This evaluation should include the following:

_____ A thorough physical examination, looking for any physical factor that might lead to depression

_____ A complete discussion of family history and relationships

_____ A meeting between parents and health care providers

_____ A meeting between health care providers and the child for the purposes of observation

After the evaluation the health care providers will give us their diagnosis along with a plan for arresting the depression and initiating treatment. If, for any reason, we feel uncomfortable with their diagnosis or plan of treatment, we should seek a second opinion. We will need to be intimately involved in the treatment program. Therefore, we must feel a strong degree of trust, experience open communication with the health care providers, have our questions answered clearly, and feel confident in the prescribed plan of treatment.

We Must Assemble a Constellation of Support for Them.

We can expedite their recovery by arranging for as much support as possible in all areas of their lives. We may find it helpful to meet with the teachers at school, the Sunday school teacher, the troop leader, and other significant adults to apprise them of the stresses our children are under and ask for their understanding and support. The children may not want their "problem" openly discussed, so we will need to be sensitive to their fear of embarrassment and use discretion.

CONCLUSION

Parenting in the nineties is tougher than anyone ever imagined. As parents, we face many situations that seem impossible, but somehow we make it through them. We must never forget how badly our children need us to be involved with them. We must accept responsibility when they need our help. More than anything else we must be healthy; we must take care of ourselves if we are to take care of them.

One of our children's favorite games is follow the leader. They play it a lot. And when they are not playing it, they are doing it. The scary thing for many of us is that they are following us. We have a special challenge and responsibility to our children to be what they need us to be. We have an obligation to work through our own pain so that we can free them from theirs.

Notes

1. "Suicide: An Update," *Statistical Bulletin,* April–June 1986, p. 18.
2. John W. James and Frank Cherry, *The Grief Recovery Handbook* (New York: Harper Collins, 1989).
3. Grace Letterman, *Depression Hits Every Family* (Nashville: Oliver-Nelson, 1988).
4. Anastasia Toufexis, "Struggling for Sanity," *Time,* Oct. 8, 1990, p. 48.

Section 2

SUICIDE

Chapter 6

◆

THE SEEDS OF SELF-DESTRUCTION

Dr. Clarence Hemingway was forty years old when his second child was born, the boy he had longed for. His passion for outdoor sports and exploration was something he intended to share with his son. It wasn't long after the boy was able to walk that little Ernest was romping through field and forest with his father. He learned early how to handle a rifle. Their annual hunting and fishing excursions bonded the two together in ways Ernest's older sister—and the three other sisters who were yet to be—would never understand. It might have been primitive male bonding at its best . . . or it might have been more. Perhaps Dr. Clarence Hemingway and Ernest shared much more in common than a love of nature. Some believe they shared common elements in their nature, seeds of self-destruction, that would outweigh all other similarities between father and son.

The family grew to include six children in all, four girls and two boys. No one would have guessed from looking at the family during the early years the tremendous weight of tragedy to come. Father and Mother were happy then, even though Mother had occasional spells of anxiety. They loved each other and their children. Dr. Hemingway's practice was growing, and when things became too pressured, they escaped from the hot suburb of Chicago to their cottage by the lake.

During the first decade of the 1900s, the natural beauty was still unspoiled. Lake and stream, field and forest, the cottage nestled in the midst of the deep greens and browns of nature, took them in and rejuvenated their weary souls. The damp, earthy aromas began to revive the spirit with each long, deep breath. The retreat became a place of adventure for Ernest and his father, a place where they could escape together. The boy adored his father and treasured the special times they spent in each other's company: up at the crack of dawn, seated on the cold earth, silently sharing the anticipation of the first tug on their taut fishing lines; wading thigh deep into the rushes, guns poised, absolutely still, ready to bring down any duck fated to meet with their well-aimed shots; hidden together behind the trunk of an ancient fallen tree, awaiting any movement in the brush that might signal that the buck they were stalking was about to appear in their sights. Ernest Hemingway loved his father deeply. His boyish understanding of life left him ill-prepared to suddenly lose the closeness they shared to an invisible intruder.

When the boy became a man, he would gravitate toward the great outdoors in an attempt to reclaim the solace known during his boyhood times at the cottage—the solace that his father began to lose touch with when Ernest was twelve, the solace that would elude Ernest in his later years, just as it had eluded his father.

Ernest tried to understand why his father was distancing himself from him. He remembered times, twice before, when the doctor had gone away alone for a fortnight. Ernest knew that his father was wrestling with a spell of depression, although no one talked about it outright. His uncle had experienced similar struggles, and it seemed to be something no one spoke of. A man needed some time away to restore the soul; that was all. Mother had always filled the void, attending to and entertaining the children as a form of distraction from her own worries about her troubled husband. Ernest remembered the notes and letters that would arrive daily while Father was away. He knew they were from his father. On occasion he had caught the disturbed look in his mother's eyes, the rare wash of tears quickly wiped away, as the note was hastily stuffed into an apron pocket. Mother's ready smile appeared the instant she realized the children were watching her reaction. When Father returned, the depression had lifted, and everyone went on as though nothing was wrong.

Later the children would remember times of harmony and contentment. The dark and foreboding signs were swept away like so much dust that threatened to mar their tidy, reasonably happy and respectable lives. There were eccentricities, to be sure—Father's passion for collecting and cataloging the most minute detail of everything he explored, his compulsive stream of notes and letters whenever he was away, Mother's strong denial and compensation for the unexplained absences—but there was still little to signal the approach of more than life's expected offering of trouble.

Something must have happened in 1912. The doctor went alone to the woods and the lake more often, leaving Ernest feeling abandoned and confused. Little by little the doctor surrendered the pursuits and relationships he once enjoyed. He seemed lost in moods of detachment, anxiety, and depression. Each summer, when the family retreated to the cottage at the lake, Father joined them less often. As the boy was emerging into adolescence, needing his father's strong presence more than ever, he had it less and less. Without explanation, Dr. Hemingway relinquished the son he loved. The boy was left with a void where his father's strength and companionship had been.

Ernest left for the Great War in 1918. It was a year of death. The swine flu took its toll at home, and the war left its bloody stain abroad. He returned home the following year, wounded in body and weary at heart. Needing consolation, he immediately sought out the comforting world of the cottage. He again followed in his father's footsteps, escaping to the cottage alone. In those first years of manhood, he watched as the seeds of self-destruction began to take root and sprout visibly within his family.

A young woman named Ruth had lived with the family for more than ten years. She originally came to study voice with Ernest's mother. In exchange, she helped out with household chores and became a source of friendship and comfort to Mrs. Hemingway. Although the primary relationship was between Ruth and Mrs. Hemingway, she became a well-loved and accepted part of the family. The girls considered her one of them. Each year, the family's summer home was hers as well. No one would dare conceive of not including her.

The summer of 1919 was different. Dr. Hemingway banished Ruth from joining them. That came as a terrible shock to them all. The doctor had become insanely jealous. He accused Ruth of supplanting him in his wife's affections. His delusions of her sinister intent to separate him from the love of his wife made him resolute. His teenage daughters could not understand his irrational ravings. They tried to ignore his strange behavior for a time, but in the end they fought back. The last straw was his attack on Ruth.

Mother had gone to the cottage without them. At home Father's criticisms and vagaries of mood became unbearable. That summer, Mother received a letter from her daughters. They described their father as "excited and exacting." To make matters worse, they were perplexed because he was unaware that his behavior was in any way abnormal. The summer of 1919 might have been what Ernest recalled as the breaking point. His father's condition grew steadily worse after that point.

In December 1928, according to some historians, Dr. Clarence Hemingway picked up the rifle that had been his companion when life was something to be explored, not simply endured. The rifle would be his companion to the end. He closed the door to his bedroom and ended his life.

It isn't clear who picked up the beloved rifle and wiped away the evidence of the gruesome death . . . but someone did. The rifle was kept in the family for years. For some unknown reason, perhaps because she knew that the rifle represented the bond between father and son, Mrs. Hemingway bequeathed the rifle to Ernest.[1]

Cleaning up the emotional debris of the suicide might have felt natural for the family, which had been living in denial for years. His wife said that the good doctor took his life "for financial reasons." According to his brother, Clarence killed himself because of ill health, diabetes and angina, to be specific. Ernest didn't speak of blame right away. Years later, the son who had so willingly and warmly bonded with his father, and who had witnessed the progressive changes over the years, blamed his mother for the man's death. He was never willing to call into question the condition of his father's keen mind.

Perhaps it was too shameful to acknowledge the truth, or perhaps too frightful to face, especially if the children had already begun to notice the seeds of self-destruction as they grew up, stretching and clinging like deadly vines around the family tree.

Clarence Hemingway's brother, Alfred, suffered from insomnia and nervous problems. Clarence's wife, Grace Hall Hemingway, suffered from milder forms of insomnia and nervous conditions along with serious headaches. Her uncle was a chronic insomniac. As time marched on, three (some say four) of Clarence and Grace Hemingway's six children would commit suicide.

Surely, Mrs. Hemingway could not have foreseen that the darkness that finally engulfed her husband would billow into the next generation. Surely, she placed the rifle into the hands of her elder son to memorialize the good times associated with the early years—the times father and son had spent together in the wild with rifle in hand, the times when life was still something to be cherished. Surely, she would have been horrified, as any mother would, if she had known the rifle would become powerfully symbolic of the fact that Clarence Hemingway had passed down the darkness with the light, seeds of self-destruction along with intellectual brilliance and a sensitive ability to appreciate the wonders of nature.

Ernest Hemingway was twenty-eight when his father died. He lived to be sixty-one. In the years between the deaths of father and son, a familiar pattern of depression and paranoia developed in Ernest's life.[2] The pattern echoed across the chasm of thirty-three years as clearly as an echo reverberates after a voice in the wild, almost re-creating the original cry.

Some historians focus on the inescapable alcoholism as the key to the suicide of Ernest Hemingway, and alcoholism certainly had him in its forceful grip. Others believe the alcohol was a form of self-medication used to fend off the more terrifying specter of depression.[3] In any case, at least one companion during the 1950s observed that when not drinking, Hemingway was "morose, silent and depressed." When he was drunk, the same companion noted, "he became merrier, more lovable," and more grandiose.[4] There is no question that as the years passed, he became more and more depressed as he drank less and less. He was hospitalized twice at Mayo Clinic in Rochester, Minnesota—not for alcoholism but for depression and paranoia. Despite two courses of electroconvulsive shock therapy, neither the depression nor the delusions were relieved.[5]

The Hemingway family had been plagued for generations with both depression and suicide, along with related conditions. Ernest did not escape the family despair. Hemingway called alcohol his "Giant Killer."[6] Alcohol might have masked Hemingway's depression and eased his aggressive tendencies, leaving him with a perceived choice toward the end of his life: endure the physical deterioration and suffering caused by the alcohol addiction, or return to the unbearable "unmedicated" state of depression and unrest.[7]

Perhaps he finally came to understand his father's abandonment of him as a young man and his father's abandonment of life. Under such conditions, we, too, might find it easier to understand how suicide could be perceived as the only way out.

By his mid-fifties, alcohol, the Giant Killer, was killing more than the depression. It was taking its toll on Ernest Hemingway's physical well-being. During the last few years of his life, he cut down on his nonstop maintenance drinking under doctor's orders; he drank elaborate combinations of three or four drinks per day but never completely abstained. The reduction in his alcohol consumption was, perhaps, enough to rule out alcohol as the cause of the depression and paranoia for which he was hospitalized and treated in his last months.

Ernest Hemingway's father committed suicide while struggling with severe depression. Later in life, Ernest experienced wild mood swings, sometimes violent, which had already evoked recurrent thoughts of suicide. He had become a living replica of his father, from the list of his physical and mental ailments to peculiarities of habit and personality.[8] Within days after his last hospital stay, which did little to relieve the dreaded bouts of depression, he came to a decision. He returned to the familiar. Again he took up the rifle and headed out into the woods in search of solace. We will never know if he ever found the depth of solace he had known as a little boy, tromping along those wild dusty trails, following in his father's footsteps.

It was thirty-three years after the death of his father when Ernest Hemingway took up what some believe was the same rifle that his mother had bequeathed to him after that fateful day and took his own life. His sister Marcelline's death, two years after Ernest's, was said to be of natural causes. However, her brother voiced his suspicion that it was a suicide as well. Ernest's sister, Ursula, died within five years, and his younger brother sixteen years after that. Both were suicides. All had suffered unbearable headaches, insomnia, irregular blood pressure, and severe depression. One of Marcelline's children succumbed as a teenager to depression, insomnia, loss of memory, and hysteria. Ernest Hemingway's granddaughter made headlines in recent years while in recovery for bulimia and severe depression.[9]

I said in the preface that the problems discussed in this book are connected in complex and powerful ways. No story could illustrate that claim any more strongly than the one you have just read. The alcoholism, depression, and suicides of the Hemingway family were not three discrete problems. The mere facts themselves convince us that the three must have interacted somehow. Current research on the indicators of suicide support this impression. Both depression and alcoholism, two conditions for which there is a comparatively large amount of evidence for involvement of genetic factors, carry with them a dramatic increase in risk for suicide.[10]

RISK FACTORS ASSOCIATED WITH SUICIDE

If we are concerned about someone we love, the following list may help us assess how serious the problem may be:

1. *Sex.* In 1950, four times as many men committed suicide as women. Today males commit twice as many suicides as females. But suicides are *attempted* three times more often by females than by males.
2. *Race.* More whites than blacks commit suicide.

3. *Age.* Suicide rates increase throughout life for males. For females, suicide rates are highest between the ages of forty and sixty.
4. *Living conditions.* Suicide risk is increased with unresolved family conflict.
5. *Physical condition.* Illness or disability increases suicide risk.
6. *Personal loss or failure.* For males, loss of job or socioeconomic status increases suicide risk. For females, increased risk results from lack or loss of personally significant relationships. Risk is also increased by lack of community involvement or personal interests.
7. *Grief or isolation.* Males who are divorced, separated, or widowed have a very high rate of suicide.
8. *Time of year.* In springtime, especially April, suicide rates reach a peak.
9. *Behavioral indicators.* Previous suicide attempts, communication of intent (e.g., note), and a history of alcohol abuse increase risk of suicide.
10. *Psychiatric diagnosis.* Personal or family history of alcoholism, suicide, or depressive disorders indicates major risk for suicide.[11]

By all accounts, Ernest Hemingway was indisputably at risk for suicide. Many of the factors, both environmental and inherited, known to heighten the risk of suicide were apparent in his life. He was a white male, an American of European descent, over the age of fifty-five, and a frequently depressed creative writer with a family history of depression (perhaps manic-depression), suicide, and other nervous disorders. He was alcoholic and ill. Powerfully bonded to his father, a role model for suicide, the son experienced losing him while yet a young man. Late in life, he found himself caught in what seemed a hopeless situation, feeling helpless to change it. He had easy access to a weapon and the skill to use it. In addition, there seemed little recourse for immediate relief of his physical and emotional pain, and he was less and less able to function in life in a way he found meaningful. Biologically, psychologically, and physically, Ernest Hemingway was ripe for suicide.

Hemingway's story is not as unusual as we might think. Of all the many states of body and mind known to be associated with an increased risk of suicide, a family or personal history of depressive disorder is the most potentially lethal. Second in line for the "dishonor" of predisposing one to suicide is alcoholism, or family history of alcoholism.[12] Together, they are associated with most of what may be considered an inherited predisposition to suicide.

Could it be that Ernest Hemingway, along with his father, brother, and two sisters, was caught in a biological and environmental trap not entirely of his own making? Could it be that a better understanding of the biological and environmental components of this human tragedy might have brought about a different ending to the story? Substantial evidence today suggests that might be the case. That their lives seem to have followed a marked family pattern strongly indicates that environmental and genetically inherited predispositions might have culminated in their suicidal tendencies.

Perhaps gaining an understanding of suicidal tendencies in the full scope of their biological and social contexts may save your life or the life of someone you know and love. As you read the following chapters, I hope you will gain the understanding you need to help yourself or someone you love.

Notes

1. "Why 30,000 Americans Will Commit Suicide This Year," *U.S. News & World Report,* April 2, 1984, p. 48.

2. Donald W. Goodwin, *Alcohol and the Writer* (Kansas City, Mo.: Andrews and McMeel, 1988), pp. 50–72.

3. Goodwin, *Alcohol and the Writer,* pp. 50–72.

4. Quoted in Goodwin, *Alcohol and the Writer,* p. 71.

5. Goodwin, *Alcohol and the Writer,* pp. 50–71.

6. Goodwin, *Alcohol and the Writer,* pp. 50–72.

7. Goodwin, *Alcohol and the Writer,* p. 88.

8. Michael S. Reynolds, "Hemingway's Home: Depression and Suicide," *American Literature* 57 (Dec. 1985): 610.

9. Anthony Burgess, "Bottle Demons and Spirits of Invention," *The Independent,* March 9, 1990.

10. Lee Willerman and David B. Cohen, *Psychopathology* (New York: McGraw-Hill, 1990), p. 387.

11. Compiled from Willerman and Cohen, *Psychopathology,* pp. 360, 386; N. C. Andreason, "Creativity and Mental Illness: Prevalence Rates in Writers and Their First Degree Relatives," *American Journal of Psychiatry* 144 (Oct. 1987): 288–92.

12. Willerman and Cohen, *Psychopathology,* p. 387.

Chapter 7

———— ◆ ————

THE LARGER PICTURE OF SUICIDE

JENNIFER

The little girl worked the crowd at her mother's party like a pro. She smiled impishly, brushed her shiny blonde hair over her shoulder, batted her big blue eyes, and tried to pretend she was one of the invited guests. She was used to having to try to get attention. Mommy was always busy . . . if she wasn't drunk. Daddy didn't come around anymore. So, five-year-old Jennifer learned to be witty, cute, adorable—whatever it took to get the occasional hug or pat on the head that made her feel special.

Tonight she wasn't having much luck, even though she was trying very hard. Every time she tugged on a shirt sleeve or asked someone to get her a piece of chicken from the barbecue, the adult shooed her away. Some of them were nice enough to say, "Not now, sweetie. You go and play now." Most of them just brushed her away without a thought. Tired of trying to make new friends, she went back to her mom, whining, "Mommy, I'm bored." She was told not to interrupt the party. Mommy was busy being friendly to a man Jennifer didn't know. "Go get ready for bed," her mother barked. And that's what she thought Jennifer had done . . . until she walked by the pool and saw the lifeless little form of her daughter at the bottom.

Paramedics could not restart the heart that had been broken long ago from neglect and a lack of nurturing. There was no note. Jennifer hadn't learned to write her letters very well yet. One can only surmise what made her get into the pool on that lonely night since she couldn't swim. Surely, she was just trying to get someone's attention. Surely, a child that young couldn't attempt suicide! Or could she?

In 1950, only 40 suicides had been reported for children under the age of fifteen. By 1980, the number of reported suicides for those under age fifteen had reached a total of 142. By 1986, the number of childhood suicides came close to 300.[1] These facts cry out for explanation since the precious children whose lives are represented by the cold statistics can no longer cry out for themselves.

MR. BETTELHEIM

Bruno Bettelheim was a survivor. He survived the death camps at Buchenwald and Dachau without losing hope. He looked death in the face and refused to succumb. He held on to his belief in human dignity. He saw beyond the suffering to find the meaning. After the war, he drew deeply from the pain in his life, studying to become a psychoanalyst and child psychologist. He became renowned at bringing life out of death, hope out of horror. He worked with institutionalized children who were mentally ill, emotionally and psychologically wounded. His persistent care, his gentle coaxing, and his determined love for children that society had devalued and forgotten brought hope and health into their bleak existence. It was as if he was defying death and disrespect for human life all over again. He had defied the Nazi assertion that he and others deemed "unfit or unprofitable" to society should be eliminated. His life and work became a living monument to the value of every human life, no matter how frail, how "productive," how "defective," how young or old. He knew how to convey dignity and respect for human life to patients and colleagues alike.

Bruno Bettelheim loved fairy tales, perhaps because in the stories good always triumphs over evil in the end. His favorite fairy tale was about Hansel and Gretel. He said he loved the story "because they needed each other." He knew about needing people and being needed. When his aged wife died, he experienced a great loss, the kind of loss that can only be known by one who has traversed the seas of life with a dear companion, through storm and calm, night and day, hunger and thirst. However, even after her passing, there were still many who needed him. Family, friends, students, and associates continued to look to his example and experience, seeking out his leadership and advice.

Although he was eighty-six, he retained a crisp, unfaltering mind. His physical health was failing somewhat, but his body was still functional.

Surely, the noble man of such strong character would live out his days like the Jewish patriarchs of old, like father Abraham who "breathed his last and died in a good old age, an old man and full of years, and was gathered to his people" (Gen. 25:8). Or would he?

On a bright spring day in 1990 the nurse headed for Mr. Bettelheim's room, looking forward to the lively conversation she enjoyed with him. Instead of the respectful repartee she expected, she found the remains of a great man who had deliberately taken his own life. One can only wonder and be perplexed that a man who had endured the most grotesque suffering of the twentieth century, and brought hope to so many, could end his own life in that way. His suicide shocked much of the world and caused many to ponder why so many senior citizens are choosing suicide.[2]

Since 1980, suicides in those over age sixty-five have risen by 25 percent and represent about 25 percent of all reported suicides. This age group now accounts for 11 percent of the total U.S. population.[3]

TEEN SUICIDE

The TV movie *Surviving* told the story of two teenagers who committed suicide together. Molly Ringwald, who gained recognition for her acting in the movies *Sixteen Candles, The Breakfast Club,* and *Pretty in Pink,* gave a superb performance as the teenage girl. She and her fictional boyfriend became disillusioned with life and killed themselves by running the motor of a parent's car in a locked garage. While waiting for death to come, they held hands and listened to their favorite rock station on the car radio. The carbon monoxide fumes had their deadly effect before the parents came home from work.

The focus of the movie was not only on the suicides and what might have led up to the deadly choice but also how the two families grappled with the aftermath of the suicides. The producers were careful to provide information for families to use to identify teens at risk and to contact support groups for family members who survive the suicide of a loved one. The movie was a brave attempt to stem the tide of teen suicides and to comfort the families left behind.

Some communities noted a sudden increase in the rate of teen suicides immediately following the showing of the movie. No one was able to prove a direct link, but there was some suggestion that the movie had the opposite effect from what was intended. Could kids have seen the suffering of the TV parents and wanted to inflict the same kind of pain on their parents? Did they want the same level of attention? Did they want someone to cry for them the way the friends of the fictional characters had grieved over their loss? Were they clinically depressed and the movie just pushed them further in the direction their physiological predisposition was already leading them? As in the case of most suicides, there were more haunting questions than clear-cut answers.

We do know that suicide is quickly becoming a primary cause of death for young people. Suicide is now the third most common cause of death among adolescents, after murder in the number two spot. The leading cause of death for teens is automobile accident, and authorities suspect that many deaths reported from single-car accidents may really be uncounted suicides.[4] There is no doubt that self-destructive behavior among teens is an even greater problem than is indicated by current statistics. Statistics from the National Center for Health indicate that one American teenager tries to kill himself or herself every seventy-eight seconds.[5] Why?

INCREASED SUICIDE RATES

I've highlighted these three groups—children, the elderly, and teens—because they are the three segments of the population in which the rate of suicide has dramatically risen since World War II. In following the theory that suicidal tendencies can be influenced by genetic predisposition, we must deal with the question of why there have been dramatic suicide increases in these age groups when there have not been corresponding changes in the gene pool over the course of the last forty-five years.

Obviously, suicide is not solely influenced by genetic predisposition. But neither does the rapid rate of increase in suicides disprove the possibility of biological influences playing a significant role in suicide cases. When an issue has such life-and-death consequences, we need to do our best to make sure that we understand all the possible influences that leave us or our loved ones at risk.

I believe there are people in every generation whose genetic makeup predisposes them to certain conditions that make it difficult to cope with life. Whether or not they have been diagnosed, their internal perspective is clouded, and their emotional responses are influenced by their physiological condition. When people live with this genetic predisposition in a society that gives them external influences that protect against suicide, fewer of them will actually attempt suicide. When the societal safeguards are taken away, and they must rely on internal coping abilities, those who are less able to cope will succumb more readily to suicidal tendencies.

Everyone who commits suicide is not predisposed to do so, just as everyone who abuses alcohol is not an alcoholic. In other words, sometimes it is more a case of secondhand emotions rather than hand-me-down genes that is the driving force of self-destruction. Societal changes have a dramatic effect on suicide rates, regardless of whether or not the person is predisposed to suicidal tendencies. However, when a society sees that suicide rates are spiraling upward, as is the case in American society today, those who are genetically at risk for suicide face a greater risk than at other times. Whatever societal influences affect the rate of suicide in the general population, they also increase the risk for those who have a diminished internal ability to cope with life under even the best of circumstances.

In our societal climate that seems to breed growing suicide rates, we need to look at what the causes may be to find an approach that deals with the many facets of why individuals would try to kill themselves. If ever there were an issue where we need to cover all the bases of prevention, including the possibility of genetic predisposition, it is the issue of suicide. Our society has made such a dramatic change in its view of the importance of life, it is no wonder that so many take theirs in desperation.

HUMAN RESOURCES OR HUMAN REFUSE?

The one thing that these three groups at increasing risk for suicide have in common is that they are seen as lacking value in our culture. Children, the elderly, and teenagers are considered key contributors to "social problems." In our postindustrialized society they are an unnecessary burden. They are devalued, often left alone, and certainly cut off from contributing meaningfully to society as a whole. Whereas children were seen as an asset in an agricultural society and the elderly as a source of wisdom and experience, in our society children are a financial drain (no matter how precious), and the elderly need care that most families are unable to provide. Many of these attitudes are due to secondhand emotions that have gone unresolved. In addition, our extended families have splintered as our ability to travel has opened up new opportunities. Our divorce from the land has also had the effect of divorcing one generation from the next. When a whole segment of society has no useful place in the avenues of power, its members will have to cope with feelings of societal worthlessness. They may be seen as human refuse rather than human resources. Other societal attitudes have changed our view of life and the importance of the individual.

These attitudinal changes have occurred since World Wars I and II. They reflect a deterioration in the belief in God and human beings as the center point of creation. They influence all of us and the way we feel about ourselves and others. For those who already have a predisposition to suicide, a lack of self-worth can be the final factor in making the decision to cross the line toward death. Let's take a look at the source of the erosion in individual self-worth.

WHERE DID WE COME FROM AND WHERE ARE WE GOING?

Before 1925, American schoolchildren were taught that they were created by God with a special purpose for their lives. The biblical view of humanity was the basis of the self-concept. In the Scopes trial of 1925, the American justice system was asked to rule on whether children could be taught Darwin's theory of evolution as a part of their standard education. The new message being taught was that human beings were not creations of divine design but another form of animal life that had originally crawled out of the primordial ooze. We were no longer to see ourselves as just a little bit lower than the angels. Instead, we were to see ourselves as just a little bit higher than the apes.

In 1968, the Supreme Court of the United States ruled that antievolution laws, which sought to prohibit the teaching of evolutionary theory, were unconstitutional. Although evolution was called a theory, the fact that powerful authority figures, including teachers, lawyers, and Supreme Court justices, upheld the theory over the belief in creation gave evolution acceptance as truth in the minds of many children.

The belief that a person is a unique creation of God—a work of art, an eternal being made in the image of God, destined to live forever, designed to accomplish great things to the glory of God—was relegated to Sunday school teaching. The "made in the image of God" self-image was socially placed in the same category as the tooth fairy and Mickey Mouse. Our public educational system has reduced children to little more than cosmic accidents instead of grand creations.

When we believe that we are grand creations, our value is inherent in who we are, even if we can't *do* anything, even if we have a handicapping condition, even if we are weak. When we see ourselves as survivors in the evolutionary process, our value must come from what we do, how productive, how strong, how connected we are to what is needed in our society. Remember, it's the survival of the fittest. It therefore follows that those who grow up believing they do not have inherent value as persons, created in the image of God, will judge their lives on what they can do and their value to their society. Is it any wonder that those least needed—children, the elderly, and adolescents—would be ending their lives at ever increasing rates?

WHO NEEDS US?

In the movie *Surviving* referred to at the beginning of the chapter, there is a captivating scene just before the two teens go into the garage to carry out their suicide plans. Molly Ringwald's character has been taking care of a tiny kitten. As she is about to enter the garage, she hears the kitten meowing. The kitten runs to her and nuzzles up to her ankle. She picks it up and seems to hesitate about going through with the suicide. The kitten needs her. She talks to the kitten and asks her boyfriend what will happen to the kitten if she is gone. He convinces her that someone else will take care of it. For a moment there I felt hope that she might have the will to live because the tiny kitten needed her. In the final analysis, she concluded that she wasn't really needed even for that. She placed the kitten back down on the driveway and patted its head for the last time.

SOCIETAL INFLUENCES

Feeling needed in society is theorized to have a significant influence on suicidal behavior. In the nineteenth century, the behavioral sociologist Emile Durkheim was among the first scientists to develop a formal theory, based on statistics, to explain suicide. He believed that suicide was primarily a result of environmental ills, such as migration, economic collapse, and other conditions involved in undermining the supports and constraints in society that undergird mental health. The term he used to describe such an environment was *anomie,* the absence of normal social controls that inhibit human impulse.[6]

Suicide, Durkheim believed, could be *anomic* (resulting from loss) or *egoistic* (resulting from deficiency—the failure of individuals to form psychological attachments to their society due to society's failure to encourage such attachments). In other words, people didn't feel needed or otherwise attached to their society. This theory basically blames suicide on society's failure to find a place for everyone to fit snugly and securely into the social order.

The major criticism of Durkheim's theory has been that it cannot account for the "rarity and heritability" of suicide. In other words, critics say that if there is a problem with society that causes people to commit suicide, why don't most people in the same society kill themselves? Why can two people who grow up in the same town with basically the same societal environment choose to respond to life in very different ways? Also, this theory does not acknowledge or account for the statistics that show suicidal tendencies do run genetically in families.

Durkheim's theory is useful in explaining why those who are needed the least, and are the least directly connected to the fabric of society, commit suicide in the greatest numbers. Children, the elderly, and adolescents aren't socially connected to society in their own right as they were in preindustrialized American society when they were needed to help run the farm. Instead, they are primarily connected to society through the family unit, which is rapidly breaking down. For the most part they are left with caretakers or left alone at home without a sense of being needed, without a valuable place, and without necessary support. In this regard, Durkheim's theory does make some sense.

Other behavioral explanations of suicide include theories about the influence of direct positive or negative conditioning of such behavior by elements in the environment. I would like to point out ways our social environment may condition people to find suicide an acceptable solution to their perceived problems.

WHEN IS A LIFE REALLY A LIFE?

This generation has witnessed a revolution in our social consciousness regarding life. Human life in America had historically been acknowledged and protected in the womb until the 1973 *Roe v. Wade* Supreme Court decision made abortion legal. That decision marked the beginning of a battle over our understanding of the nature and value of human life. Those promoting the right to abortion have sought to convince us all that the unborn child is no more than a ''mass of cells'' or ''pregnancy tissue.'' After the first trimester, they concede to call ''it'' a fetus. To them, the issue is the pregnant woman's right to choose what to do with her body. The unborn child is not even acknowledged as having a body! Some persons promote the right to abortion as long as the fetus is unable to live outside the womb. Again, that reinforces the belief that our ability, not our essence, gives us the right to live in our society.

The unborn child has been systematically devalued, redefined as not even being a person. With the lawful allowance that a human fetus is not necessarily a human being, we have devalued all human life. When a pregnant woman asserts her ''right'' to dispose of her human fetus on the basis that it really isn't valued as a human life, it interferes with her plans, every child should be a wanted child (and this one isn't), or a child is too expensive, too much trouble, or too inconvenient, we are sending a message about the value of all life.

Is it any wonder that a generation of children and young people struggle with feeling that they are unworthy of life; that they are just interferences in someone else's busy schedule; that they may not be wanted; that they aren't worth the expense, the trouble, the inconvenience they present to their parents? Could some of the attempted suicides be an outcry of a generation asking to find out if anyone really does value their lives?

Some very interesting studies associate abortion and birth traumas with adolescent suicidal tendencies. Although the research is ongoing and clear conclusions have not yet been drawn, it is well worth considering at this point. One study has produced evidence that fetuses who survive an abortion attempt also register the experience as birth trauma and are at higher risk of suicide. Andrew Feldmar, a Canadian therapist, examined the cases of four adolescents who tried to end their lives every year at the same time of year. After interviewing their mothers, Feldmar discovered that each had tried to abort her child at the very same time of year (the children were unaware of this).[7]

Lee Salk, a psychologist at the Cornell University Medical School in New York City, began to suspect that the dramatic increase in adolescent and young adult suicides since World War II might have more than sociological and psychological explanations behind it. Salk observed that the heroic measures now in use in neonatal intensive care units were primarily developments of the last thirty years, and that the rate of infant mortality had begun to drop dramatically about fifteen years prior to the start of significant increases in teen suicide rates. He also noted that birth complications are more common in males than females, and men commit suicide more frequently than women. To test his theory, Salk compared the birth records of 52 adolescents born between 1957 and 1967, who had ended their lives in suicide, with the birth records of 104 nonsuicidal controls. Among the suicides, three characteristics consistently reappeared: (1) respiratory distress at birth for a period of over one hour, (2) a chronically ill mother during pregnancy, and (3) no prenatal care before the end of the fifth month of pregnancy.[8]

A second study, conducted in the U.S. by Dr. Bertil Jacobson of Sweden, found that suicide was linked more closely with birth trauma than with any of the other eleven tested risk factors, including parental alcoholism. In another study in Sweden, Jacobson also found that the kind of birth trauma and the method used to commit suicide were correlated (e.g., those who had asphyxiated themselves were four times more likely to have suffered oxygen deficiency at birth as were controls). He observed that birth trauma that was not life threatening might even have a link to suicide.[9]

Peter, a fifteen-year-old boy, showed none of the usual warning signs for adolescent depression and suicide. He did well at school and seemed to be navigating the waters of adolescence with little trouble. He was active in the youth organization at his church and had solid friendships. When he hanged himself from the rafters of his parents' garage in 1987, no one could come close to explaining why. A number of researchers have begun to suspect that the tendency of some people to end their lives, and end them in particular ways, is associated with events they experienced as traumatic at birth. Could that have something to do with Peter's unexpected suicide? He had been born with the umbilical cord tightened around his neck and had required emergency resuscitation to save his life, already nearly extinguished.[10]

Attempted explanations for the birth trauma/suicide phenomenon range from imprinting to cellular memory to weakened resilience to the allure of near-death experiences remembered from birth (which may eradicate a fear of death). However, there is not yet enough evidence to fully satisfy any of these theories. Of course, experiencing birth trauma does not cause suicide any more than being an adolescent boy causes suicide, but these studies are interesting and help us focus on the importance of the early years of development.

ENCOURAGING SUICIDE

Behavioral theorists note that a society that encourages suicide will see greater rates of suicide as a result. That conclusion seems fairly obvious. In this regard, is it any wonder that many are alarmed that the book *Final Exit,* which condones euthanasia and gives detailed how-to suicide instructions, has made it to the number one spot on the *New York Times* best-seller list in the hardcover advice category? The author asserts that the book is designed to assist in "self-deliverance" for those who are already terminally ill and wish to "die with dignity." He does not intend to promote suicide among the depressed or among adolescents and does not believe that the book will do so.

I believe the underlying beliefs that allow a society to accept euthanasia also undermine the societal influences that would discourage suicide in the population as a whole and in those who are genetically predisposed in particular.

The elderly are cut off from society; they are "retired" and "put away." They no longer hold the honored position they once did when families stayed together for generations. They may be seen as having outlived their usefulness, having become a burden to the family.

When these attitudes pervade a society, reinforcing the belief that life is valued only by what a person contributes, it follows that those who don't see themselves as valuable may see themselves as doing the world a favor by relieving it of the burden.

FATALISM

This is the last social issue we will examine in hopes of understanding why the rate of suicide has risen dramatically since World War II. After August 6, 1945, the world entered a new era from which we cannot retreat. When the Americans dropped the first atomic bomb on Hiroshima, Japan, we realized for the first time that humankind had the power to destroy all life as we know it. Unless this knowledge is combined with a strong sense of hope, or a strong faith in God and His divine plan for the future of humankind, one may grow up with a sense of futility about life.

Going back to the Molly Ringwald movie, just before the suicide, she remarked, "What difference does it make? It's all just going to blow up anyway." With the environmentalists' concerns that our earth may be doomed if we don't get our global act together, the prophets of doom predicting the end of the world, and the sense that human beings have never before been able to resist using a weapon once its power was in their hands, life can look bleak.

Life is a struggle for all of us. It holds its share of pain for everyone. When a generation grows up believing that there is a very real threat of obliteration, the determination to endure the struggle and pain that are normal parts of life may be undermined. When a hopeless feeling of being unable to succeed is added, the chance for an increase in suicide escalates. We live in an age of despair. Those who are in the thick of it need to know there is hope and there is reason to endure.

Those who lose all hope and come to believe it would be better to die than live come to that fatal decision for many reasons, with numerous factors contributing to the risk. Most researchers recognize that no simple solutions are likely to be forthcoming. Rather, most agree that any explanation of vulnerability to suicidal behavior is likely to involve integration of the many different approaches to the problem, and the solution is likely to be many faceted as well. The search for a biological link to suicide helps from the perspective of prevention and treatment. If it runs in the family, we know there is a greater need to counter the forces. Additionally, if it is familial, people may better be able to accept that is not something they will grow out of but something they must address throughout life. This point is especially important since the risk increases with age.

Notes

1. "Suicide: An Update," *Statistical Bulletin,* April–June 1986, p. 18.

2. Celeste Fremon, "Love and Death," *Los Angeles Times Magazine,* Jan. 27, 1991, pp. 17–21.

3. Fremon, "Love and Death," p. 17.

4. Polly Joan, *Preventing Teenage Suicide* (New York: Humanities Press, 1986), p. 37.

5. Sherry Baker, "Born Under a Bad Sign," *Omni,* Nov. 1988, p. 26.

6. Emile Durkheim, quoted in Lee Willerman and David B. Cohen, *Psychopathology* (New York: McGraw-Hill, 1990), p. 390.

7. Baker, "Born Under a Bad Sign," p. 100.

8. Baker, "Born Under a Bad Sign," p. 26.

9. Baker, "Born Under a Bad Sign," pp. 26, 100.

10. Baker, "Born Under a Bad Sign," p. 26.

Chapter 8

◆

THE CASE FOR PREDISPOSITION

Perhaps the most famous of all suicides was carried out by the betrayer of Jesus. Shortly after Judas Iscariot turned Jesus over to the Roman authorities, he killed himself. His need to destroy himself was an obvious result of the guilt, shame, and remorse he experienced after committing the horrid sin of being Christ's traitor. With such a glaring example of immorality leading to suicide, many have concluded that the suicidal pattern established by Judas can be found in all suicides today. There is evidence that this is too simplistic an evaluation of what causes suicide. Sometimes persons who possess the highest integrity, living up to high standards of morality and character, kill themselves. The Amish provide us with an example of suicide in the midst of morality.

The Amish people live in the lovely rolling hills of Pennsylvania where the vibrant greens and rich reddish browns of the farmland meet skies bright as flame. Their well-kept barns dotting the landscape and the neatly furrowed rows, plowed by hand or horse, speak of their well-ordered way of life. It is a way of life ordered by strict interpretation of the Bible, generations steeped in tradition, and the approval or disapproval of the community. The Amish are a God-fearing, morally cautious sect of Christianity, who adhere to simplicity in all their ways. They are known for their austerity, relying on God, their hard work, the tight-knit community, and the rich soil to provide all they need for this life.

Visiting Amish country is an experience in contrasts; the archaic tucked away from the contemporary, the dark fabrics of their clothing and buggies against the brightness of the fertile land. It is like taking a step backward into the 1800s. They dress primarily in black, so as not to fall prey to the vanity of worldly fashions. The men wear long black frocks and black hats, reminiscent of orthodox Jews, who also seek to dedicate themselves wholly to God. The women wear black as well, except for their simple white bonnets symbolic of their submission to God. The Amish are known for their antiquated mode of transportation, choosing to use horse-drawn carriages rather than modern automobiles. The snap of the harnesses and the pounding of the horses' hooves sound a persistent call to a more tranquil way of life—a life of serenity, purity, devotion to God, and commitment to family and community.

You may be familiar with the Amish from their portrayal in the movie *Witness,* starring Harrison Ford. In the movie the serenity of Amish culture was used as the backdrop for a violent murder witnessed by a young Amish boy. Just as that kind of violence seemed especially out of place among such peace-loving people, so, too, does the alarming rate of suicide among Amish families. The Amish have become a focus of attention for research scientists studying how suicides may run in families. A surprising pattern of suicide has been noted in this small interconnected, isolated segment of the American population.

Because of the strict religious beliefs regarding life-style, the Amish tend to marry others of their faith and marry into families that have carried on the Amish traditions for generations. This practice limits the gene pool and makes the Amish good candidates for studies relating to inherited traits. One study revealed that within the Amish community, there have been twenty-six reported suicides over the last one hundred years. This number is lower than the national average, which is understandable because of the stability of the family unit and the close-knit network of support within the community. The unusual fact is that nineteen of the twenty-six suicides (or 73 percent) occurred within four families. The four families comprised only 16 percent of the total Amish population. The statistics indicate that certain inherited traits may predispose someone from a particular family to exhibit suicidal tendencies.[1] In chapter 6 we saw how suicide was prevalent in one family. These studies highlight the fact that suicide may run in what one might consider the most religious of families.

THE DEPRESSION-SUICIDE FAMILY LINK

The familial link here is thought to be tied to clinical depression. Of those in the Amish families who committed suicide, 90 percent had been previously diagnosed with a clinical mood disorder.[2] The most common mood disorders among them were major depression and manic-depression. (You may recall that major depression involves recurrent bouts of depression unrelated to the normal circumstances of life, being caused by biochemical imbalances in the brain. Manic-depressive persons swing from emotional highs to the lows of depression; these highs and lows are also generated by chemical imbalances in the brain and are unrelated to the normal ups and downs of life.)

Countless observations over the course of medical history point to serious depression as the most likely indicator of suicide. That is, suicide is more prevalent among those who suffer from clinical depression than among other groups of people. Hippocrates and Aristotle recognized that before the time of Christ. Medieval doctors and churchmen acknowledged the link. As early as 1621, Robert Burton wrote about it in his work *Anatomy of Melancholy,* as did many scientists of the eighteenth and nineteenth centuries. Current research continues to confirm the link between depression and suicide.

At least 15 percent of those who are significantly depressed commit suicide. An estimated 30 to 70 percent of completed suicides have been previously diagnosed with major depression.[3] These figures are considered conservative since many may destroy themselves before seeking diagnosis for their mood disorder. The overall rate of suicide in the United States is around 15 per 100,000. The lifetime risk for the average American is about 1 in 100 (1 percent), but among those who are clinically depressed, the risk at any given time is 15 or 16 per 100 (15 or 16 percent).[4] Since it is generally accepted that people can be genetically predisposed to clinical depression, it would follow that the suicidal tendencies linked to depression could be seen as predisposing them to a higher risk of suicide as well.

EVIDENCE FROM ADOPTION STUDIES

Adoption research on depression, alcoholism, and suicide has provided substantial reason to believe that at least some of the increased vulnerability to suicide in certain individuals is inherited. Biological relatives of adoptees who have been diagnosed with major depression or manic-depression are fifteen times more likely to commit suicide than relatives of those with no history of clinical mood disorders. The biological relatives of those who commit suicide also show an increased risk of suicide. However, the adopted children of those who commit suicide with no genetic link show no increased risk of suicide over the general population.[5] Thus, genetics has more of an influence toward suicidal tendencies than environmental influences, that is, the trauma of dealing with the deaths of family members who have committed suicide.

In 1963, a Harvard Medical School researcher investigated the public adoption-psychiatric-population records of Denmark. He hoped to unravel genetic riddles believed to underlie certain psychiatric conditions. Ever since Seymour Kety used those documents in his investigation of possible genetic factors involved in schizophrenia, scientists have tapped the same reliable source for research on other psychiatric disorders. A group of persons with depressive disorders, some of them twins, has been isolated and compared with a control group of nondepressed persons with similar backgrounds. Among the close relatives of both the depressed and the control groups, eighteen committed suicide. Of those eighteen, fifteen were among biological relatives of the depressed group.[6] This study and others of a similar nature indicate a measurable link between the susceptibility to suicidal tendencies and genetic predisposition to clinical depression.

When bouts of manic-depression begin in adolescence, there is a greater degree of risk for suicide in both men and women. The suicide risk is greatest during the mood transitions, entering or leaving times of severe depression. More young men than young women actually kill themselves during these transitional times.[7]

THE ALCOHOL-SUICIDE FAMILY LINK

After depression, the condition most frequently cited in conjunction with risk for suicide is alcoholism. In one major research effort, 134 suicides in and around St. Louis, Missouri, were categorized according to diagnosed psychiatric disorder. Though a small percentage were related to various other disorders, 47 percent were depression related, and 25 percent were alcoholism related.[8]

THE ANXIETY DISORDER-SUICIDE LINK

There seems to be a strong connection between panic disorder and risk for suicide. Myrna Weissman and her colleagues concluded that persons diagnosed with panic disorder have a higher rate of suicide attempts than seriously depressed persons. Even when figures were adjusted to account for those who were also clinically depressed or who abused alcohol, the panic disorder sufferers reported more suicidal thoughts and attempts. And if they did abuse drugs or alcohol, they were at even higher risk for attempted suicide. Members of a group that experienced less frequent panic attacks showed an increased likelihood of attempting suicide if they also had problems with depression and/or alcohol abuse.[9]

CAN WE PREDICT VULNERABILITY?

A rise in the rate of adolescent depression also corresponds to the sharp rise in adolescent suicide. Susan Blumenthal of the National Institute of Mental Health believes that undiagnosed mood disorders are among the most significant risk factors in adolescent suicide. She estimates that one-third of the teens who succeed in killing themselves have a mood disorder that has never been diagnosed or treated.[10]

Connected with the depression-suicide link is the discovery that both depression and suicide are associated with low levels of the neurotransmitter serotonin in the synapses, or spaces, between nerve cells in the brain. Serotonin, like other neurotransmitters, facilitates communication between these nerve cells. When these neurotransmitters are lacking, depression is the result.

Sufficient levels of serotonin and other neurotransmitters are vital to the proper functioning of the mind and emotions. Abnormal levels of serotonin, in particular, have been indicated in many types of abnormal behavior, including depression, schizophrenia, alcoholism, aggressive behavior, and suicide. Low levels of serotonin are associated with high levels of depression, impulsiveness, and aggression.

Self-destructive behavior can be directly linked to biochemical predictors. Among adolescents, boys with low serotonin levels tend to commit suicide, while girls with low serotonin levels have a much higher incidence of bulimia, a serious eating disorder. In 50 to 70 percent of those with bulimia, low levels of serotonin and the resulting mood disorder have also been diagnosed. In these cases, certain antidepressant medications that raise serotonin levels in the brain also decrease or eliminate the eating binges that characterize bulimia.[11]

Low serotonin levels may be a common denominator for suicide occurring in conjunction with other psychiatric disorders, such as depression, alcoholism, and some personality disorders. Swedish researcher Marie Asberg found that of hospitalized patients admitted for a suicide attempt who also had low levels of serotonin in their spinal fluid, 22 percent ended their lives within a year of their admission.[12]

This biochemical connection to the increased risk of suicide gives us hope of being able to medically predict suicide risk in some cases. In between the nerve cells of the brain, certain brain chemicals act as messengers taking the mental messages across the gap, or synapse, to the nerve ending on the other side. One of these brain chemicals is imipramine. For the message to get completely across to the other nerve ending, there must be receptors to receive it on the other side. This receptivity for imipramine is believed to reflect the brain's usage of serotonin. Fewer numbers of imipramine-binding sites may be a trait marker for vulnerability to suicide. *One day,* screening for potential suicidal tendencies may be a possibility by testing for imipramine levels in the blood. This type of testing done on persons who died by suicide shows a reduced number of imipramine receptor sites in the brain.[13]

The mounting evidence points to a suicidal predisposition unrelated to character. Those who continue in deep dark sins, such as Judas, will of natural consequence self-destruct. But those are but a fraction of the persons who take their lives. The evidence points to a "wiring" problem or, perhaps more accurately, a chemistry problem. If it is a problem of physiology, there is hope for detection and prevention. That could eventually lead to lower rates of suicide and fewer families left holding the emotional bags of those who die too young.

THE BIOCHEMICAL LINK BETWEEN ALCOHOLISM AND SUICIDE

Another biochemical abnormality is common in certain forms of alcoholism and in persons with suicidal tendencies. It involves the brain chemical 5-hydroxyindoleacetic acid (5-HIAA for short). When the human body uses serotonin, one of the by-products is 5-HIAA, which can be measured in a person's spinal fluid. Researchers have repeatedly noted an association between low levels of 5-HIAA, major depression, alcoholism, and suicide. In a study reported in 1976, a group of hospitalized depressed patients with low levels of 5-HIAA in their cerebral spinal fluid committed suicide (within a year of admission) significantly more often than those with high 5-HIAA. Other studies have since confirmed these findings. In a summary analysis of the studies, 5-HIAA was observed to be low in impulsive-aggressive persons, in those with a history of suicide attempts, and in schizophrenics who were also suicidal. Low measurements of 5-HIAA in those with episodes of major depression may be useful as a trait marker for suicidal behavior, especially violent, aggressive, or impulsive suicidal behavior. However, a low level of 5-HIAA is not a marker for those who are manic-depressive.[14]

At least one other brain chemical has been implicated in predisposition to suicide. The enzyme MAO (monoamine oxidase) is responsible for "reuptake" of certain neurotransmitters. In other words, once the chemical messengers between nerve cells take the message across the synapse, MAO reabsorbs or removes the neurotransmitter that has completed its mission. This reuptake of the neurotransmitters maintains a proper balance in brain chemistry. When too much or not enough of the neurotransmitter is removed, problems may result from the imbalance. High levels of MAO may inhibit nerve transmissions, while low levels may create an environment of nonstop stimulation of nerve cells in the brain. Drugs that inhibit MAO when the levels are too high are effective in treating some forms of depression. Low levels of MAO, however, have been shown to be associated with chronic schizophrenia and manic-depression. Men with low MAO activity, and the families of these men, have a suicide rate that is eight times higher than the suicide rate for men with high MAO activity. Enzymes such as MAO, which play a significant role in the transmission of nerve impulses in the brain, may also play a significant role in abnormal behavior, including suicide. This indication contributes to the growing weight of evidence that physical influences may promote suicidal tendencies.[15]

CONCLUSION

What if we are to conclude that there can be a genetic connection to suicidal tendencies? How can this understanding be integrated with the moral and interpersonal issues related to the taking of one's life? Certainly, the conclusion must *not* be that those who are so predisposed are, in effect, predestined to commit suicide. Neither does this information lead us to conclude that persons are not responsible for their actions. This information is presented so that those who may be physiologically inclined to life-destroying behavior will recognize the nature of the problem and get appropriate help.

This information may also reduce the shame that often keeps the family from seeking help when one member shows warning signs associated with suicide. A statement quoted earlier in our discussion of depression bears repeating: "According to a report issued in June (of 1990) by a commission formed by the American Medical Association and the National Association of State Boards of Education, about 10% of teenage boys and 18% of girls try to kill themselves at least once. Despite the urgency of the problems, only 1 in 5 children who need therapy receives it."[16] There is no other explanation for this fatally low response to assistance other than the shame or ignorance at the heart of not getting help.

According to *The Youth Ministry Resource Book,* "About 90 percent of suicidal teenagers feel their families don't understand them. And when they express their feelings of unhappiness, frustration, or failure, the teenagers say their families either ignore, deny, or attack those feelings."[17]

These facts display the paralyzing effect that shame and confusion can have. When we don't know exactly what to do—and especially when we are deeply ashamed to admit that the family could have such a serious problem, one that would make life not worth living for one member—we may stay in denial . . . until it's too late.

With the understanding that part of the problem may be physical or biochemical, the shame can be reduced, and we can broaden our perspective to look into an array of possible causes for this life-threatening condition. I hope that those who battle with suicidal tendencies and those who love them will explore the possibilities and take action that can bring freedom.

Notes

1. Egeland Sussex (1985), cited in Lee Willerman and David B. Cohen, *Psychopathology* (New York: McGraw-Hill, 1990), p. 389.

2. Egeland and Sussex (1985), in Willerman and Cohen, *Psychopathology,* p. 389.

3. Brana Lobel and Robert M. A. Hirschfeld, "Depression: What We Know," National Institute of Mental Health, Pub. no. AMD84-1318, 1984, p. 49, cited in Archibald D. Hart, *Counseling the Depressed* (Dallas: Word, 1987), p. 232.

4. Wender et al. (1986), cited in McGuffin and Katz, 1989, p. 296.

5. Willerman and Cohen, *Psychopathology,* pp. 388–89.

6. Zolt Harsanyi and Richard Hutton, *Genetic Prophecy: Beyond the Double Helix* (New York: Rawson, Wade, 1981), pp. 194–200.

7. Harsanyi and Hutton, *Genetic Prophecy,* pp. 194–200.

8. Robins (1981), in Willerman and Cohen, *Psychopathology,* p. 387.

9. B. Bower, "Panic Attacks Increase Suicide Attempts," *Science News,* Nov. 4, 1989, p. 293.

10. Joseph Alper, "Depression at an Early Age," *Science,* May 1986, pp. 40–50.

11. Alper, "Depression at an Early Age," pp. 40–50.

12. J. Greenberg, "Suicide Linked to Brain Chemical Deficit," *Science News,* May 29, 1982, p. 355.

13. Greenberg, "Suicide Linked to Brain Chemical Deficit," p. 355.

14. William E. Bunney, Jr., et al., "Biological Markers in Depression," *Psychopathology* 19, suppl. 2 (1986): 74, and Maya Pines, "Suicide Signals," *Science,* Oct. 1983, pp. 55–58.

15. Harasanyi and Hutton, *Genetic Prophecy,* pp. 209–10.

16. Anastasia Toufexis, "Struggling for Sanity," *Time,* Oct. 8, 1990, p. 48.

17. Nancy H. Allen and Michael L. Peck as quoted in *The Youth Ministry Resource Book* (Loveland, Colo.: Group Books, 1988), p. 168, from Nancy H. Allen and Michael L. Peck, "Suicide in Young People," (West Point, PA: American Association of Suicidology), p. 2.

Chapter 9

◆

FREEING OURSELVES FROM RISK

As I explained at the beginning of the book, suicide is a reality in my family. I believe hand-me-down genes and secondhand emotions leave me vulnerable to the same forces that infected my family two generations ago. I do not go blindly through life without the realization that I could end up victimizing myself and my family through this selfish means of removing pain. So I do what it takes to ensure that my depression remains in check. I also have to make sure that my behavior is such that I do not add shame to an already difficult life. Anyone with suicide in the family should do the same for his sake and the sake of generations to come.

Even though there is evidence that suicides run in families, and that there may be a genetic influence due to predisposition to depression or alcoholism, no one is born to commit suicide. More than any other topic touched on in this book, the act of suicide hinges on the choice of the individual. Conditions and influences can color our perspective as we make choices related to living or dying. However, we are human beings with the God-given will to choose, not helpless players playing out a predetermined role without choice.

Much can be done *before a crisis occurs* to minimize the dark influences that would lead someone to choose suicide. Steps can be taken to minimize risk when someone is suicidal or exhibits warning signs that may indicate an immediate risk for suicide.

If suicide has been an issue in the family, we know the stark terror, the silenced fear, that it could happen (or happen again). When we courageously face the "unthinkable" possibility that suicide could strike the family and examine possible contributing factors, we will gain power and no longer remain immobilized by fear. Shedding the light of understanding on the underlying factors and considering ways to deal with each of them can bring hope into a dark and frightening situation.

If someone we love has committed suicide, we may reprimand ourselves as though we were partially responsible for the death because we didn't do the things described in this chapter for the person. This type of guilt and second-guessing is a normal part of grieving a suicide, but *we cannot be responsible for things we did not understand at the time.* We did the best we could with what we knew. In the final analysis, the weight of moral responsibility for a suicide remains with the person who committed suicide.

This chapter will give concrete steps to free ourselves or a loved one from contributing factors that increase the risk of suicide before and at a crisis point.

What can be done before a crisis occurs?

1. Deal with physiological predisposition (for the contributing factors of depression and alcohol/drug addiction).
2. Deal with family patterns and systems that can contribute to desperate behavior.
3. Deal with issues involving shame and fear of exposure.

It is also important to know what warning signs indicate an immediate risk and what steps need to be taken if the threat of suicide seems imminent.

DEALING WITH PREDISPOSITIONS THAT CONTRIBUTE TO SUICIDE

As stated in the previous chapter, depression and alcoholism are the two most highly recognized factors associated with suicide. Both physiological predispositions can be dealt with through a program of recovery that addresses the needs of the whole person in physical, mental, spiritual, and social contexts. When dealing with the problems of depression or alcoholism (that is, physiological conditions inherent in our genetic makeup), we cannot settle for incomplete treatment. It is not enough to address the spiritual issues without taking care of the physical realities as well.

In the chapters on depression and alcoholism there is a detailed plan for addressing each area of concern. Leaving depression or alcoholism untreated is a choice to leave the person at risk for suicide. It's that simple.

Choosing to get help for these conditions is also a simple choice, although certainly not an easy one. We may have to overcome our previous misconceptions, our shame at admitting these conditions exist in the family, and our denial. We may have to talk about issues that are painful and pervasively intertwined around the roots and branches of the family tree. We may have to reexamine our faith in God and be willing to stand up to the criticism that may come from well-meaning people who believe that God works only their way. Granted, we face real obstacles when we consider getting professional help for clinical depression or alcoholism. For those who have a family history of depression or alcoholism, the question that must be asked is this: When my life or the life of a loved one is at risk, is it worth finding the resources and strength needed to overcome every obstacle? Denial will be the natural inclination; we'll tell ourselves that the problem really isn't that bad. Statistics prove otherwise. If there is a family history of depression or alcoholism and someone in the family currently suffers from these conditions, the person is at risk and needs help. The best thing that can be done to reduce the risk of suicide is to address these conditions head-on and get help that works.

Look for Signs of Hormonal Imbalance

A physiological condition that may contribute to the risk of suicide in some women is depression affected by hormone imbalances. It may prove helpful to get a professional evaluation of how hormonal imbalances may be contributing to depression. Most women notice mood alterations accompanying the body's hormonal changes. According to Holly Anderson, founder and director of the PMS Treatment Clinic in Arcadia, California, hormonal imbalance can produce depression that sometimes can be severe enough to trigger suicidal tendencies. It is most noticeable during times of premenstrual syndrome (PMS), postpartum adjustment, the onset of menstruation, the onset of menopause, or following a hysterectomy, tubal ligation, or miscarriage. Holly declares, "This is not an emotional disorder; it's a physical disorder."

In the ten years the clinic has been administering natural progesterone therapy, it has documented a 90 percent success rate. Blood tests verify that hormonal balance has been restored and women experience relief from disturbing physical and emotional symptoms. Treatment is not an instant cure. Recovery usually takes between one and three years, depending on the severity of the condition and other factors.

Acknowledging the relationship between fluctuating female hormones and depression should not intimate that "hormone-crazed females are more prone toward suicide than men. Statistics show that although women attempt suicide more often, three times as many men actually took their own lives (from 1950 to 1985)."[1]

DEALING WITH FAMILY SYSTEMS THAT CONTRIBUTE TO DESPERATE BEHAVIOR

Janice was a beautiful girl of sixteen. Her mother and stepfather appeared to have a close relationship with each other and with Janice. They had been married since Janice was four and had come through a lot together. They credited God with having rescued their family from the despair that came with their previous life of drug and alcohol addiction. The mother and stepfather had been addicts for many years before entering recovery and surrendering their "old life" to Jesus Christ when Janice was nine. They were shining examples of what the Lord can do when we submit our lives to His care. They were often invited to speak to various groups on the dangers of addiction and to give their testimony of how they found freedom from drugs and alcohol. They volunteered to head up a twelve-step group for their local church and were often called on to counsel families struggling with issues related to addiction.

Janice attended the church youth group faithfully and was active in a youth recovery group as well. She and her parents were admired for their successful recovery from extremely difficult circumstances. Janice appeared basically happy, given the normal fluctuation of emotions teenage girls are prone to having. She was accepted by the other girls and was quite popular with the boys.

On the surface everything was fine. The family portrait, seen by those on the outside, made a pretty picture. That's why many people were puzzled when Janice attempted suicide. She was taken to get counseling at their church. Her answers to the pastor's questions were vague. Everything was really fine, she said. She was just upset. She didn't really want to kill herself. The answers pleased her parents and relieved the pastor. Then came the second attempt . . . then the car accident when she drove off an embankment while alone. She was taken to speak with the youth pastor. He was supposed to understand these things. When he promised to keep her confession to himself, she told him that she had been sexually molested by her stepfather and couldn't live with herself.

After several closed-door conferences between pastors and Janice, between pastors and her parents, the stepfather admitted that once many years before, while he was drunk, he had been involved in inappropriate behavior with Janice, who was eight years old at the time. Mother, Stepfather, and Janice sat down together with the pastor to hear what he had to say. As he went over what he knew, how it had all happened so long ago . . . before they had begun their new life in Christ . . . Janice exchanged a defiant glance with her mother. She knew what Mom's look meant. She had better go along with this version of the story. Janice looked back to the pastor, hoping that he would see through their pretense, hoping that he would come to her rescue. The pastor, not realizing he'd been misled, went on, "Since it was all in the past, you need to forget those things that are behind."

Janice couldn't say a word. She nodded her head obediently as she felt the icy grip of despair lay hold of her. She couldn't tell the pastor the truth—that it had gone on as recently as a year ago, when she was in eighth grade. She couldn't ruin her parents' reputation. She couldn't end their ministry that was helping so many people. Maybe she should just let it go. But she couldn't because she had never really dealt with it honestly. It was still a present reality for her. She felt utterly trapped. Maybe they were right, and she was the one with the problem. Whatever the case, she would have to try harder to keep up the pretense that kept the family together and happy . . . until it became unbearable again.

Janice is an example of someone who is at risk because of a dysfunctional family system that constitutes environmental predisposition. The family unit forms a system where relationships are delicately balanced to protect the whole family. Each member plays a specific role in maintaining the family balance, relating to one another in ways that are expected within the system. In a healthy family, individual members grow, communicate freely, and learn to develop into adults who are capable of breaking away from the family to live their own lives. In a dysfunctional family, individual members are prohibited from breaking away from the role they play in the family. Each one is frozen into a set role and kept from developing a whole person. In a dysfunctional family, where there is a cycle of shame, addiction, or abuse, the members are not allowed the freedom to get the help they need if it would upset the family balance or expose a family secret.

In her family, Janice was not free to get help for the effects of the sexual abuse because it would have drastically affected her parents' lives and the image of respectability they needed. They had overcome the substance abuse, and perhaps Janice was afraid that the stress of dealing honestly with the issue of the sexual abuse would have destroyed them all. Apart from this one issue, the family made Janice feel safe.

Those stuck in a dysfunctional family system, which keeps them from being able to meet their needs, may experience a sense of desperation. They believe there's no way out without destroying the people they love and depend on. This sense of desperation may set the stage for suicide as a way out. Denial and self-deception are two characteristics of a dysfunctional family that can warp everyone's perspective; family members may live in the presence of all the classic warning signs for suicide and remain blind to them. In the economics of familial emotions, there are times when family members can't afford to look carefully at what suicidal tendencies may point to within the family as a whole. That was the case with Janice's family and perhaps even in the larger context of their church family. It would have cost too much emotionally for them to admit that Janice's suicide attempts were more than teenage "pranks" to get attention.

Research has shown that adolescent suicides tend to come from families unable to tolerate crisis and given to patterns of repeated yelling, hostility, and nagging. The families rarely demonstrate affection. There is often either too much discipline or too little. These families also make autonomy extremely difficult or impossible for a child, creating "symbiotic relationships" between the parent and the child. Mothers of suicidal children tend to be more depressed and/or dominant, often neglecting their children. Their families tend to be frequently uprooted, and the children lose the social networks that support them.[2]

Family Counseling

Someone in the family who is in this kind of double bind needs help, help to see that the needs are valid and help to get the needs met without destroying the family. The participation of other family members in family counseling with a professional can be beneficial. A good counselor will help each family member find a way to get the help needed without having to sacrifice life and personality on the family altar.

If we feel that we are in this kind of trapped relational situation and other family members will not cooperate, we must take steps to get help for ourselves. We must find a professional who understands our spiritual convictions, our love for the family, and the destructive effect of dysfunctional family patterns. We must keep telling our story until we find someone who will listen and help us get the care we need.

Support Groups

If a specific issue is tormenting us, which we feel we must keep secret because of family considerations, we need to look for a support group of people who understand the particular issue we are dealing with. In a support group we will make connections with others so that we don't feel so alienated and helpless. Our sense of shame will be relieved when we realize that we are not the only ones. We will realize that we are not hopeless when others share their experience, strength, and hope with us.

To find a support group in the area, we can call the local hospital, churches, psychiatric treatment clinics, twelve-step groups, radio talk show information lines, or recovery bookstores. These communication networks should be helpful in locating almost any type of support group imaginable. If we are unable to find a support group already in operation, we may be able to find a few other people dealing with similar issues and begin meeting together for mutual support. Please note that a support group is just that; it is not an adequate substitute for professional care. Although there is a great deal of comfort in meeting with others who really understand, there is also the danger of ending up with the blind leading the blind.

DEALING WITH SHAME-RELATED ISSUES

It seems that many unsuspected suicides are the result of a perceived choice between death and dishonor. For those who are immobilized by shame or secret self-hatred, the fear of exposure or the weariness of maintaining two separate lives may lead to suicide. When they can't find the strength to face dishonor, death becomes the victor by default. Since that has been such a persistent and powerful influence historically, it seemed appropriate to address the subject of shame reduction as a means of self-preservation.

Shakespeare immortalized the story of Lucrece, a Roman woman who was raped by the Roman general, Sextus Tarquinius. Afterward, she called her husband and family together, told them the story, and killed herself to prove her honor and that of her family. The disgrace seemed too much to bear. She is a glaring example of art imitating life or, more appropriately, death.

Throughout history, people who were otherwise stable and not recognized as being at risk for suicide have taken their lives in response to the sudden exposure or fear of exposure of something that was overwhelmingly shameful. They are examples that not everyone who commits suicide is suffering from mental illness or living a sinful life alienated from God. They made a decision either to maintain honor or to avoid public shame and ridicule. Here are some examples of shame-related suicides.

Masada: The Stand for Honor

Perhaps the most famous of all mass suicides is the Jewish self-massacre that took place at Masada. In A.D. 70, a large community of Jewish Zealots, along with their families, took refuge from the Romans at the fortress of Masada on the high plateaus above the Dead Sea. For three years they lived under siege until their supplies were nearly exhausted. True to a mutual pact they had made never to submit to the dishonor of becoming Roman slaves, the soldiers at Masada first killed their wives and children and then killed one another—960 people in all—to avoid capture and preserve the purity of their souls. Even the callous Romans were awed and appalled.[3]

Indian "Braves"

The Indian culture of North America provides a more recent example of suicide for honor. Among the Cheyenne Indians, males were provided an institutionalized means of recovering lost honor. A disgraced warrior could place himself in a life-threatening situation, take risks, act bravely on behalf of the tribe, and even inflict pain on himself directly. If he survived, his self-esteem and honor were restored. If not, he was considered to have died an honorable death.[4]

The Indian who wanted to recover his honor or avoid shame placed himself in the midst of high-risk behavior. That same behavior is played out today in many different forms. When I was growing up, my father had a friend who piloted his plane in all sorts of horrible weather. Many said of him that he had some sort of death wish. He seemed to have confirmed that to his friends one night as he confessed that if he had known for sure he could go to heaven after committing suicide, he would have done it a long time ago. A few years later, he died while piloting his plane into the side of a mountain with three of his family members on board.

There are other more common high-risk and suicidal behaviors today. The person who takes drugs while drinking or drives while intoxicated is participating in high-risk behavior that is potentially self-destructive. At some level the person is suicidal. With the rapid spread of HIV, individuals sharing needles or having multiple sex partners must have little regard for their own lives. In this era, few participate out of lack of awareness or stupidity.

Homosexuality and Suicide

Although AIDS is not just a disease of the gay community, it is in that arena that I have had the most contact with people with AIDS. My brother died from AIDS on June 13, 1988. He moved to Laguna Beach at exactly the same time as patient zero, the supposed flight attendant who was most responsible for the rapid spread of the virus in North America among the gay population. Back then no one knew what AIDS was. No one knew that having sex with multiple partners was more dangerous than playing Russian roulette. Today it is different. Some people participate in this high-risk behavior, and they are both consciously and unconsciously committing suicide with every act of sex.

Before you accuse me of being outrageous, let me tell you about a man who admitted to doing just that on national television when he appeared with me on "Geraldo." I knew his story before he appeared, but it was still shocking to hear him go through it again. For quite some time he had struggled with feelings of homosexuality. He had reached out to help many in the gay community, and as he did, he found himself relating more to them than to his wife. The feelings of guilt and shame tormented him until he began to act out sexually. When he did, he said he purposely sought out those he believed to be HIV positive. He was so desperate he hoped the virus would do what his own hand could not: end his life. Indeed, one of his sex partners was positive for the virus, and today the man is HIV positive.

Since that time of desperation he has had a spiritual awakening. He wishes he could undo the damage he did. He has longed to have his wife back, but there is no hope for that. Now his goal is to do as much as he can until he dies of natural causes or the virus. Although he is an example of suicide through high-risk behavior, today he has a smile on his face and a new purpose in his heart.

That man was just one of many who have struggled with sexual identity issues and considered suicide as a way out. The story of Lawrence is another. The essay he turned in to his eleventh-grade English teacher was cryptic. His fantasy of death was dark and brooding, filled with the pain of living, alluding to the confusion over who he was and "what he was." The young idealistic teacher tried not to think about their recent conversation. She noticed that Lawrence seemed shy and reclusive. The few friends he had were girls, and the other boys rejected him outright. She suspected that things were troubled at home, but he never spoke of his family. Judging him by his effeminate mannerisms, she tried to help the young man make peace with himself. She had taken it upon herself to talk to him about the numerous famous men who had made valuable contributions to society even though they were homosexual. He caught her drift. Lawrence was not yet sexually active. He was struggling intensely with his emerging sexual desires and heart-wrenching confusion relating to his gender. Fighting back angry tears, he insisted, "I'm not gay! I would rather be dead!'' Reading his essay again, she corrected the grammar, changed the punctuation in a few places, and returned the paper with a *B*.

She feared that perhaps she had driven him to the brink by stating the obvious. She had read the statistics showing that as a group, homosexuals committed suicide more often than the general population. She thought it best not to meddle further. She didn't dare to look deeper or cross the line into a family situation that had symptoms of pervasive problems. Lawrence finished out the school year without ever looking her in the eye again. There was an unspoken understanding that the discussion was closed permanently. He graduated the following year, and she never knew what became of him. She only knew that his personal struggles with homosexual issues and the shame associated with being labeled homosexual posed a risk of suicide for the young man.

Homosexuals are among those groups considered to have a high tendency for suicidal behavior. A high percentage of those who have contemplated, threatened, or attempted suicide are homosexual or are concerned about homosexuality.

Alienation from oneself or others is often cited as a cause for grief, anger, and frustration, leading to suicide. Emotional alienation from family and mainstream culture is frequently cited as a reason for increased vulnerability to suicide among gays. Dr. Herbert Hendin notes that "unresolved separation anxiety" is a common characteristic in both homosexuality and suicidal behavior, suicide being an expression of rage at having been rejected. Also, homosexuals seem to be particularly vulnerable to all forms of rejection and must typically cope with a greater amount of emotional isolation.[5]

Several studies lend support to these observations. Schneider, Farberow, and Kruks recently found that 19 percent of a group of college-age homosexual men and 23 percent of a group of male homosexuals from the surrounding community had made past attempts to commit suicide. By comparison, 6 percent of nonhomosexual college men reported prior suicide attempts. Suicide attempts among homosexuals were further linked to those critical developmental stages where homosexuality was a central issue. Another research group, from Washington University, demonstrated a connection between overt male and female homosexuality and attempted suicide. True to the prevailing pattern, 23 percent of female homosexuals had attempted suicide compared with 5 percent of the single female heterosexual controls, 7 percent of male homosexuals, and none of the male heterosexual controls. The homosexual group did not have a significantly higher percentage of emotional disorders but had higher rates of suicide, drug abuse, and problem drinking. In yet another study by Dr. Hendin, a group of black suicidal males was examined. About 33 percent of the seriously suicidal black men studied were homosexual, compared with the rate of homosexuality among white males in general, which is estimated at 5 to 10 percent. Among all black males, the rate is even lower. Schneider and colleagues also found that a higher percentage of homosexual men from minority races reported having attempted suicide (69 percent compared to 31 percent of whites).[6]

Not every homosexual who commits suicide does so because of homosexuality. Homosexuals are whole human beings whose lives involve more than just their sexuality. However, someone who struggles with deep shame associated with homosexuality, or experiences a sense of desperation at feeling trapped into a sexual mold, can be at greater risk for suicide. Something needs to be done to address the issue of homosexuality in a way that gives hope.

That is what finally happened with Lawrence. It took many years for him to face the fact that although he was a Christian and morally rejected the homosexual life-style, he had homosexual tendencies he had to deal with. Ignoring them didn't make them go away. He went through seasons of giving in to his homosexual desires followed by seasons of repentance and sexual abstinence. He married and put homosexuality completely out of his life for several years until, at a moment of emotional vulnerability, he gave in to a temptation that presented itself. He considered whether there was any hope for him. He dearly loved his wife and children; at the same time he felt trapped by the desire to be sexually involved in behavior that was clearly contrary to his Christian commitment. He was tired of disappointing everyone: God, himself, his wife, his pastor. He was in incredible pain, overwhelmed by guilt and shame. He could no longer pretend that prayer and willpower would erase the pervasive craving, but he would not give up his Christian convictions and the family he loved dearly. He found himself in a double bind and saw no way out. The unresolved struggle developed into a crisis when he was thirty-two, and he came very close to suicide. In desperation he admitted himself to a psychiatric hospital. There, through hard work and tough choices, he was able to make peace with himself, his homosexuality, his wife, and God.

Lawrence came to the conclusion that whether it was nature or nurture, homosexuality was something he would have to accept as being a part of him (his version of the apostle Paul's "thorn in the flesh"); but he also realized that just because it was part of his makeup didn't mean that he had to live the homosexual life-style. In other words, the desires that were within him from childhood were there due to neglect from his father. He could not erase that part of his development, but he did not have to sexualize the meeting of that need. He tried to heal the wound of his father rather than take the advice of his gay friends and act out sexually. He came to see it in much the same way alcoholics come to accept that the body is predisposed to alcoholism. That doesn't mean they are destined to live a life of drunkenness. Lawrence takes life one day at a time; by the grace of God, he is growing as a whole person. He remains in counseling to deal with issues related to his gender confusion and marital issues. He no longer feels trapped. He doesn't have to pretend that he doesn't have homosexual feelings, and yet he has the freedom to choose the life he desires, being faithful to his wife and to God.

Quite frankly, I realize that many people in and out of the Christian community do not want to admit there are those who have had homosexual desires and have now rectified those feelings. They think that anyone saying that homosexual behavior is wrong is stupid or old-fashioned. I would caution those who value the freedom to live this life-style that they must also allow those who do not want to live it to choose otherwise. If a married man has homosexual feelings but wants to work through them and resolve certain issues so that he can be the husband of his wife and father to his children, he deserves to have that opportunity.

There are also organizations available to help those who have been involved with homosexual behavior but don't want to be anymore. Exodus International is a referral network of Christian organizations nationwide. The number is (415) 454-1017.

The Killer Secret

Norman Larkin was the model of respectability. He was stable, accomplished in his chosen profession, revered by colleagues and friends. He was a dedicated Christian from the time he was a child. As an adult he held positions of church leadership for more years than most people in his home fellowship of Christians could remember. Around their church, Brother Larkin (as he was affectionately called by everyone who had ever graduated from his Sunday school class) was a pillar of the faith. He was always there, greeting visitors at the door on Sunday mornings, leading worship for the men's meeting. So many people looked up to him. So many people turned to him when they needed godly counsel. Just spending time with him gave one the sense of being able to make it in the Christian walk.

His wife, children, and grandchildren seemed to settle down comfortably in the shade of his dependable character. They all found their place in the church family and in the church pew, seated together every Sunday morning third row from the front, to the left of the altar. There was always the empty space in the pew, right on the aisle, next to Mrs. Larkin. The well-worn brown leather Bible rested on the seat, "saving a place" for Mr. Larkin when he finished greeting those coming through the doors.

One Sunday, the Larkin family was conspicuously absent from the pew. No one sat there; it just didn't seem right. Had the Larkins gone on vacation? No one had mentioned it. Hmmm . . . odd. More than a few took note of the absence but gave it no more than a passing thought. It just seemed like their church family was incomplete. When the pastor appeared from the side door and approached the pulpit with reddened eyes, no one linked the two oddities. The announcement of Norman Larkin's sudden death was felt like a physical blow to the congregation as a whole. To each member there was the confusing emotional grappling that goes on when someone tells you the unbelievable and you juggle the thoughts and emotions trying to figure out what the loss means to your life. Because Mr. Larkin had given so generously of himself for so many years, the waves of loss began to swell up across the sea of faces, breaking with gasps and sobs as the realization of the announcement came crashing down.

How did it happen? Was it an accident? The minister was discreet in comforting the grieving congregation and preserving the dignity of his longtime friend and colaborer in the work of God. The congregation never knew of the letter he left behind. In the letter he told how he had grappled with an overpowering area of sin in his life. Sin that was so far from all he loved and held dear, it made him wonder if there were two of him. He had fought as best he knew how. He had used *every* scriptural strategy he knew. He had seasons of freedom, but with each relapse into his secret life his self-hatred grew. He had vowed time and again that this last time was *the* last time . . . only to fall again. He was so sorry for all the people he would leave and disappoint, but he couldn't live with himself anymore. He couldn't go on being a disgrace to God. He chose to condemn himself to death for his sin and pray to God that the grace of Jesus would cover him and let him find peace and forgiveness.

The one thing Norman Larkin did not do, which the Bible tells us to do, was to reach out for the loving help of others, to confess his sins to those who would pray for him and lend him support as he sought healing. That part of his life was too dark, too diabolical. He dare not let anyone ever know. His deep sense of shame, that he was utterly flawed at the depth of his being, immobilized him. The shame kept him in bondage and signed his death warrant.

Whenever we allow any part of our lives to be kept forever in the darkness, vowing never to bring it into the light, there is great danger. If we go on living with the fear that if anyone ever knew the awful truth about us, we would be utterly destroyed, we live at risk. It's been said that guilt is the healthy response to wrong behavior that tells us we need to seek forgiveness and change our ways. Shame is the unhealthy conviction that we *are* defective human beings, unable to change. Shame tells us that our only hope is to hide, to spend our lives trying to do enough good deeds to make up for the darkness of who we really are. When this type of shame is at the core of our self-concept, we are at risk. If somehow we are exposed or if the weight of the double life becomes too much to bear, we may conclude that suicide is both the way out of the pain and the rightful judgment for someone so abhorrent.

If shame has a grip on some area of our lives, we need to take it seriously and get treatment. It may be wise to turn to a professional who will be sworn to keep our confidence as the person helps restore the brokenness of the soul rather than to someone we know personally. If we tell Church leaders, we should make sure that they will guard our confidence and not add to the problem by publicly exposing the sin being confessed. That can add to the stress dramatically and even trigger self-destructive behavior. If it is a deep problem, we need to remove ourselves from public responsibilities as much as possible and seek treatment. Once the power of the shame has been diffused and the shameful or sinful behavior is under control, we may want to cautiously share our need for ongoing support with a trustworthy confidant or spiritual mentor.

WARNING SIGNS

The practical steps discussed earlier in this chapter can reduce the risk of suicide. There are also some specific things to do if suicide seems imminent. There are warning signs that can sometimes be recognized before a suicide attempt. All warning signs should be taken seriously and responded to with action. Here's a list of commonly recognized warning signs:

1. Direct verbal warnings; statements of intention ("I might as well kill myself. There's no way out for me. My life is over.")
2. Depression (see the list of symptoms in chapter 2), especially signs of hopelessness
3. Experience of separation, loss, or bereavement
4. Fears related to severe illness ("I'd rather die than go through that . . .")
5. Giving away valued possessions; setting affairs in order
6. Noticeable change in eating and sleeping habits

7. Communication breakdown; withdrawal from friends and family
8. Moodiness; despair; marked behavioral changes
9. Expressing feelings of being unwanted
10. Violence, recklessness, or rebellious behavior
11. A calm after a season of emotional struggle (Once the decision has been made, he may seem "back to normal." He may appear to snap out of a spell of depression, but what has really happened is that he has finally made the firm decision to end his life.)
12. Drug/alcohol abuse
13. Unusual neglect of personal appearance
14. Radical personality change
15. Difficulty concentrating on anything
16. Psychosomatic or physical complaints

If someone we know exhibits any combination of these warning signs, we need to *get help now.* We may want to ask her if she has ever considered suicide. If she admits to considering the possibility, we need to discover how she would go about it. If she has thought things through enough to have a particular plan in mind, there is *immediate* danger. In any case, it is better to err in getting her help too soon rather than to assume that the warning signs don't mean anything and risk losing her.

FINDING HELP

If a person we care about exhibits the warning signs, we must not under any circumstance leave him alone for one moment. We may call the counselors at New Life Treatment Centers and let them direct our efforts. They will find a resource we can afford. Whatever we do, we cannot just pray or hope this will go away. Too many have died because someone has not acted.

We may also consider calling the National Suicide Prevention Hotline at (800) 333-4444. The counselors can be of immediate assistance or answer more general questions.

Suicidal people need us to protect them from themselves. To fail to do so may be interpreted as a confirmation that their lives really aren't worth saving. If we think that they are just trying to get attention, we may be right. However, many people have actually died while desperately crying out for attention with a suicide attempt. They are literally dying for attention. If we are aware of the need, we must respond by getting them attention that will help.

Notes

1. "Suicide: An Update," *Statistical Bulletin,* April–June 1986, p. 18.

2. Glen Evans, *The Encyclopedia of Suicide* (New York: Facts on File, 1988), p. 122.

3. Evans, *Encyclopedia of Suicide,* p. 122.

4. Evans, *Encyclopedia of Suicide,* p. 122.

5. Evans, *Encyclopedia of Suicide,* pp. 151–52.

6. Evans, *Encyclopedia of Suicide,* pp. 151–52.

Chapter 10

◆

FREEING OUR CHILDREN FROM SUICIDE

What could produce a more frightening thought for any parent than the possibility that a child would commit suicide? The sheer horror of the prospect may cause us to hide from the truth that each year thousands of parents wake up to this grim nightmare too late.

If we have children who are at risk, we are to be commended for the courage it takes to allow ourselves to grapple with the chilling fact that we live in a society where our young people are killing themselves in increasing numbers; the chilling fact is that *every* parent needs to take precautions.

THE SCOPE OF THE PROBLEM

On April 1, 1991, a Cable News Network Prime News report stated that approximately 2,500 teens commit suicide annually in the U.S.[1] That, as we saw earlier, makes suicide the third leading cause of death for teenagers (accidents rank first, and homicides rank second).[2] In March 1991, George Gallup, Jr., released the findings of what he called "the most important poll conducted by our organization in the last 50 years." It was the Gallup Poll on teen suicide in America. The disconcerting results disclose that 1 out of 5 American teens come close to or attempt suicide. A different poll of a cross-section of 1,100 teens nationwide yielded these results: Those who . . .

—Know someone who attempted or committed suicide 60%
—Have considered suicide themselves 33%
—Have attempted suicide . . . . 6%[3]

Of those who considered or attempted suicide, they cited the cause as

—Family problems 47%
—Depression 23%
—Problems with friends 22%
—Low self-esteem 18%
—Boy/Girl relationships 16%

No particular group seems to be exempt from the peril of suicide. An October 1990 release of a poll of "Who's Who among American High School Students" gives ample cause for concern. This poll surveyed teens ranked as high achievers, all *A* and *B* students; economically, they were middle- to upper-class; 76 percent had parents with their original marriage still intact. These are the kids we wouldn't consider prone to suicide. However, results show that they aren't exempt. Here are the results of the poll of high achievers:

—Those who know a young person who has tried to commit
or has committed suicide 61%
—Have considered suicide 26%
—Have attempted suicide . . . . 3%[4]

Apparently, it's not enough to give them a comfortable economic situation, a good education, and a family that looks good on the surface. What can we do?

There are steps we can take to reduce the risk of suicide for our children. The remainder of the chapter will cover these five steps:

1. Decide to act now on the information we have rather than regret later that we waited too long or did not do enough.
2. Take preventive action to deal with family predispositions to depression, obesity, and alcoholism.
3. Make sure that we are not blinded to seeing the warning signs of suicide when they are present.
4. Build up values and beliefs that are shown to be deterrents to suicidal behavior.
5. Develop a family system where members are given the freedom and power that equip them to face life and survive.

EYES TO SEE . . . BUT THEY SEE NOT

Unfortunately, many parents of children who commit suicide are caught completely off guard. In some cases there aren't obvious signs that would automatically sound the alarm. However, in other cases parents look back on the days and weeks preceding a suicide and are horrified to admit that there were warning signs, but they failed to see them. If we are going to be able to protect our children from this risk, we need to check our ability to see the signs. We need to consider whether we are prepared to recognize the warning signs and get help for our children should the indicators present themselves.

WARNING SIGNS

Here is the list of commonly recognized warning signs as they might be manifested in children:

1. When the child makes statements of intention ("I might as well kill myself; there's no way out for me; my life is over"), the parent should consider them direct verbal warnings.
2. The child seems to be depressed all the time, lacks energy, and appears hopeless in many circumstances.
3. The child experiences separation, loss, or bereavement, such as the death of a favorite pet, a best friend, or a close family member.
4. The child has fears related to severe illness ("I'd rather die than go through that . . ."). A child facing the loss of a limb or cancer may choose death rather than live what is perceived to be an abnormal life.
5. When the child gives away favorite possessions, it may be a way of getting affairs in order.
6. Eating and sleeping habits change noticeably.
7. The child stops talking to friends and family and seems to completely withdraw from others.
8. Moodiness, despair, and behavioral changes become evident.
9. The child openly expresses feeling unloved or unwanted.
10. The child begins to act out in violent ways, recklessly demonstrating rebellious behavior.
11. A calm occurs after a season of emotional struggle. If the child seems to have an instant cure for the depression, it could mean that a decision has been made for suicide, and the burden of reality has been lifted.

12. Since about 70 percent of suicides occur under the influence of alcohol or drugs, signs of abuse could mean suicidal tendencies or the need to medicate pain.
13. The child neglects personal appearance, which is unusual.
14. Radical personality change takes place.
15. The child's attention span seems shorter than normal, and the child has obvious difficulty concentrating on anything.
16. The child becomes sickly, complaining about health and constant pains.

We should be aware of these warnings and keep an eye open to any changes in our children's moods and behavior. If several show up in our children now, we should act immediately. In some cases, only one of the symptoms, such as discussing the wish to die, is enough to warrant immediate action on our part.

TRYING TO SEE REALITY

It is not always easy to see the reality of the problems before us. We may be blocking out information due to a feeling of inadequacy to deal with them. We may be in denial for reasons we are not aware. The following self-quiz is provided for us to evaluate whether there are unresolved issues in our lives that may inhibit our ability to recognize the warning signs and take protective action for our children.

1. Have you ever noticed any of the suicidal warning signs and told yourself and others not to pay attention to them (for any reason)?
For example, when a fifteen-year-old says, "I might as well kill myself! No one around here cares about my feelings!" the parents decide, "Let's not make a big deal out of her dramatics and tantrums. It will only encourage her to act that way."

2. Do you pretend that everything is fine when inside you know it's not and you feel that you have to cover up the truth about your child's behavior?
For example, there has been evidence of substance abuse, recklessness, and a dramatic change in your child's mood. However, you try to hide the evidence from other family members or friends: "If your father knew about this, it would kill him. Just go to your room until you feel better." Or you think to yourself, *What would they think of me if they knew my child has such deep problems?* Or to church members, you say, "Oh, he's doing great. He's just very busy with schoolwork and sports," but in reality the child is in deep depression and can't face anyone.

3. Do you devalue, negate, or ignore your child's feelings when he tries to express them?

For example, he tells you that he is despondent over a romantic breakup, and you respond, "Oh, honey, everyone has a broken heart at least once. It's just part of growing up." Or if he expresses "unpleasant" emotions such as anger, you respond, "Don't you ever yell at me. Just go to your room until you can be civil."

4. Do you try to control her through rewards and punishments to convince her that she *shouldn't* feel the way she does?

For example, you say, "Let's just have some ice cream and we can go out for pizza later. You'll feel better then, and we can just forget about all of this unpleasantness," or "I know you're upset that Dad and I are getting divorced, but it will be better. We can give you the large bedroom all to yourself . . . and we'll get you a car."

5. Do you focus more attention on the problems of others outside your family than you do on the problems within your family?

For example, you are consumed with work-related problems to the extent that when your child needs your full attention and emotional support, you are already drained. You volunteer your time to church or civic organizations or are out every evening for various worthwhile meetings, but you are too busy to focus on your problems or your child's problems.

6. Do you feel a strong aversion to seeing a family counselor, do you have a list of reasons why your family doesn't need counseling, or are you rigidly determined that even a credentialed Christian counselor should not be seen?

For example, you tell people that God uses preachers, not counselors, to reveal the truth. (If there was really nothing to hide, what would it hurt to try family counseling to address suicidal tendencies?)

7. Do you fear any admission that your family needs help or strongly object to any outside "meddling" in your family?

For example, you declare, "What can some outsiders tell us about how we're supposed to live? What do they know anyway? Their lives are probably more messed up than ours."

8. Are you consciously aware that a family problem exists (abuse, molestation, addiction, severe depression, etc.) and feel powerless to get your child the help he needs for fear that the family secret may be revealed?

For example, you know that your child has been abused physically by your spouse, but you fear that going for help would mean that the child would be removed from your home. Or you suspect sexual improprieties when your husband tucks your child into bed but feel immobilized to know any more, so you do nothing.

If we said a reluctant yes to *any* of the previous questions, we may be blinded to the warnings if our children were truly at risk. The first step to freeing them from the risk of suicidal tendencies is to courageously face and deal with the issues that cause us to live in denial and take away our power to protect them.

INSTILLING VALUES AND BELIEFS THAT REDUCE THE RISK OF SUICIDE

Some deterrents are common among people who do not opt for suicide, even though they may be depressed:

1. A sense that life is meaningful, pleasurable, and manageable.
2. A sense of responsibility to family and children.
3. Moral and religious objections to suicide.
4. Fear of the physical and existential consequences of the suicidal act.[5]

All of these deterrents are rooted in the realm of morality, values, and religion. As parents, we have the right and the power to strongly influence our children to develop a healthy, morally sound view of life. Security and confidence come from having clearly defined guidelines for living. We have the opportunity to instill this sense of security in the lives of our children by teaching them clear-cut moral instructions regarding what is right and wrong. The Bible tells us that this part of our parenting role is a solemn responsibility that can preserve our children's very lives.

Immediately after Moses had read the Ten Commandments to the people of Israel, God gave these instructions to the people:

> So keep these commandments carefully in mind. Tie them to your hand to remind you to obey them, and tie them to your forehead between your eyes! *Teach them to your children.* Talk about them when you are sitting at home, when you are out walking, at bedtime, and before breakfast! Write them upon the doors of your houses and upon your gates, so that as long as there is sky above the earth, *you and your children will enjoy the good life* awaiting you in the land the Lord has promised you (Deut. 11:18–21 TLB, emphasis added).

To be able to enjoy life, our children need the security of clearly defined boundaries. The boundaries of moral teachings and strong biblical values will give them a framework for understanding life and for making their own choices. The Ten Commandments, which form the basis of law and socially acceptable conduct in our society, were given by God as a way parents could help their children face life successfully. Many parents shy away from "preaching" their values to their children, perhaps because parents of this generation are still recovering from the rebellion of the 1960s and vows they made never to preach the way their parents preached to them. In any case, our children need to learn what our values are in order to test them out and develop their own values. If we fail to communicate clear standards of belief and conduct for living, they may take that to mean we don't value them enough to protect them in this way.

Giving our children a clear understanding of right and wrong, and allowing them to experience the consequences of their choices, is a form of protection. The result will be a greater sense of freedom in their lives. These guidelines and boundaries could be seen as a moral fence around their lives. In a study conducted with school-age children, two groups were told that they could play wherever they wanted within the playground area. One group had their play area enclosed with a fence. The other group had no such physical boundary to limit their play. The group with the firm boundary of the fence felt the freedom to roam all over the area without concern. The group left without the firm boundary apparently didn't feel the same sense of freedom. The children congregated together near the center of the play area. Without the firm boundary, they lacked the security to roam freely. In the same way, when we give our children clearly defined limits for their beliefs and behaviors, they will grow secure in their understanding of life and enjoy life more fully without fear that they may be crossing danger lines they cannot see or feel.

We all need a framework of values from which to make our decisions about life . . . and death. If we neglect our responsibility to teach our children life-preserving values, they will more easily adopt the values being proclaimed by our society. The media never cease advancing the values of this humanistic and materialistic age: the values that may be contributing to the soaring suicide rates in our society; the beliefs that undermine the value of human life and remove societal deterrents to suicide; the beliefs that tell young people their lives don't really matter and suicide is an acceptable response to pain. Can we honestly afford to default on such a vital responsibility?

As a summary of some beliefs and values we may want to focus on as our children grow and learn, consider the following:

- Every human life matters. It is our *being,* not our *doing,* that makes our lives worthwhile.

- Every human life is created in the image of God with a special purpose. We are much more than just another kind of animal in the world's "ecosystem."
- Each person has a contribution to make in this life that matters in the eternal scheme of things, regardless of how long our world will continue before the end of the age.
- We are never completely alone. God is with us, and we can always turn to each other for love, forgiveness, and support when we feel all alone.
- Everyone sins, and forgiveness is available. We can do nothing so horrible that God can't forgive us and we can't forgive one another. Love covers a multitude of sins.
- We are accountable to God for our actions.
- Suffering will be a part of life, but pain doesn't have to destroy us. Suffering can make us stronger and more compassionate people.

MONITORING OUTSIDE INFLUENCES

As parents, we not only need to communicate values but also must be vigilant about monitoring the other sources of information that influence our children. The popular motivational speaker Zig Ziglar says, "You are where you are, you are what you are, because of what has gone into your mind. You can change where you are, you can change what you are, by changing what goes into your mind." This statement is important to consider in our endeavor to protect our children from suicidal tendencies. An overwhelming amount of information goes into their minds. We are not the only ones influencing our children's thinking. Their minds are being filled with input from teachers, television programming, music, advertising, peers, books, magazines, and so forth. We must know what is going into their minds and take an active role in helping them monitor it and interpret it in healthy ways.

There are sensational and tragic stories of parents bringing lawsuits against record companies and rock musicians after their teenage child has committed suicide. They attribute the decision to commit suicide to be a response to the lyrics of a song that openly glorified suicide. One boy was listening to the music tape when he killed himself.

There are also reports of young people who killed themselves accidentally while trying to imitate perverse sexual behavior described in hard-core pornography. One young boy "found a copy of *Hustler* magazine and read the article 'Orgasm of Death.' Out of curiosity, the boy set up the sexual experiment just the way the magazine prescribed, followed the instructions, and wound up dead. The *Hustler* August

1981 article was lying at his feet when his mother found his cold body."[6]

Certainly, these overtly dangerous influences on our children's thoughts, perceptions, and behavior need to be thwarted, but there are also far more innocent influences that we need to be aware of and help our children understand in the context of building up their self-esteem and valuing their lives. Here is an example of this type of "innocent" incident. The mother of a second-grade student in a public grade school was picking her daughter up from school. She went into the classroom and noticed a large poster depicting the relationship between animals and the environment. She asked her child, "Where are the people in the poster?" The child replied, "Oh, we're just one of the animals so we don't have to be in the picture." The response gave the mother an opportunity to explain that people are much more than just "one of the animals" and that public school teachers aren't allowed to explain anything about God in the classroom. The parent was able to help the child integrate potentially confusing and conflicting information relating to how she would grow to see herself. If each of us is just one of the animals, we are in big trouble. I believe we have a higher calling than to just graze on the earth. With all of the self-esteem problems our children have, the last thing we want them to believe is that they are no more important than animals.

BUILDING UP THEIR SELF-CONCEPT

On a regular basis we should affirm our children. We should keep on the lookout for what is unique and special about them and affirm those things. We should identify their talents and give them opportunities to develop those particular abilities. We should help them learn to succeed and allow them to fail without concluding that *they* are failures.

Our words hold tremendous power for our children. We need to be careful not to characterize them in negative terms but to separate exhibiting poor behavior from being a bad person. For example, when a child makes a serious mistake, the response should be, "That was not a wise choice," rather than, "You idiot! How could you be so stupid?" As we learn to use our words to build them up while identifying poor choices and unacceptable behavior, they will grow to distance themselves from the belief that they are worthless.

Self-concept is also undermined by overprotection. Our children need to know that they have the capability of solving their own problems and that we are aware of their capability. Every time we step in to fix something that they could fix or need to fix, we lead them to believe that we feel they are incompetent. If we tell them what to eat, what to wear, when to study, and a thousand other things they can figure out for themselves, they get the message of their incompetence loud and clear. We are doing these things for the right reason: we love our children. But that kind of overprotective love will produce irresponsible children who have not experienced the consequences of poor decisions until later in life. It's better for a child to get an *F* today because of lack of study than to get fired tomorrow because of lack of preparation. A parent who shields a child from the *F* today sets up the firing for tomorrow. And on the dismissal summary that will be placed in the child's employment folder will probably be a note indicating an employee who was irresponsible and had a low self-concept.

The extreme ramification of this low self-concept is suicide. Children who grow up feeling incompetent and worthless may choose to take their lives. Often those who attempted suicide say things like they really didn't mean to die or they had no idea they really would die. Those are the words of kids who have no understanding of consequences of their behavior.

DEVELOPING A HEALTHY FAMILY SYSTEM

According to the 1991 Gallup Poll referred to earlier, 47 percent of teens who have considered or attempted suicide cited family problems as the cause. As our families grow healthier, the risk of suicide will decrease. However, if there is a suicide in a family, we should not conclude that it was necessarily the fault of the family. It's just that a strong, loving support system can help each family member endure and overcome the difficulties all families face. Here are some things we can do.

1. Having a Healthy Marriage

Marriages can't stay together just for the kids. If they are anything for the kids, they are loving relationships. When a marriage is on the rocks, children's emotions are rocky, also. They are very insecure when they do not believe their parents are in love with each other. If parents are having a difficult time in marriage, the best thing they could do for children is to seek out a good marriage counselor. I have seen very few marriages that could not be fixed. The tough part is getting two people to give up on their selfish issues so they can accomplish a greater thing, that of creating a healthy marriage. No effort will have a greater impact on children than the effort to create a great marriage.

2. Spending Time Together

Spending time together as a family and one on one with each child builds strong relationships. It is important to make sure that our time commitments reflect our personal commitments to the welfare of our children. During the time together, we need to work to maintain open communication. That includes allowing the child to express thoughts, feelings, questions, concerns, hopes, and dreams. The open lines of communication may be a lifeline during a troubled time.

There has been a lot of talk about quality time versus quantity time. We can't have quality time with a child unless there is a lot of it. As parents, we need to be creative in the way we develop opportunities to have fun with our children. We also need to find a way to have times of teaching and instruction. Parents who take the time to spend quality and quantity time with their children never regret it. I have never heard a parent say, "I wish we hadn't spent so much time with our children when they were younger." It is always the other way around.

3. Providing Protection from Abuse

Another factor frequently involved in the experience of those who commit suicide is childhood abuse. In a study conducted by the National Institute of Justice, 1,575 children were observed over a period of twenty years. Approximately half had been victims of abuse or neglect. After recently interviewing 500 of the original subjects, now mostly in their twenties, researchers concluded that 18 percent of the adults who had been abused or neglected in childhood later attempted suicide. That was true of only 7.5 percent of nonabused children followed in the study and only 3 percent of the general population. Consistent with current statistics, abused girls were more likely to attempt suicide than abused boys.[7]

If any type of abuse is occurring in the home, the family needs help. We can call Childhelp USA Child Abuse Hotline (800) 422-4453 to talk to someone anonymously about our problem. We are not alone. Child abuse is a problem for families all across the nation. We need to reach out for help for our own sake and the sake of our children. Parents Anonymous offers free anonymous consultation, professional help, and support related to a host of parenting issues, including child abuse. The group's toll-free number is (800) 421-0353.

4. Getting Help for Family Secrets

Just as a shameful personal secret can leave an individual at risk for suicide, a shameful family secret can leave our children at risk. By getting help for family secrets and dysfunctional family patterns, we are acting to protect our children in many ways. So often the shame of family secrets drives children to commit suicide rather than reveal what cannot be hidden anymore. The burden of guilt and shame becomes too great for them to carry.

We need to free our children from these burdens we created. It is a different day. People are more open about their problems, and there is less rejection of those who have them. If we have been keeping a family secret from the world and expecting our children to do the same, we might have placed upon them a burden they cannot bear. They may free themselves from the burden by taking their own lives.

Thousands of families have done the right thing and the brave thing and received treatment for their secrets. Their families stand as examples of what can be accomplished when we humble ourselves, swallow our pride, and allow God and professionals to heal our families.

5. Giving Credence to Children's Feelings

As stated earlier, the *Youth Ministry Resource Book* reports, "About 90 percent of suicidal teenagers feel their families don't understand them. And when they express their feelings of unhappiness, frustration, or failure, the teenagers say their families either ignore, deny, or attack those feelings."[8]

We need to listen carefully to our children and truly hear their pain from their perspective. Often teen suicide is a last-ditch effort to stop the pain of living. Before they reach this point, kids will usually make attempts to let someone know that they are hurting. The danger comes when those around them minimize the pain just because the kids' reaction to the situation seems out of proportion or because parents can't handle the emotional intensity of the kids' grief.

6. Helping Them Navigate Their Grief

If children despair over some loss important to them, we need to help them grieve their losses and move beyond them. If we have never learned to grieve our own losses, that may be extremely difficult for us. If we just ignore their pain and cries for help, they may feel desperate to do something to stop the pain. Their youth may not allow them to realize that the pain will pass and that they will be happy again someday.

Suicide may be their attempt to make the pain stop, their way of shutting off the whole painful world. G. K. Chesterton said, "The man who kills a man kills a man. The man who kills himself kills all men. As far as he is concerned, he wipes out the world."[9] Like the child who closes her eyes and thinks that no one can see her, the child who commits suicide is often trying to close himself off from everyone who may hurt him; he is trying to stop the world and the pain of living from touching him.

Our children need an open line of communication with us, not just a one-way connection. We can help them avoid feeling so trapped emotionally by listening to their cries, affirming the validity of their feelings, assuring them that life will get better and they can make it. They need support as they try to navigate the emotionally turbulent tides of adolescence.

Two books may prove helpful in this regard: *The Grief Recovery Handbook* by John W. James and Frank Cherry and *Surviving Adolescence* by Jim Burns. During times of loss, the worst thing we can do is to pretend that everything is fine. They need us to help them acknowledge their losses honestly, grieve their losses, and learn to cope.

7. Choosing Our Battles Wisely

As Dr. James Dobson points out in the title of his recent book, "Parenting isn't for cowards." It takes courage to face the challenges of parenting in our stress-filled world. If we don't want to forget the joy of parenting in our desire to protect our children, we need to choose our battles wisely. We don't have to fight over everything in their lives, from the length of their hair to how they decorate their rooms. We do need to be prepared to fight for those things that have the power to threaten their lives.

CONCLUSION

Suicide. What a horribly negative thing to have to think about! It seems that life is too short to go about focusing on the negatives like suicide, but the world is too full of stress not to. If we love our children, we have laid a foundation so that the last thing they would ever consider is suicide. If we love our children, we have let them know that their behavior produces negative and positive consequences for themselves, but it never affects our love. We will also allow them to fail. And they will know that there is always a way back from failure. Our children will know that God the creator and Mom and Dad can forgive and provide a way to start over. If we love our children, we will do all this and more. We will set an example of healthy living that motivates them to live life to the fullest. Those who are doing that have no time to think about suicide.

Notes

1. Gallup Poll on teen suicide, March 1991 release date, presented at the New York Forum on Teen Suicide, April 1, 1991, as reported on CNN Prime News, April 1, 1991.

2. Eugene Roehlkepartain, ed., *The Youth Ministry Resource Book* (Loveland, Colo.: Group Books, 1988), p. 166.

3. Summary, *Who's Who Among American High School Students, Twenty-First Annual Survey of High Achievers' Views on Education, Careers, Social Issues, Sexual Issues, Drugs* (Lake Forest, Ill.: Educational Communications, October 1990).

4. Summary, *Who's Who.*

5. Lee Willerman and David B. Cohen, *Psychopathology* (New York: McGraw-Hill, 1990), p. 363.

6. Dr. Jerry R. Kirk, *The Power of the Picture: How Pornography Harms* (Pomona, Calif.: Focus on the Family, 1989), p. 7.

7. Thomas H. Maugh II, "Studies Link Childhood Abuse to Adult Social Dysfunction," *Los Angeles Times, Orange County Edition,* Feb. 17, 1991, section A, p. 5.

8. *The Youth Ministry Resource Book,* p. 168, from Nancy H. Allen and Michael L. Peck, "Suicide in Young People" (West Point, PA: American Association of Suicidology), p. 2.

9. G. K. Chesterton, quoted in Glen Evans, *The Encyclopedia of Suicide* (New York: Facts on File, 1988).

Section 3

◆

OBESITY

Chapter 11

◆

THE DILEMMA OF OBESITY

THE RIDICULE OF BROTHERS

A line from a popular song of the fifties caused me more problems than any other piece of music ever written. The sonata I messed up at my piano recital produced less misery than that first line from "Peggy Sue." You see, I was a fat child—much plumper than my lean two older brothers. So they converted the first line of the song and sang those words to me in a new rendition over and over again. I can still hear them today, "Piggy Sue, Piggy Sue, piggy piggy . . ." and on and on it went, along with their deep laughter of ridicule. They really thought they were something.

When you are fat, ridicule is something you have to learn to live with. I was tortured for something I could not figure out. I did not eat more than my brothers. We all subsisted on our Texas diet high in fat from a lot of beef and fried vegetables, such as okra and green tomatoes. When they ate, the food became muscle. When I ate, it became fat through no fault of my own. I know there are many others who have experienced the same frustration just because the body seemed to be programmed differently from birth.

If you have not experienced this phenomenon personally, you probably know someone who obviously has a marked difference in metabolism. For someone overweight, there are few things as frustrating as watching a person eat all the fried chicken, biscuits, and gravy that he wants and still remain thin. It just doesn't seem fair. But it is reality. Twinkies for one person are entirely different from Twinkies for another person. One is predisposed to thinness, and the other is predisposed to heavy weight problems.

When we look at a fat person, we often think of irresponsibility or wonder what underlying problem is being self-medicated with food. But upon watching a thin eater devour three hamburgers, we seldom question the person's mental health. The fact is, many thin people use food as medication just as many heavy people do. It is just that for one group, the consequences are much more obvious. It doesn't seem fair, and like many other areas of life, it isn't.

REEXAMINING THE CASE OF MR. AND MRS. SPRAT

The unfairness of it all has been written about down through the ages. This nursery rhyme points to the differences in two people who lived in never-never land:

> Jack Sprat could eat no fat,
> His wife could eat no lean;
> So 'twixt them both they cleared the cloth,
> And licked the platter clean.

Evidence may prove that Mrs. Jack Sprat is one of the most grossly misunderstood women of all time! You remember Mrs. Sprat, the image of the "fat lady" in Mother Goose nursery rhymes. There she sits at the dinner table across from her painfully thin husband. She's reaching her pudgy arm back to the serving tray to get another helping of that juicy meat. We can almost imagine her double chin jiggling as she "chews the fat," savoring each bite. The tiny stool seems to strain under the weight of her massive frame. Her husband sits up straight and tall over his empty plate, his thin profile in stark contrast to her portly one.

Today, we might caption the picture from the storybook, "You are what you eat!" All these years we've been led to believe that the reason Mrs. Sprat was fat and Jack was thin was strictly because of their diets. Okay, they didn't come right out and say it, but that's the point of the story, isn't it? Scientific research reveals that this approach isn't fair to Mrs. Sprat. It's far too simplistic.

What if Jack and the Mrs. ate the same foods, but her body stored the energy as fat, while Jack's revved up its engine and burned all those extra calories? It wouldn't seem quite fair, but that very well could have been the case. Some people are born with bodies that are inclined to store fat, and others are born with bodies that are inclined to burn it.

For a moment, let's imagine the suffering, conflict, and shame Mrs. Sprat endured. Perhaps we don't need to imagine it. We may be modern-day versions of Mrs. Sprat. It seems that everything we eat turns to fat. We struggle to diet; and when we allow ourselves to splurge the least little bit, the food appears to be applied directly to the tummy or thighs! Yet, we may sit across the table from people who can eat anything they want, in copious amounts, and they never seem to gain an ounce.

While we receive smirks and snide remarks from the opposite sex, they are viewed with approval. While we sit on the sidelines because of embarrassment and physical limitations, they run, jump, and play with ease. We're passed over for the front office job, while their healthful looks seem to open doors. We are left wondering if our spouse's lack of interest has to do with our weight (and heap guilt on ourselves), while they are free to focus on a host of possible reasons for marital difficulties without assuming the blame. While we may shy away from participating at our children's school functions for fear of subjecting them to the cruel taunts of other children, they never give it a second thought. We're sick and tired of being sick and tired, and yet, they have energy to burn!

This tendency to gain weight is hazardous in many ways. It can lead to health problems, self-hatred, low self-esteem, deep shame, relational difficulties, depression, marital problems, discrimination, interference with career plans, eating disorders, social limitations, resentment, and bitterness. The most debilitating result is the deep depression that comes from living as outcasts or second-rate humans in our eyes and the eyes of others.

THE TRUTH ABOUT OUR STRUGGLE WITH OBESITY

We are born with a certain predisposition for how the body processes food energy (calories). It is metabolism, which can set us up with an inclination toward obesity. Metabolism can also change in response to many factors and affect how the body burns or stores food energy. The food energy stored in the body takes the form we affectionately call fat.

This section will explain how two individuals can eat the same foods and one can't gain weight if he wants to, but the other stores away the fat involuntarily. This is not to say that one is doomed to obesity if predisposed in this way. It does mean that some people have to be more careful than others to keep their bodies at a healthy weight. This understanding can help us become more compassionate and less judgmental of anyone who is overweight or obese (including ourselves).

There are plenty who fall into these categories. The numbers of people who carry around excess weight are growing. Anthropologist George Armelagos says that Americans carry 2.3 trillion pounds of stored fat. According to a U.S. government survey, almost two out of every three Americans (61 percent) are somewhat overweight, and about one in five is obese (weighing 20 percent or more over "desirable" weight). Twenty-three million Americans are classified as obese; eleven million are severely obese (weighing 40 percent over their "desirable" weight). A conservative estimate gauges that one of ten American children is obese. That means a lot of fat people live in a culture where thin is the ultimate virtue. The weight standards generally used are compiled by the Metropolitan Life Insurance Company to help actuaries assess the health risks associated with obesity.[1]

In modern Western culture, people seem desperate to measure up to the "thin is in" standard of beauty, and yet as a population, we continue to gain excess weight. In a world where millions are starving, Americans are driven to spend billions of dollars each year on weight control programs. From 1970 to 1980 there was a 500 percent increase in the sales of weight control goods and services; in 1980 it was estimated that seventy million Americans were dieting.[2]

If we're spending all this money and doing all this dieting and still gaining weight, something must be missing in our approach to the problem. Before we can solve a problem, we need to have an accurate understanding of the causes so that we can deal with the *real* problem. Perhaps gaining an accurate understanding of the causes of our weight problem will relieve some of our shame and prompt us to adjust the way we go about trying to rid ourselves of the excess weight.

For example, if we assume that our obesity is primarily caused by a lack of willpower, we will focus our attention on gaining control of ourselves. If this assumption is too simplistic and doesn't deal with the whole problem, we will be frustrated in our attempts to lose weight. We'll spend much time and emotional energy tearing ourselves down for repeated failures instead of using our energy in identifying and solving the real problem.

It's like caring for an infant. An infant has many needs: to stay dry, to be fed, to be held, and to be kept at a comfortable temperature. If we realized that the baby cries when it is hungry and drew the conclusion that whenever the baby cries, it must be hungry, we would set ourselves up as failures in the realm of child care. If we focused all our attention on that one area of concern, we would be frustrated (not to mention the poor baby). We would find ourselves dealing with a screaming infant who was cold, wet, and emotionally needy. We would be left wondering why our attempts to feed the baby didn't seem to work. This situation can parallel our frustrated attempts to deal with obesity if we make assumptions about the condition without considering the whole picture. These assumptions and preconceived notions also affect the way we see other people who struggle with weight control.

Depending on the approach one takes and the individual being considered, obesity may be seen from four primary perspectives:

1. A disease—not the kind one catches from a germ but a developmental one that progresses over time. It is a medical condition with physical as well as emotional symptoms and consequences. As with other diseases, it requires and responds to medical treatment. The disease could be caused by a lifelong hereditary tendency or a temporary biochemical/hormonal imbalance.
2. An addiction—a dysfunction of the mind and body with characteristic patterns that are similar to those of other known addictions, such as alcohol and drug addiction.
3. A psychological problem—resulting from unresolved inner conflict, skewed thought patterns, or emotional reliance upon food to feed a deep emotional need.
4. A behavioral dysfunction—learned behaviors that were shaped by environmental factors. A set of "bad habits" that we learned growing up set us up to continue in life patterns that lead to obesity.

The approach we take in viewing any problem (including obesity) will determine the approach we take to solving the problem.

IT'S AN ELEPHANT OF A PROBLEM

The story is told of a group of blind men arguing about what an elephant is like. They all know because they have experienced the elephant for themselves. One man who reached out his hand and took the animal by the tail swears that it's like a rope. The man who happened to slam into its massive side is determined that the elephant is like a wall. The man who ran his hands up and down the squirming trunk and felt the spray of water coming out with great force knows that the elephant is more like a fire hose than anything else imaginable. The short man who felt the sturdy mass of the animal's leg asserts that the elephant is like a tree trunk. The fellow who was swatted by the large flat ear says it is like a fan. Is it any wonder that a hearty argument ensued?

Our beliefs and arguments about obesity may parallel this account. We have drawn conclusions from our own real but limited experience.

We have sought to deal with the "whole animal" on the basis of our assumptions gained from what we know about the part that has touched our lives or the part we have explored. We may in fact be blind to the other factors that influence the tendency to gain weight through a lack of information (or even denial if our obesity is related to deep emotional scars or unresolved inner conflicts).

Obesity is an elephant of a problem with many facets and seemingly contradictory parts. It's a human problem. It crosses over our intellectual concepts of being exclusively a problem of the body, mind, or spirit. It deeply affects and involves all of our being. The body is obviously involved. The mind participates by bringing all that we have learned into the approach we take to eating and trying to control our weight. The spirit (defined here as the seat of the will and emotions) is involved as we often use food as a source of comfort and pleasure in response to inner turmoil and as we struggle with the issues of self-control and "moral strength" or willpower.

The ones who view obesity as primarily a physical problem may think that learned habits and inner conflicts have nothing to do with it. It's just that they have a "hormone imbalance" or have trapped their bodies into the vicious cycle of yo-yo weight gains by repeated attempts at crash dieting. One simplistic solution used by those who view the problem as purely physical might be to resort to the use of drugs to try to deal with the body chemistry or to use liposuction to physically remove the excess fat.

The ones who see obesity as primarily the result of learned behavior may focus all their attempts at weight control on behavior modification (chewing each bite one hundred times, always eating at the dining table instead of in front of the TV, etc.) without addressing possible physical conditions or spiritual needs being fed by eating food.

The ones who see obesity as merely a moral dilemma will view those who are overweight as being weak willed. They might be overheard to say, "The only exercise they need is to push themselves away from the table." If we try to battle our own weight problem exclusively in the moral/spiritual realm, we may assume that we gain weight because we eat when we want to feel loved or because our willpower needs to be exercised more. We may beat ourselves up with guilt and condemn ourselves mercilessly because we don't keep our eating and weight under control. Those who see the problem simply as a moral/spiritual problem may neglect the real possibility that the cause may lie in physical, biochemical, and/or behavioral areas.

NO ONE ISOLATED CAUSE

Obesity is one example of what scientists call a heterogeneous condition. Many elements are involved in causing it, and various factors may play a part in making some people more vulnerable than others. In fact, there are probably several different sorts of obesity, each linked to different kinds and combinations of vulnerability factors.

Those who have dedicated themselves to the study of obesity see the threads making up the fabric of the problem to be a complex mix of human elements. They involve body, mind, *and* spirit. To attempt to address the problem in only one area will probably yield short-term results, if any. One psychologist voices this opinion: "I believe . . . predispositions toward overweight are inherited but that environment—a person's family, peers, ethnic makeup, and so on—help shape those predispositions."

Poor Mrs. Sprat might have been predisposed to store fat even if she were the one eating only the "lean." Maybe we were wrong about her all along. We may want to take a moment to consider some of our attitudes toward the Mrs. Sprats we know. Have we made some unfair assumptions about them (or ourselves) on the basis of our limited knowledge? Have we been too hard on them? Is there hope for the Mrs. Sprats of the world to find a way to live in a body that maintains a healthy weight, whether or not they are predisposed to obesity?

Notes

1. "As Seventy Million Americans Try to Shed Weight," *U.S. News & World Report,* Dec. 22, 1980, p. 61.
2. "As Seventy Million Americans Try to Shed Weight," p. 61.

Chapter 12

◆

THE CASE FOR PREDISPOSITION

To make the case for predisposition, I have provided a quiz with detailed answers. The quiz will identify some misconceptions, thus opening up and enlarging the understanding of obesity. I hope this broader understanding will better enable us to free ourselves and our children from obesity. At the least, we will have information to help us form a more compassionate opinion of those we might have misjudged previously.

FAT FACTS QUIZ

Circle true or false in response to each statement.

1. Obesity has been officially declared a disease.

   True   False

2. There is strong scientific evidence that proves some people are genetically predisposed to obesity.

   True   False

3. Obesity is listed as the third most significant health problem in America.

   True   False

4. Two groups of people can overeat the exact food and the exact number of extra calories; while one group gains weight at a rapid

rate, the other group gains much less weight from the same number of excess calories.

True   False

5. Studies show that obese people generally eat more than people who maintain an average weight.

True   False

6. Having a body that has a tendency to store fat or to burn fat rapidly is an inborn genetic trait.

True   False

7. In studies of twins, separated at birth and raised in different families, results show that environment is as influential in predicting obesity as is the person's genetic makeup.

True   False

8. Becoming overweight or underweight is something that runs in families.

True   False

9. An obese person who faithfully follows a strict low-calorie diet will lose weight slowly but steadily.

True   False

10. Studies show that our genetic makeup influences the types of foods we crave.

True   False

11. Differences in the rate at which the body burns fat are inherited.

True   False

12. All people burn approximately the same number of calories while they are resting.

True   False

13. Some people's bodies change to burn calories faster when they overeat, making it difficult for them to gain weight when they want to.

True   False

14. Exercise not only burns calories, but it causes the body to change so that it burns calories at a higher rate (even when not exercising).

True   False

15. Our bodies add fat cells throughout life, particularly when we over-eat.

   True   False

16. The number and size of our fat cells can increase but never de-crease.

   True   False

17. The fat cells created by overeating are different from those created naturally.

   True   False

18. Fat cells created by a high-calorie diet accumulate fat more quickly and don't lose fat as easily as fat cells formed naturally.

   True   False

19. Our diet and type of exercise routine determine where our bodies tend to store excess weight.

   True   False

20. Men and women tend to store fat in different places on the body.

   True   False

21. People who store fat in the upper body are prone to fewer health risks than those who store fat in the lower abdomen and pelvic areas.

   True   False

22. Some obesity has been proven to be caused by diseases.

   True   False

23. A hormonal imbalance can trigger obesity in people who have been thin for most of their lives.

   True   False

24. Changes in the way a man's body processes food to energy can cause him to start putting on weight in his late thirties and early forties, even though his diet doesn't change at all.

   True   False

25. A carefully planned program of rewards and punishments has been shown to help people lose weight.

   True   False

26. The most successful treatment programs for obesity focus primarily on dietary and behavioral changes.
    True   False

27. A biochemical impairment or imbalance in the brain can set us up to experience constant cravings and never feel full.
    True   False

28. Clinical research shows that obese people eat more frequent meals than those who maintain a normal weight.
    True   False

29. Obesity that begins in childhood doesn't respond as well to treatment as obesity that begins later in life.
    True   False

ANSWERS TO THE FAT FACTS QUIZ

1. Obesity has been officially declared a disease.
   TRUE

In early 1985, obesity was declared a disease by the National Institute of Mental Health. Whatever else it is, being severely overweight seems to be a biological problem involving physical changes in metabolism, neurochemistry, and physiology that do significant damage to both body and mind. The disease of obesity and its related health problems are very expensive in terms of collective health costs and often in a premature loss of life.

2. There is strong scientific evidence that proves some people are genetically predisposed to obesity.
   TRUE

The genetic basis for obesity has been thoroughly documented in animals since the 1960s. Some of the earliest experiments performed to discern genetic factors in obesity involve mice. Certain strains of mice are born fat—often as much as ten times fatter than a normal-size mouse. They suffer from many of the same medical complications observed in obese humans (e.g., diabetes). These mice have two copies of a gene that has been labeled *ob*. Their litter mates whose only distinguishing characteristic is the lack of an *ob* gene remain normal in size. Researchers found that if they fed the obese mice a diet identical to that of normal mice in caloric content, the obese mice stored a greater than normal amount of those calories as fat. They were genetically equipped to store greater amounts of energy.

Scientists also used these strains of genetically obese mice to determine the biochemical processes involved in genetic obesity and to compare the differences between inherited obesity and that caused by overeating. Real physical and biochemical differences distinguished the body systems of the two groups.

Mice prone to obesity, determined by the *ob* gene, had a defect in what is called the sodium pump (it pumps sodium and potassium through the cell walls). The physiological defect made their bodies decrease the level of energy they would expend. Their metabolism slowed down, burning less energy and storing more as fat. This animal research is clear evidence that some tendency toward obesity can be genetically inherited.[1]

At the annual meeting of the American Heart Association, described in the January 1990 *Journal of the American Medical Association,* several studies were reported to support a genetic basis for obesity. Recent studies (over the last three decades) have upheld the evidence for genetic involvement in obesity, and most investigators have been satisfied to say that some of the reason for increased vulnerability to obesity involves inherited traits.

Twin and adoption studies have long been used in the attempt to separate the roles of nature and nurture in family diseases. Research on family and twin and adoption studies gives evidence that genetic factors in people can set up a predisposition to obesity.

In early 1987, Albert Stunkard and his colleagues announced the results of a study they had been involved with the past thirty years. Studying four thousand pairs of male twins (two thousand pairs were identical; the other two thousand pairs were fraternal), the researchers examined the height and weight of the twins at the time of their induction into the army twenty-five years earlier, and again when they were in their forties and fifties.

At the time of their induction physicals, the identical twins were found to have the same level of obesity twice as often as the fraternal twins, who are not genetically identical. Furthermore, when their levels of obesity were again compared, after twenty-five years, many more of the twin pairs had developed a problem with excess weight, but the identical twins were still two times more likely to have the same obesity level as were fraternal twins.

After complex calculations to determine *heritability* (that's scientific jargon for how much inherited genes were found to be the cause of the obesity), Stunkard's group of investigators found that up to 30 percent of the excess in weight carried by the identical twins could be attributed to genetic factors. They concluded that a strong genetic component is present in determining human obesity, which means that children of obese parents are predisposed by their inherited genetic makeup to storing excess fat and becoming obese.[2]

In May 1990, Albert Stunkard again reported the results of a study involving weight and height records for adopted identical and fraternal twins from Sweden and the U.S., raised either together or apart. Participating in the study were 93 pairs of identical twins raised apart, 154 pairs of identical twins raised together, 208 pairs of fraternal twins raised apart, and 218 pairs of fraternal twins raised together.

The body mass index of both groups of identical twins was more similar between twins in each pair than among the pairs of twins, and similarity between twins raised apart was nearly the same as that between twins who grew up in the same environment. In the pairs of fraternal twins, body mass index was not as closely matched. This finding indicates that regardless of the eating habits and activity levels in the home they grew up in, the identical twins were genetically programmed to store fat in similar degree and in the same areas of the body.[3]

Five percent of the United States population are estimated to have inherited a predisposition for obesity, according to Trudy Burns of the University of Iowa. Burns and her colleagues calculated the body mass index of 277 high-school students and 1,303 of their first-degree relatives (parents, siblings, first cousins, aunts, and uncles). They discovered a pattern in family body mass levels that follows the expected pattern for inheritance through a single recessive gene.[4] The only way to inherit the recessive gene that predisposes someone to obesity is to receive the recessive gene from each parent. Five percent of the population are predicted by Burns's model to carry two recessive genes for obesity. These people are more likely to be among the heaviest in our population.

People can also be predisposed to an average or a less than normal weight level. Thirty-four percent are likely to carry both an obese gene and a slimness gene, which means that they would be predisposed to maintain an average weight. The remaining 61 percent carry two genes for slimness, which means they are predisposed to burn energy rather than store it as fat. The same predictable pattern that correlated genetics with obesity was seen in families whose genetic makeup tended toward slimness or average weight levels.

3. Obesity is listed as the third most significant health problem in America.

FALSE

Obesity has been called the nation's number one health problem. Dr. William Castelli, who has directed the now forty-year-old Framingham Heart Study on longevity in Framingham, Massachusetts, warned that his studies have shown that every pound gained over one's ideal weight range on the 1959 Metropolitan Life Insurance tables increases the probability of death during the next twenty-six years by 2 percent.[5]

Only comparatively recently have we begun to believe the considerable evidence that obesity is a serious health problem. Those who carry excess fat have three times the incidence of high blood pressure and diabetes as that found in the population in general. They also have more risk for heart disease. Their risk of developing respiratory disorders is very high, and risks are elevated for arthritis and certain cancers.

In very obese women, five times the normal rate for cancer of the uterine lining and increased risks for breast and cervical cancer have been found. In men who are obese, there is an increased chance of developing cancers of the colon, prostate, and rectum.

4. Two groups of people can overeat the exact food and the exact number of extra calories; while one group gains weight at a rapid rate, the other group gains much less weight from the same number of excess calories.

TRUE

Scientific research has proven this to be the case (even though it's not fair!). A study by Claude Bouchard and his colleagues at Laval University in Quebec, reported in May 1990, investigated twelve pairs of identical twins who actually lived in their research unit for four months. All the young men were fairly inactive. For the first two weeks of the study the twins were allowed to eat as they pleased while researchers closely monitored their body metabolism and other functions. During the following stage of the experiment, they were overfed (more than the intake of calories found to be usual for them during the previous two weeks of monitoring) with one thousand extra calories per day, six days per week, over a period of one hundred days. After that period, their body fat distribution and weight gains were recorded and studied. Some pairs of twins gained about nine pounds, while others gained up to twenty-nine pounds.[6]

5. Studies show that obese people generally eat more than people who maintain an average weight.

FALSE

There is no convincing evidence that obese people consume more daily calories than do people of average weight. In fact, scientific research comparing groups of obese people to groups of people of average weight found that overweight people do not generally eat larger quantities (more calories) than their normal weight counterparts.[7]

6. Having a body that has a tendency to store fat or to burn fat rapidly is an inborn genetic trait.

TRUE

There is a difference in how a person's body is predisposed to either storing or burning fat. In Claude Bouchard's May 1990 Canadian study of twins, remarkably, the metabolism of those pairs who gained the most weight turned the excess energy almost exclusively into fat, while in those who gained lesser amounts, only a slightly greater amount of fat gain than muscle gain was observed. Bouchard and his fellow researchers are convinced that genetic factors are involved in determining the *results* of overfeeding. The tendency to store extra energy as either fat or muscle tissue, as well as resting metabolic rates, and the location of accumulated fat were found to be likely to be inherited to some degree. As Bouchard commented, "These differences reflect something very fundamental in the body controlling the form that extra energy takes."[8]

7. In studies of twins, separated at birth and raised in different families, results show that environment is as influential in predicting obesity as is the person's genetic makeup.

FALSE

By 1978, at least a few studies had given evidence of a genetic basis for obesity. The studies involved identical twins separated from each other at birth and adopted or placed in foster homes. Their weights turned out to be more similar to their other twin (identical twins have identical genetic makeup) and their natural parents than to their adoptive siblings and parents.[9]

In January 1986, Dr. Albert J. Stunkard, director of the Obesity Research Group at the University of Pennsylvania, and his colleagues from Copenhagen and Houston, Texas, reported the results of a large study, which used meticulous Danish adoption records. Five hundred forty Danish adoptees were questioned via mail and the results analyzed for data on height and weight. Using a height-weight formula, the researchers calculated the body mass index for each adoptee and identified each as thin, median weight, overweight, or obese. They did the same calculations for adoptive and biological parents of each adoptee.

Examining the data, Stunkard found a strong connection between the adoptees and their biological parents, especially the mothers, in all four categories of body mass, including the obese group. To his surprise, he found no relationship at all between adoptees and their adoptive parents when levels of obesity, overweight, median weight, and thinness were compared. This finding clearly indicates that genetics are far more influential in predicting a tendency toward obesity than the home environment we grow up in.[10]

8. Becoming overweight or underweight is something that runs in families.

TRUE

Children with a single obese parent have a 40 percent chance of being overweight. If both parents are obese, the children have an 80 percent chance of being obese.[11] Determining how much of this tendency is due to environmental factors, such as poor diet or learned behavior, and how much can legitimately be attributed to genes is not as clearly defined.

At the 1990 American Medical Association meeting, several studies focused on obesity in families. In one revealing study, researchers observed a family whose members always remained at an ideal weight, despite consuming 3,500 calories per day. That's enough to store one pound of fat if no energy is expended. Half of the calories consumed came from fats, and even though the family members exercised very little, they still did not gain weight! (I know . . . it isn't fair.) Even without a predisposition to obesity, most of us would have gained weight rapidly if we overate like that.

The family was found to have an extremely high level of high-density lipoprotein (HDL), a type of cholesterol that seems to discourage fat storage, and low levels of low-density lipoprotein (LDL), which is associated with increased fat storage. This is strong evidence that the rate at which each person's body processes food may be inherited. The family of nearly one hundred members continues under observation and may give researchers more important information about the mechanisms involved in gaining, maintaining, and losing weight.[12]

9. An obese person who faithfully follows a strict low-calorie diet will lose weight slowly but steadily.

   FALSE

Chemicals within the body systems regulate how much fat the body reserves in storage. When an obese person goes on a strict diet, the body may interpret it as a starvation threat and increase the chemical that regulates the rate at which the body stores fat, in essence telling the body, "Oops! There seems to be a lack of food. We better save more of it as fat." The biochemical that sends this message to the body is abbreviated LPL.

Philip Kern and company tested LPL activity in nine extremely obese subjects (235 to 385 pounds) both before and after dieting. The subjects lost an average of 94 pounds on a very low-calorie diet. After their large weight losses, the subjects were observed to have significantly increased activity levels of LPL. Those who were most overweight to begin with also had a greater increase in levels of LPL. This mechanism, operating in the very obese after drastic dieting, might favor increased fat storage and, therefore, work against any additional weight loss.[13]

Still other changes in the resting metabolic rate (RMR, the rate at which the body burns calories while resting) can occur in response to severe dieting or starvation. This "starvation reflex" can slow rates of metabolism by 20 to 35 percent, rendering consistent weight loss and maintenance, especially in the very obese, an extremely trying affair. After just a few weeks of dieting, they must again decrease their intake of calories by the same percentage by which RMR has dropped simply to *maintain* their previous weight loss. Furthermore, when normal eating patterns are resumed, a higher percentage of food is converted to fat rather than lean mass, and the body is found to contain a higher percentage of stored fat and less lean tissue than it did before dieting began.

10. Studies show that our genetic make up influences the types of foods we crave.

    TRUE

Newborn children of a group of obese parents were compared with newborns of nonobese parents to see if certain preferences come with being born to certain moms and dads. Researchers observed that if the parents are fat, children are more likely to prefer sweet tastes when someone gives them a choice. They are also more likely to get excited over tastes and sights in general.[14]

Still another study of eight thousand twins by researchers at the Medical College of Virginia "suggests obese people are genetically pro-grammed to eat a high fat, high salt, diet."

11. Differences in the rate at which the body burns fat are inherited.
    TRUE

In a recent study involving rates of metabolism, the subjects were children of six lean and twelve obese mothers. Researcher Susan B. Roberts of Tufts University measured energy intake and expenditure of these children at three different ages. The first measurements were taken in the first few days of life. At that point, no differences were observed in the metabolic rates of the infants. At three months, mea-surements were again taken—with no difference evident in energy in-take but with significant differences in energy expenditure. At one year, 50 percent of the children of obese mothers and none of the children of lean mothers were overweight. The overweight children registered an energy expenditure 20.7 percent lower than infants who did not be-come overweight.[15]

The difference in energy expenditure could account for the difference in weight gain between the two groups. Studies done with the Pima Indians showed that some of us are predisposed to "fidgeting" (moving around) more than others when we are not involved in a specific activity. This fidgeting level influences how much energy we use while resting and how many calories we burn up on a regular basis. Since our fidget-ing level is set by genetics, it follows that the rate at which the body burns energy is also inherited.[16]

12. All people burn approximately the same number of calories while they are resting.
    FALSE

Many studies of obesity have used individual resting metabolic rate measurements to determine differences in body metabolism. Each per-son inherits a set rate at which the body will burn food energy (calories) while at rest. This resting metabolic rate can also be influenced by exer-cise and by hormonal/biochemical changes in the body. Research in this area reveals important clues about why some bodies store up an excess of body fat. For instance, RMRs in women are lower than those in men (meaning that a woman's body tends to burn energy at a lower rate, burning fewer calories overall and allowing more energy to be stored—more fat). RMR also declines dramatically with age (about 2 percent per decade after age twenty), encouraging additional accumulation of fat.[17]

Those who live in cold climates have higher RMRs to meet their bodies' need for more heat.[18]

The average person at complete rest uses between fifteen hundred and eighteen hundred calories per day. But certain people use their energy more efficiently, or more slowly, and some burn far more energy than they need to get the job done.

> 13. Some people's bodies change to burn calories faster when they overeat, making it difficult for them to gain weight when they want to.
>
> TRUE

In one study conducted at the University of Vermont, a group of thin men and a group of obese men ate an extra thousand calories per day over a three-week period. Measuring the resting metabolic rate of each subject both before and after the start of the experiment, the researchers found that the thin men developed higher RMRs in response to the increase in calorie intake whereas the obese men experienced no change in RMR. The obese men gained weight, but the thin men did not. Some of the thin men increased their daily intake of calories between six thousand and eight thousand over their energy requirements before they began to gain weight! The differences were believed to be linked with inherited traits.[19]

> 14. Exercise not only burns calories, but it causes the body to change so that it burns calories at a higher rate (even when not exercising).
>
> TRUE

Exercise has been repeatedly shown to raise resting metabolic rates not only while the exercise is being performed but also for as long as fifteen hours afterward. That is why exercise can be doubly effective in helping us gain control of our weight. It not only burns up calories but actually changes the body so that it burns up a higher rate of calories for up to fifteen hours after we stop exercising.[20]

> 15. Our bodies add fat cells throughout life, particularly when we overeat.
>
> FALSE

Fat cells (adipocytes) usually increase in numbers only during infancy and adolescence, especially if a child is overfed. There are some rare instances when they will multiply during prolonged overeating in adulthood.

16. The number and size of our fat cells can increase but never decrease.

    TRUE (Yes, sad . . . but true!)

The number of fat cells, though it may increase, will never decrease. Fat cells may shrink when less fat is stored in them, but they will never grow fewer in number.

17. The fat cells created by overeating are different from those created naturally.

    TRUE

Fat cells added due to high caloric intake tend to act differently from those formed at other times.

18. Fat cells created by a high-calorie diet accumulate fat more quickly and don't lose fat as easily as fat cells formed naturally.

    TRUE

Fat cells formed by overeating don't lose their fat as easily and are likely to form new fat deposits more quickly after dieting.

19. Our diet and type of exercise routine determine where our bodies tend to store excess weight.

    FALSE

Not only are there inherited tendencies toward gaining weight, there are also tendencies that determine *where* we gain weight. (No, we weren't crazy when we suspected that piece of chocolate cake was headed directly toward our thighs!) There are actually patterns of genetically determined body shapes. That means that if we were to become overweight, our genes would tell the body where to store the fat.

Our bodies are genetically preprogrammed as to where on the body to store excess fat. In the study of twins by Claude Bouchard of Quebec's Laval University, the twins in each pair shared a tendency to accumulate fat in the same places—some mostly in the abdominal region, others on the hips and thighs.[21] This and other clinical research confirms that the body's genetic program has a predominant say in where our bodies store the excess fat. Our diet and exercise routine can help determine how much extra fat there is for the body to store away and how firm our muscle tone is in a specific area of the body.

20. Men and women tend to store fat in different places on the body.
    TRUE

Gender can influence where the body tends to store fat. In general, women tend to accumulate fat in the lower abdomen and pelvic area (taking on a pear shape), and men tend to accumulate fat in their arms and upper chest (taking on an apple shape). Researchers have lately referred to persons with these patterns of sex-related obesity as having an applelike shape or a pearlike shape. Some men, however, may resemble the pear shape, and some women the apple shape.[22]

21. People who store fat in the upper body are prone to fewer health risks than those who store fat in the lower abdomen and pelvic areas.
    FALSE

Genetically determined shape can influence how much of a health risk results from whatever excess fat we carry. Although all obesity carries elevated risk of sickness and premature death, those with the apple-shaped body have a much greater risk for certain health problems than those with the pear-shaped body. The tendency to accumulate abdominal fat has been linked to various medical problems, such as diabetes, high blood pressure, and high levels of blood cholesterol. Some researchers believe that the apple-shaped body tends to accumulate more fat inside the abdomen rather than just under the skin, possibly interfering with internal organs and metabolism.[23]

22. Some obesity has been proven to be caused by diseases.
    TRUE

Approximately 1 percent of all obesity is caused by other medical conditions. Even though the chances of becoming obese because of a related disease are very small, it is important that they be recognized. For instance, if our obesity is caused by diabetes and we neglect getting medical care, it could cost us our lives. Diabetes is a defect in glucose (sugar) metabolism that leads to dangerous or fatal levels of sugar in the blood. Hypoglycemia is a related problem involving low levels of blood sugar. Both throw off the body's energy balance mechanisms, often resulting in substantial increases in fat storage and obesity. However, obesity also causes diabetes, and it is often difficult to identify the primary problem. Either way, treatment is more than just a matter of desiring an attractive body; it becomes a matter of life and death.

23. A hormonal imbalance can trigger obesity in people who have been thin for most of their lives.

TRUE

Changes in hormonal balance can trigger the onset of obesity in people who have never before had a weight problem. Underproduction of some sex hormones is sometimes involved in predisposing an individual to obesity, as is overproduction of estrogen, the hormone responsible for increasing a woman's fat stores in adolescence and pregnancy. That may be why some women become obese at the time of pregnancy or puberty.

Obesity is also associated with diseases of the endocrine system, such as thyroid hormone deficiency. (It is more rare than people claim, but it does have the potential to create metabolic obesity in those who really are affected.)

24. Changes in the way a man's body processes food to energy can cause him to start putting on weight in his late thirties and early forties, even though his diet doesn't change at all.

FALSE (But don't breathe easy just yet.)

A man's metabolism tends to slow down in his late twenties and early thirties (not his late thirties and early forties). So he starts putting on extra pounds, even though his diet hasn't changed a bit.

Our tendency to gain weight changes with age. Our bodies seem to alter the way they process food into energy during the changing phases of life. Women tend to experience this metabolism change in their forties and fifties.[24]

25. A carefully planned program of rewards and punishments has been shown to help people lose weight.

FALSE

One source notes, "There has been surprisingly little evidence to demonstrate that reinforcement and/or punishment has much influence in the development of factors influencing weight gain."[25] It's not just a matter of wanting to gain a reward if we lose weight or to avoid some set punishment that allows us to lose weight. Anyone who has suffered with obesity knows that the desire to be at a healthy weight is reward enough and the pain of living in an obese body within our culture is already punishment enough.

26. The most successful treatment programs for obesity focus primarily on dietary and behavioral changes.

FALSE

The most successful treatment programs take a comprehensive approach to weight control, including recovery from addictive-compulsive cycles, behavioral changes, dietary changes, exercise, and group support. However, there is no one surefire treatment program to help every obese person. That makes sense because of the various factors involved in why one person may struggle with excess weight compared with why someone else does. Each person needs individual assessment of the problem and an individualized plan to deal with the elements affecting the body.

27. A biochemical impairment or imbalance in the brain can set us up to experience constant cravings and never feel full.

TRUE

Serotonin is one of the chemicals produced in the brain that regulates hunger and appetite. When levels of serotonin drop, we are prompted to eat and also prompted as to what kind of food to eat. When the serotonin level rises to a certain point, we reach a point of satiety and experience a feeling of fullness. The amino acid tryptophan is the basic material from which serotonin is formed. In most people, increasing levels of tryptophan in the diet will increase serotonin levels. Tryptophan is found primarily in carbohydrates. In a healthy body, eating carbohydrates increases the level of tryptophan, which in turn causes the body to produce higher levels of serotonin. Serotonin will then cause a sensation of satiety for carbohydrates, encouraging us to eat proteins. The proteins, having less tryptophan, cause serotonin levels to drop again, prompting us to again eat carbohydrates. In this way, a balance in the levels of serotonin is maintained.

In clinical settings when serotonin production is blocked with drugs (as in some forms of depression), weight gain is experienced. Also, the antidepressant drug d-fenfluramine raises serotonin levels and sometimes reduces persons' consumption of carbohydrates (since they don't have an appetite for them).

In obese people, the interaction of tryptophan and serotonin seems to be impaired so that not enough serotonin is manufactured. The levels of serotonin are not corrected naturally, and the persons continue to crave the carbohydrates that would, under normal circumstances, correct the problem. Without the normal signals of satiety (feeling full), the persons crave a constant flow of carbohydrates. In this way, the persons are set up by the body to live in a state of constant craving and hunger. When they respond to the body's signals to satisfy the perceived hunger, they are set up to become or remain obese.

28. Clinical research shows that obese people eat more frequent meals than those who maintain a normal weight.

    FALSE

Frequency of meals has been shown to be associated with obesity— but not in the way we might expect. Among schoolchildren, those who had less frequent meals had *increased* levels of excess weight and more fat in their skinfold thickness measures.[26] Fewer meals are associated with an increase in fat storage, higher cholesterol levels, and lower glucose tolerance.

29. Obesity that begins in childhood doesn't respond as well to treatment as obesity that begins later in life.

    TRUE

Obesity that begins in childhood is more likely to involve abnormal numbers of fat cells (to be hyperplastic) and is more difficult to resolve than obesity that begins in adolescence or adulthood. Obesity beginning in adulthood is usually characterized by an increase in fat cell size (hypertrophic) and has a better response to treatment.

CONCLUSION

With all these facts, we can better help those who have a weight problem by understanding it is much more than just a case of low willpower. We can free ourselves from the dilemma of obesity since the battles we will fight will produce results rather than more frustration. We can free our children by helping them develop attitudes, habits, and understanding that will lead to a life free of obesity. Before we work with our kids or others, however, it is best that we free ourselves.

Notes

1. Zolt Harsanyi and Richard Hutton, *Genetic Prophecy: Beyond the Double Helix* (New York: Rawson, Wade, 1981), pp. 125–26.

2. Albert J. Stunkard and Bill Lauren, "Family Fat," *Health,* Feb. 1987, p. 8.

3. Albert J. Stunkard et al., "The Body-Mass Index of Twins Who Have Been Reared Apart," *New England Journal of Medicine* 322 (1990): 1483–87; Steven Findlay, "The 10 Top Developments of the Year," *U.S. News & World Report,* June 18,

1990, p. 78; "Chubby? Blame Those Genes: Heredity Plays the Pivotal Role in Weight Control," *Time,* June 4, 1990, p. 80; and Ethan A. H. Sims, ed., "Destiny Rides Again as Twins Overeat," *New England Journal of Medicine* 322 (1990): 1522–24.

4. K. A. Fackelmann, "Family Ties Point to Recessive 'Obesity' Gene,'" *Science News,* Nov. 18, 1989.

5. Ellie McGrath, "Girth Control: Debate over Age and Weight," *Time,* Aug. 19, 1985, p. 57.

6. Claude Bouchard et al., "The Response to Long-Term Overfeeding in Identical Twins," *New England Journal of Medicine* 322 (1990): 1477–82.

7. "Born to Be Fat?" *U.S. News & World Report,* May 14, 1990, p. 62.

8. Henry E. Adams and Patricia B. Sutker, *Comprehensive Handbook of Psychopathology* (New York: Plenum, 1984), p. 662.

9. Adams and Sutker, *Handbook of Psychopathology,* p. 662.

10. Martin Katahn, "Your Body Blueprint—Born to Be Fat?" *Mademoiselle,* Sept. 1987, p. 337.

11. Catherine Houck, "Programmed to Be Fat?" *Cosmopolitan,* June 1987, p. 58, and "Chubby? Blame Those Genes," p. 80.

12. Martha F. Goldsmith, "Heart Disease Researchers Tailor New Theories—Now Maybe It's Genes That Make People Fat," *Journal of the American Medical Association* 263 (1990): 17–18.

13. Philip A. Kern et al., "The Effect of Weight Loss on Activity and Expression of Adipose Tissue Lipoprotein Lipase in Very Obese Humans," *New England Journal of Medicine* 322 (1990): 1053–59.

14. Adams and Sutker, *Handbook of Psychopathology,* pp. 671–72.

15. Susan B. Roberts et al., "Energy Expenditure and Intake in Infants Born to Lean and Overweight Mothers," *New England Journal of Medicine* 318 (1988): 461–66.

16. Diane D. Edwards, "Metabolism Studies Predict Obesity," *Science News,* Nov. 14, 1987, p. 309.

17. Ruth Papazian, "Transitions," *Weight Watchers Magazine,* May 1990, p. 65.

18. "Taking the Mystery Out of Metabolism" *Current Health,* Feb. 1985, p. 24; and Adams and Sutker, *Handbook of Psychopathology,* p. 662.

19. "Taking the Mystery Out of Metabolism," p. 24.

20. *Encyclopedia Americana,* s.v. "Metabolism."

21. Bouchard et al., "Response in Identical Twins," pp. 1477–82.

22. Lee Weidman, "The Testosterone Connection: Women with Upper-Body Fat May Have Extra Male Hormones," *Health,* Nov. 1983, pp. 10–11.

23. "Apple-Shaped People Beware," *USA Today,* Oct. 1990, pp. 4–5.

24. Goldblatt, Moore, and Stunkard (1965), in Adams and Sutker, *Handbook of Psychopathology,* p. 653.

25. Adams and Sutker, *Handbook of Psychopathology,* p. 671.

26. Falry et al. (1964), in Adams and Sutker, *Handbook of Psychopathology,* pp. 666–69.

Chapter 13

◆

FREEING OURSELVES FROM OBESITY

Eating became one of the most pleasant activities I could find to fill the lonely hours, and I ate and drank with abandon. The large amounts of food I ate were a substitute for everything I felt I was lacking in my life. After a while, [it] became my only consuming interest. I thought I looked okay, because those fleeting glimpses [in the mirror] were self-deluding. I was dying. But I never said anything because I didn't want anyone to know.[1]

If we take a moment to ponder the life of the woman speaking, few of us would lack sympathy for her. I can feel for her because at times in my life, those could have been my words. That was how I felt, and that was what I did. We can sense the desperation, the emptiness, and the intense pain. We see a real live model of the addictive-compulsive cycle and the devastation it brings. We realize the deep shame involved in an ongoing struggle with obesity. We probably feel sorry for her. Imagine . . . feeling sorry for Elizabeth Taylor!

The quote was taken from a story about Elizabeth Taylor. For years now we've kept track of her ups and downs as we noticed the photos on the front pages of the tabloids—those violet eyes staring at us as we unloaded our groceries onto the checkout counter. One time we saw her bloated and looking miserable, hardly recognizable as the beauty women all over the world have envied for decades. Another time, we saw a slim smiling Liz next to some headline that promised to reveal her latest dieting secret. The tabloids showed no compassion for the real human being trapped inside the cycle. Sure, they promised the "miracle diet of the month," but where was the promise of freedom for Elizabeth Taylor? Where was the promise of freedom for the millions of men and women who know the cruel suffering of yo-yo dieting and recurrent obesity?

JAN

"Hi, Jan. Congratulations!" the other girls echoed as they approached their lockers. Jan had just been chosen for next year's eighth-grade cheerleading squad. Although the other girls were envious, they wanted to be associated with her. After all, Jan was the only girl in the junior high to make it on to every sport team and the cheerleading squad, which virtually ensured popularity. She was the image of what every plump girl with two left feet longed to be. Puberty had been kind to Jan. Her naturally thin frame now had curves in all the right places. "Thanks," Jan said with an air of confidence.

Eighth grade passed, and Jan maintained her social status. She was sure she had a good chance to make the high-school cheerleading team next year. That should put her in a secure position of popularity on the high-school campus and give her ample opportunities to attract one of the popular guys on the football team. Her plans were set, and she was used to having things her way if she just worked hard enough.

Jan didn't make it to the cheerleading tryouts in the fall. Instead, she was sitting out in the field behind the school smoking marijuana with her new circle of friends. The group made fun of the cheerleaders and the others in the social groups where they were rejected. Why? What happened to Jan to make her abandon the plans she had worked toward for years? What made her hide behind the drugs and the ankle-length black coat she had taken to wearing almost constantly?

Between the end of eighth grade and the beginning of ninth grade, something cataclysmic happened to Jan's body. For some unexplained reason, she began gaining weight at an alarming rate. She went from five two and 105 pounds in June to five two and 155 pounds in September. There was really no point in trying out for cheerleader.

Throughout high school and college Jan fought back. She dieted, starved herself, binged, and repented to begin again. She joined a health club and Weight Watchers. She read numerous books on weight control. She bounced back and forth between 145 and 170 pounds. Well-meaning friends and relatives gave their particular formula for restoring her previously attractive figure and healthy appearance. The girls and guys she had snubbed when she was on top vented their frustration now that she had lost her qualifications for popularity. Every aspect of her life and self-concept was drastically affected.

Finally, during her last year of college, Jan broke free from the cycle of obesity. She now enjoys the freedom to eat whatever she wants and maintains a healthy weight. She never diets . . . says she doesn't have to. Is there something we can learn from her story that fits with what we've learned about predisposition to obesity? Can we learn something here that will help those of us who are trapped in the vicious cycle of obesity?

FREEDOM FOR REAL HUMAN BEINGS

What are we to make of all the evidence that indicates some of us are predisposed to obesity? What difference do all the scientific studies and clinical conclusions mean to Liz and Jan? What difference can they make in our lives as we seek freedom from obesity?

One conclusion is indisputable in light of genetic research. That is, each one of us is an individual. Each of us is created with a unique combination of genetically prescribed commands that designed who we were to be before we were ever born. There's no one else exactly like us, and there never will be. Since we are individuals, we need to discover the response to the body's unique sensitivities and conditions that will allow us a healthy life-style. It won't work to take others' response to their unique weight problem and apply it directly to ourselves (even if we do wish we could look exactly like them).

Remember the illustration of the blind men examining the elephant and drawing their conclusions on the basis of their limited perspective? Well, chances are that we had drawn our own conclusions about obesity before reading this book. They might have been based on a limited perspective as well. We may be experiencing some confusion now if the facts we've read about obesity dispel some of our previous beliefs. If we are to gain any lasting help from the information, we need to be able to fit it into our previous beliefs and draw some sort of plan from new conclusions.

Let's take a look at obesity from several commonly held perspectives to get a better idea of the possible solutions we should consider for our individual conditions. Some people will swear from their experience that their perspective is *the* correct view of obesity. From their viewpoint, the only way to deal effectively with a weight problem is to believe their theory and follow their prescribed solution. They know because they have experienced it for themselves, and it worked. Well, they might have experienced it for themselves, but they didn't experience it for us! They might be as sure that their view is right as one blind man was sure that the elephant was like a rope and another knew that the elephant was like a tree trunk. We must broaden our perspective before we can narrow it again to a successful solution.

THEORETICAL PERSPECTIVES

Here we will look at several commonly accepted theories, all of which undoubtedly convey a measure of truth:

1. Obesity can be caused by a physical disease or hormonal imbalance.
2. Obesity can be the result of an addiction to food used to medicate emotional pain.
3. Obesity can be the result of a moral or spiritual problem; our gluttony and lack of self-control cause us to sin by consistently eating more than we need.
4. Obesity is caused primarily by behavioral and learned responses to environmental factors.
5. Obesity can be caused by a genetic predisposition to respond to diets (artificial famines) by triggering binge eating and storing extra fat in anticipation of the next famine (diet) as a means of survival.
6. Obesity can be caused by a genetic predisposition alone to store excess fat instead of converting it to useful energy.

As we look at each theory related to current research and human experience, we will get an expanded view to help us customize a plan.

Theory #1: Obesity can be caused by a physical disease or hormonal imbalance.

Although only 1 percent of all obesity is determined to be caused by physical diseases, such as diabetes or problems with a hormone imbalance, it still needs to be considered.

One young woman condemned herself mercilessly for many months as just being fat and lazy (like her older sister always told her she was). She avoided going to the doctor. She didn't want to pay someone to tell her what her sister would tell her for free and what she "knew" about herself anyway. When she finally did see a doctor because she was falling asleep recurrently and it was interfering with her job, she was found to have a thyroid condition, which was easily treated. She began taking the medication, and the problem of "being fat and lazy" went away.

Theory #2: Obesity can be the result of an addiction to food used to medicate emotional pain.

At present, the conviction holds that some obesity, like some alcohol abuse, is a matter of addiction. That is, compulsive overeating is used as a means of escape from emotional pain. When this cycle of inappropriate eating to compensate for emotional pain is prolonged, it can result in obesity.

Figure 13.1 depicts what the food addiction cycle might look like.

Figure 13.1

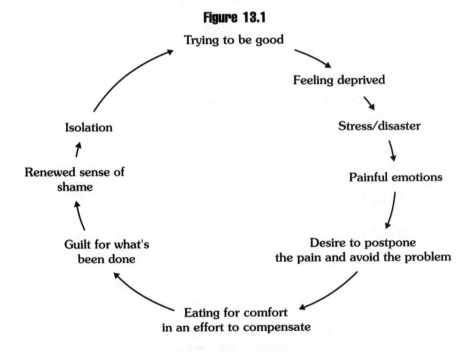

At least four clinical symptoms are recognized as diagnostic measures of both the presence and the severity of addiction. Many health care professionals and counselors find that in some cases, they do apply to compulsive overeating:

1. *Preoccupation* with a substance, when that preoccupation is prolonged and compulsive;
2. *Tolerance* of the substance: larger and larger doses are needed in order to produce the same results that formerly required a smaller dose;
3. *Dependency:* withdrawal symptoms, either physical or psycholog-

ical, are experienced when use of the substance is abruptly discontinued;

4. *Debilitation:* Both physiological and social (e.g., family, job, school) functioning is significantly impaired.[2]

The pleasure connection

Any activity or state that involves pleasure—either by stimulation or by the elimination of pain and distress—is a possible avenue for the addiction cycle to begin. When a given pleasure relieves chronic discomfort or misery (e.g., depression, anxiety, loneliness), it gives incentive to continue. The person feels driven, even though the "drug of choice" will eventually result in pain of its own making.

Those who see compulsive overeating as an addiction predict that real recovery can begin only when the pain caused by the effects of the addiction exceeds the pain the addiction is being used to medicate. Perceiving *all* obesity as an addiction can lead to a viewpoint that says, "Well, when you finally get sick and tired of being fat, you'll do something about your weight." This attitude lacks the compassion needed by anyone who struggles with obesity for any reason.

If a cycle of compulsive overeating is in effect, it may also be tied in to physiological and biochemical patterns in the brain but interpreted as *only* emotional. That is common because emotions and desires are connected to the body's appetite signals through neurotransmitters or "pleasure-connectors" in the brain.

Neurotransmitters are the messenger cells of the brain. They are linked in many ways to our experiences of emotion, pleasure, and pain. These are, of course, strong motivators and key players in the addictive process. However, exactly why neurotransmitters are implicated in risk for obesity is still unclear.

Certain types of neurotransmitters are known to have an effect on obesity or processes that may be associated with increased risk of accumulating too much fat. Excesses and deficiencies of selected *norepinephrine* neurotransmitters are known to enhance food intake, while *dopamine* neurons have been shown to be necessary for weight gain in animals with a rare defect of the hypothalamus.[3] *Serotonin* has been implicated in many common psychological disorders. In adolescent girls, low serotonin often results in bulimia, a severe eating disorder involving binge eating and purging by vomiting.

Whatever the mechanisms involved, neurotransmitters certainly play a part in some forms of obesity and are especially suspect as reinforcers of the addictive process. The *polypeptides* are a class of neurotransmitter known to have effects such as pain relief, pleasure intensification, relief from depression, and enhanced concentration and learning. Two polypeptides, *endorphins* and *enkephalins,* have been suspected to play a role in eating behavior. Enkephalins are located in areas of the brain related to eating, a clue to possible involvement with obesity.[4]

Therefore, when we conclude that it's "just an emotional thing," we may not realize that many of our emotional cycles and addiction-related behaviors are affected by very real biochemical levels within the brain. It's just that our experience of these neurotransmitters is felt most keenly in the realm of our emotions, cravings, and desires. We live in a culture that tends to minimize the validity of our feelings in favor of more tangible influences. So, we may discount a real physiological component of our obesity because the evidence of the problem comes to us through our emotions. What we term an *emotional addiction* may really be a biochemical compulsion that could respond to certain types of medication.

The addictive personality?

Although many people believe that addiction is the lot of a predisposed addictive personality, there is little evidence that such a personality exists (recovered addicts, no longer acting out their addictions, frequently appear to be completely different people from when they were under the sway of an addiction). Many professional counselors have begun to pursue a different line of thought.

Instead of the term *addictive* personality, it might be more accurate to use the term *addicted* personality. This line of thinking goes that at some point a person becomes addicted to a particular substance or behavior. Moving through life and not resolving the issues that led to the addiction, the person replaces one addiction with another. She remains addicted, and until she begins the recovery process, she will always feel the effects of the addiction.

Vulnerability to addictions

"I do not believe that any one addictive personality type exists, but that people become addicted because they are vulnerable to the *addictive process,* which is rampant in our culture," says Dr. Lawrence J. Hatterer.[5] What makes them vulnerable? Although "emotional damage or dysfunction is a key to understanding addiction," a variety of factors —genetic, biochemical, environmental—"always play roles in addiction and must be taken into account in understanding any addict."[6] Just as with alcohol addiction, predisposition to food addiction, and so to obesity, is tied in to many other familial and emotional issues. These must be dealt with in a healthy way if the need for the addictive cycle is to be broken.

Theory #3: Obesity can be the result of a moral or spiritual problem; our gluttony and lack of self-control cause us to sin by consistently eating more than we need.

This theory is based in reflection on the Bible's admonitions regarding gluttony. Proverbs 23:21 asserts, "For the drunkard and the glutton will come to poverty, and drowsiness will clothe a man with rags." Also consider Philippians 3:18–19: "For many walk, of whom I have told you often, and now tell you even weeping, that they are the enemies of the cross of Christ: whose end is destruction, whose god is their belly, and whose glory is in their shame—who set their mind on earthly things." In this passage, it seems that the gluttonous person is associated with being an enemy of Christ. That is *not* the point the apostle Paul was developing in the passage of Scripture. However, some Bible-believing people interpret the verses that way and therefore feel wary of the moral character of obese individuals.

People typically *assume* that obesity must be the result of gluttony. Therefore, they reason, the way to deal with the obesity is to repent of the sin of gluttony, gain spiritual strength and increased self-control, and begin to live the good moral life God intended. As we have seen, this theory breaks down because some people overeat with abandon and their bodies burn up all evidence of their sin! Some who exert more willpower and self-control than their skinny friends can imagine continue to gain weight. Still within our thin-loving culture, obese persons are morally suspect.

Our aversion to obesity is less involved with concerns of physical appearance than with the conviction that obesity is associated with weak moral character. In the late 1970s, William DeJong, a social psychologist, conducted research among 226 high-school girls involving opinions about the obese. He found that girls perceived as fat were also perceived as "less dynamic," and that fat girls who gave a reason for their fatness were better liked and thought to be more self-controlled, cleaner, and sweeter than those who gave no reason.[7] Most Americans, and many of their doctors, pastors, priests, and counselors, continue to think of obesity as almost entirely a problem of moral character, chiefly involving self-control.

Figure 13.2 describes what the cycle might be like for the person who sees obesity from a purely religious viewpoint.

Figure 13.2

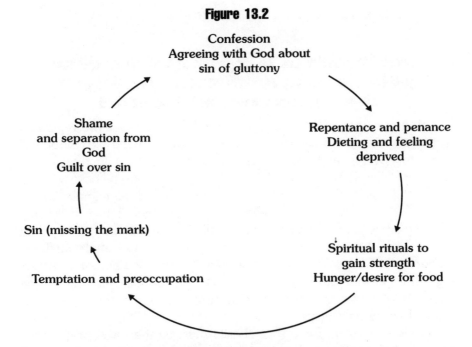

Confession
Agreeing with God about
sin of gluttony

Shame
and separation from
God
Guilt over sin

Repentance and penance
Dieting and feeling
deprived

Sin (missing the mark)

Temptation and preoccupation

Spiritual rituals to
gain strength
Hunger/desire for food

Theory #4: Obesity is caused primarily by behavioral and learned responses to environmental factors.

Dr. Thomas Wadden believes that environment influences obesity. He points out that for each dollar the surgeon general spends for the prevention and treatment of obesity, it is outmatched by a hundred dollars spent by the food industry to lure us into consuming more junk food and fat-laden foods. (Note: A Big Mac is almost 60 percent fat!)[8]

In support of his view that environment is the key player in obesity, Professor Stanley Garn cites his findings that people who are not related biologically but live together (e.g., husbands and wives) have a tendency to maintain similar levels of weight. He also points to groups of people, such as entertainers and other public figures, who manage to stay trim because they are financially at risk if they don't.[9]

That may explain why some people are obese, but if we take this view exclusively, we may conclude that all a person needs to do to overcome obesity is to work a program of behavior modification, change some factors in the environment, and develop new habits. Yet, those who approach their weight problem merely from an environmental perspective, with behavior modification as the only treatment program, have short-term results.

Theory #5: Obesity can be caused by a genetic predisposition to respond to diets (artificial famines) by triggering binge eating and storing extra fat in anticipation of the next famine (diet) as a means of survival.

This theory is based on an understanding of the theory of adaptation, which basically suggests that all creatures, including human beings, are designed to adapt to their situation in a way that ensures their survival. Our bodies are genetically predisposed to store fat to keep us alive in times when food is in short supply. Our genetic makeup determines how sensitive our systems are to the lack of food, how well they cause us to hunger for more than enough food when it's available again, and how much of that food energy is stored as fat when there's an abundance.

From this viewpoint, those of us whose bodies crave lots of food after a season of dieting and store fat in large amounts might be seen as lucky —that is, if we lived in a place where food was scarce. The genetically influenced predisposition would allow us to survive better than those "unlucky" folks whose bodies refused to store fat no matter how much they ate. But . . . alas, we live in a land of abundance, and the only famines we will survive are the ones we impose on ourselves in the form of low-calorie diets.

Low socioeconomic groups . . . high level of obesity

This theory explains why some of the lowest economic groups have the highest incidences of obesity. Both children and adults of low socio-economic class are more prone to grow obese. In women, the condition is six times more prevalent in lower socioeconomic classes.[10]

We've probably seen pictures of long lines of Russians waiting all day to get the bare essentials for their meals. They are hungry most of the time. And yet, have you looked at the bodies of the people in line? They are fat! "Sixty Minutes," the popular CBS news magazine, did a report on Russia. One segment showed sunbathers at a Russian beach. Remember our picture of Mrs. Sprat? Well, imagine hundreds of women like her, except they were wearing two-piece bathing suits. That was basically the picture. Lying on extra-large beach blankets next to them and romping in the water were rotund men with protruding bellies. Judging from the scene, the Russian population seemed to have more than enough food, at least in the form of stored fat. What's the explanation? Do they have a secret stash of goodies they're sneaking into when no one's looking? That is highly unlikely.

This paradox can be explained by the theory of adaptation. Since the bodies of the Russian people have endured hunger, they have adapted to store more of the calories they take in as excess fat. In that way they are more likely to survive in the absence of food over an extended period.

A cultural trigger for obesity

In our nation, we have plenty of food available, much more so than the Russian people. There is no socioeconomic reason that, as a population, we should be affected by this genetic survival mechanism. The key is that our bodies don't differentiate between food shortages caused by economic conditions and food shortages caused by our belief that we must go hungry (diet) to stay thin.

A sociological reason in our culture may cause some of us to gain excess weight. We live in a culture where we practically worship a flawlessly lean appearance. Our culture loathes the appearance of anyone who is overweight. Therefore, we fear being fat and respond by creating self-induced food shortages. If dieting were a disease, it would be at epidemic levels in Western culture. One study calculated that 70 million Americans were on a diet.[11] And yet, in keeping with the rate of dieting, as a population, the weight of our excess stored fat continues to increase. How can we explain this?

We who have an abundance available to us have made our bodies grow up thinking that there was always a food shortage. As a result, some of us end up looking like the men and women on extra-large Russian beach blankets. What do our bodies have in common with them, other than excess amounts of stored fat and the ability to survive a long cold winter? Whether for socioeconomic reasons or cultural reasons, our bodies have had to respond to recurrent food shortages.

Making sense of fat facts

The process of adaptation for survival explains some of the surprising facts we learned in the Fat Facts Quiz. It explains why obese people were found to eat less often and consume less food overall than their slim friends while gaining increasing amounts of weight. Those who have never been afraid of becoming overweight have consistently fed themselves when they were hungry. Their bodies never had to use their survival mechanism to store excess fat.

It also explains why some young women are thin until puberty and then get caught in a vicious cycle of dieting and gaining weight (like Jan in the opening story). Women are genetically preprogrammed to gain some weight during the onset of puberty. That is the body's response to the changing hormones that turn a little girl into a woman capable of bearing children. The extra padding is designed to prepare the young woman to nurture a baby if necessary. In our culture, adolescence is a time when peer pressure is put on the young woman to remain as thin as ever to maintain social status. It may be the first time she has suppressed her hunger in an attempt to stay socially acceptable. As a child, she ate whatever she was hungry for and stayed at a healthy weight. When dieting begins in earnest, often at menarche, the genetic predisposition to survive food shortages goes into effect. The diet-weight loss-binge-weight gain-diet cycle is set in motion.

This principle also can apply to weight gain after childbirth. Instead of accepting that bodies need the extra padding for a season, women panic and try a crash diet. If they are so predisposed, the cycle is set in motion to crave food to make up for the shortage and to store excess fat.

On a theoretical level this may even play into why women experience this struggle beginning in their fifties and sixties. Studies have shown that a woman's metabolism slows down during this stage of life resulting in a slight weight gain. If the response is panic, the cycle is set in motion.

Figure 13.3 shows what the cycle associated with this theory would look like.

Theory #6: Obesity can be caused by a genetic predisposition alone to store excess fat instead of converting it to useful energy.

As can be seen from the research, a genetic predisposition definitely affects how, where, and how much fat is stored on our bodies. The various studies of twins provide convincing evidence that genetic predisposition to obesity is more of an influence over the shape of the body than environmental factors. Some people may conclude that nothing can be done to offset this genetic predisposition and that there are no other contributing factors.

Persons who grapple with the evidence regarding genetic predisposition to obesity also must take into account a genetic predisposition woven into the fiber of every person. That is the predisposition to go on living. The human body is predisposed to survive and to avoid death under normal circumstances. When we continue to live in a way that puts our lives at risk, there is something wrong, something out of balance, within our being. Prolonged obesity leads to premature death. Therefore, concluding that our bodies are simply predisposed to remain obese goes against the accepted fact that our bodies are genetically designed for survival, not self-destruction.

Certainly, we live in an imperfect world where things are not as they

Figure 13.3

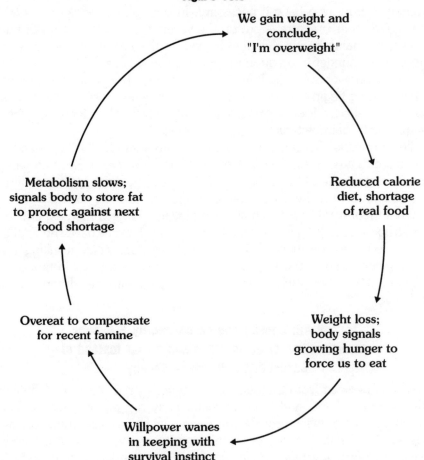

We gain weight and
conclude,
"I'm overweight"

Reduced calorie
diet, shortage
of real food

Weight loss;
body signals
growing hunger to
force us to eat

Willpower wanes
in keeping with
survival instinct

Overeat to compensate
for recent famine

Metabolism slows;
signals body to store fat
to protect against next
food shortage

should be. Babies are sometimes born with fatal birth defects. Some precious souls are born with minds that do not serve them well or mental disorders that severely limit their participation within society. Some are born addicted to drugs, through no fault of their own. Others are born with handicapping conditions. Children get cancer, and the elderly are plagued with Alzheimer's disease. So, it does seem conceivable that there may be some rare individuals whose genetic makeup works against the body's normal survival instinct by becoming and remaining obese without other contributing factors.

As mentioned before, doctors and research scientists see obesity as a heterogeneous condition, having a variety of contributing factors. All of these possible factors are considered in dealing with anyone suffering from obesity. They do not take the position that predisposition *alone* causes obesity.

DEVELOPING A PLAN TO FIND FREEDOM

Now that we have an understanding of the various perspectives taken regarding obesity, we need to know what we can do if they represent the truth of what influences our obesity. Here are guidelines for dealing with the most commonly accepted contributing factors to obesity. We need to plan to take a season of time to work through all of them.

1. Dealing with the Disease Theory

When we see a doctor, we should make sure that we are checked for possible hormonal or disease-related causes. Having a complete physical examination by a healthy doctor who is not overweight is truly important. We should be tested for all possible contributing physical/hormonal causes of obesity.

If we find we have some kind of physiological and/or hormonal condition, we must obey doctor's orders in medicating the problem. And we shouldn't stop there. Chances are that there is no single cause of our obesity. It may involve many other thought and behavior patterns as well.

2. Dealing with Addiction to Food as a Source of Emotional Comfort and Pain Avoidance

Our obesity may not be entirely an addiction to food to satisfy some unmet emotional need or to deaden some unbearable pain. However, when we are obese, it is easy to become obsessed with food. As Liz Taylor said, it is easy to allow it to become our only consuming interest. Being obese might have affected our social relationships so much that emotional deficits and unbearable pain were a result of our obesity. They can cause us to turn to food as our only reliable friend and comforter. Another way we can get drawn into an addictive cycle is that our obesity becomes such a primary problem, we can avoid other painful emotional issues while working on our recovery from obesity.

In this season of exploring solutions to our weight problem, we need to be sensitive to how our eating and even our excess weight have helped us avoid or cope with other unresolved emotional and interpersonal issues. For example, Karen, whose story was told in chapter 3, ate to comfort herself during periods of terrible depression each month.

Popular TV talk show host Oprah Winfrey has openly discussed her weight gains and losses. One issue she ties in to being overweight is being raped as a young girl. For anyone who has been sexually abused, excess weight can be an emotional protection from the advances of the opposite sex. A person who has never received professional counseling, or otherwise worked through the deep issues related to something as personally devastating as sexual abuse, must do so to be free. Chances are that when the emotional brokenness is healed and the person feels safe again, the weight loss efforts will have a much better chance of success. In this instance, the survival mechanism is working; it's just that the person is convinced that survival is helped by excess weight.

If we were thin tomorrow, what would be the next most powerful underlying issue that would demand our attention? An honest answer to the question may be that there are none we're aware of under the surface. For some of us, though, another issue that is extremely painful may be unresolved.

We need to work toward health for the whole being, not just the physical body. We need to take constructive steps to get help for the issues we fear dealing with because they are so painful. The pain in our lives is a signal that we need some care in that area. During this season of seeking health, we must get competent professional help to deal with other painful issues and resolve them.

Someone with an emotional addiction may have physiological and/or genetic factors in play that need to be treated in addition to getting psychological help to deal with the emotional pain being avoided by eating pleasure and comfort foods.

Addressing the addiction

So, what can we do if we suspect that our obesity may be linked to a form of addiction? We need to address it as an addiction. Numerous twelve-step groups deal specifically with the problem of compulsive overeating and have proved helpful to many people. The principles in the twelve steps (originally developed for use with alcoholics and now adapted to myriad other addictions) are healthy practices that can benefit anyone. If we suspect that our obesity is tied in to addictive patterns, we can avail ourselves of the numerous twelve-step workbooks, devotionals, support groups, and meetings widely available.

Working a twelve-step program brings all areas of our lives back into balance, whether or not our obesity is partially related to an emotional addiction to food. If we treat ourselves as though it may be part of the problem and it really is, we are well on the way to resolving some of the contributing factors to our obesity.

3. Dealing with Moral and/or Spiritual Factors

We are all spiritual beings created with an intricate balance of body, mind, and spirit. Our spirituality will influence how we deal with our obesity, and our obesity will influence how we deal with our spirituality.

The first thing we need to do is to dispel the effects of what I call toxic faith. If our spiritual beliefs or practices have tied us in to a cycle of self-condemnation and penance without leading us to true forgiveness and freedom, we need to reevaluate those beliefs and practices. I am a Christian, and I find a great deal of strength and moral support from my relationships within my church and my relationship with God. However, I know others who read the same Bible and seem to see only condemnation. How wonderful it would be for them to see mercy and grace as well.

Persons who see their obesity primarily as a moral problem desperately need God to help them break the cycle. Their feelings may parallel those described by the apostle Paul (the same one who penned the book of Philippians, which they use to condemn themselves). He said in Romans 7:19—8:1:

For the good that I will to do, I do not do; but the evil I will not to do, that I practice. Now if I do what I will not to do, it is no longer I who do it, but sin that dwells in me. I find then a law, that evil is present with me, the one who wills to do good. For I delight in the law of God according to the inward man. But I see another law in my members, warring against the law of my mind, and bringing me into captivity to the law of sin which is in my members. O wretched man that I am! Who will deliver me from this body of death? [We could almost imagine that this could be Walter Hudson's prayer.] I thank God—through Jesus Christ our Lord! So then, with the mind I myself serve the law of God, but with the flesh the law of sin. There is therefore now no condemnation to those who are in Christ Jesus, who do not walk according to the flesh, but according to the Spirit.

One key to breaking the cycle of sin and death in the form of obesity is to find a place of forgiveness and freedom from condemnation. Perhaps our attempts to pay for our own sins of overindulgence by severe dieting have set in operation a law within our bodies to crave even more food and store even more fat. An overall understanding of the Bible shows that God desires His children to be free from all forms of bondage. That freedom comes through accepting the free gift of salvation from Jesus Christ without having to pay for our own sins by means of

penance. Perhaps even when our penance takes the form of strict dieting, it sets in motion a vicious cycle.

The spiritual help we can draw from will be beneficial if it is not
condemning and demanding of penance. I know of one obese pastor
who was so condemned by his own theology and his congregation's
disrespect (because he was severely obese) that he came to believe he
was possessed by a "demon of fat." He then called on his congregation
to fast and pray until the demon was cast out. Since Jesus told His
disciples that some demons come out only by prayer and fasting, the
blame was switched from himself to his congregation. In essence he was
saying, "I'm not to blame. Don't condemn me. It's your fault because
you haven't fasted and prayed well enough to free me from this demon." He was right in not feeling that he should be condemned because
of his struggle with obesity. He was wrong in the sense that shifting the
blame didn't help him come any closer to resolving the problem.

People who have a relationship with God and an active faith will see
all aspects of their lives with a spiritual understanding since the Bible
gives a specific perspective on our natural lives. When we take a physical
problem and divorce it from the physical realm, isolating it as a purely
spiritual problem, we distance ourselves from the chance to gain real
help. Instead, we need to bring the spiritual help God provides (truth,
wisdom, our church family, and spiritual power) into the reality of our
physical problem.

I believe that each one of us is created with a need and a hunger for
God. We live in a fallen world and in a body that is driven, at times, by
our fallen nature. That may explain the tendency in all of us to become
ensnared in activities promising pleasure but leading us toward self-destruction. I believe that God sent His Son Jesus to identify with our plight
and pay for all our sins. (The Bible tells us that even Jesus Himself was
accused of gluttony by the religious leaders of His day!) Jesus summed
up His mission this way:

> The Spirit of the Lord is upon me;
>> he has appointed me to preach Good News to the poor; he has
>> sent me to heal the brokenhearted and to announce that captives
>> shall be released and the blind shall see, that the downtrodden shall
>> be freed from their oppressors . . . that God is ready to give bless-
>> ings to all who come to him (Luke 4:18–19 TLB).

If our spiritual experience doesn't bring us good news of forgiveness
(without paying for our own sins), healing for our broken hearts, and
freedom from bondage, it's time to make some changes. We need to

find a church where people show compassion and encourage hope for our condition. Some churches even sponsor twelve-step or support groups. If we have never entered into a relationship with God on the basis of Christ's payment for our sins, now would be a good time to give that serious consideration. Jesus came to give us freedom and demonstrated His power in His resurrection. It would help to have Him on our side in our battle against obesity.

4. Dealing with the Environmental Influences That May Affect Our Obesity

One thing we all can do is to design our living space and our life-style with as much necessary built-in movement as possible. We can rent a parking space so that we need to walk a bit farther. We can walk the kids to school instead of driving them. We can have only one permanently fixed telephone so that we have to get up and move to answer it (if there's a teenager in the home, this one choice alone could result in thousands of expended calories just answering the phone calls!). Any choice we can make to design necessary movement into the things we routinely do each day will help in the long run.

Peter D. Vash, M.D., M.P.H., is assistant clinical professor at UCLA School of Medicine. In an article in *Good Housekeeping* magazine (June 1988) he gives helpful suggestions regarding what we can do to change our habit patterns to maintain weight loss:

> Experts agree that diet plays a large role in weight loss, but other permanent habit changes are necessary to keep those excess pounds from returning.
>
> One lifelong habit everyone should develop is a regular exercise program. Dr. Vash explains, "A persistent, consistent, rational meal plan is important. But if it isn't coupled with an exercise regime, there is no hope for weight maintenance." Studies show that most people who lose weight without exercising are unable to keep the weight off.
>
> Other changes that help to control weight: SELF-MONITORING: Keep a food diary, recording not only what and when you eat, but with whom, where, why, and how. This daily record will help you become aware of your eating behavior and understand reasons for bingeing. STIMULUS CONTROL: Once you recognize the cues that trigger eating, work on ways to change your habits. For example, if you tend to snack while watching TV, take up a hobby that keeps your hands and mind occupied during viewing times.

The *Good Housekeeping* article provided other hints. We shouldn't make two different dinners. Instead, we should serve healthy balanced meals for the whole family. We can avoid desserts by asking the family to clear the table and do the dishes while we take a walk. And we shouldn't use the family as an excuse for not sticking to a healthy eating plan. It also suggested serving portions of food on a smaller plate so that we won't feel deprived by skimpy portions.

Anyone who can find help from these suggestions of behavioral changes should use them. However, if the walk around the block after dinner leads us straight to the nearest ice-cream parlor to sneak a hot fudge sundae, there is more to our problem than just environment.

5. Dealing with a Possible Predisposition to Respond to Food Shortages by Craving More Food and Storing an Excessive Amount as Fat

An excellent book that discusses this theory in depth is *The Anti-Diet Book: How to Become Naturally Thin by Eating More* by Jean Antonello, R.N., B.S.N. We would do well to read it and try following her guidelines for healthy eating.

People who have a problem with excess weight have heard that they should visit a doctor, follow a balanced diet, get involved in some form of exercise, and take their time to lose weight permanently. I know very few people who have actually followed these recommendations. Most who consider themselves overweight lack the confidence in this approach necessary to follow it. Most people feel compelled to lose weight rapidly. The more excess weight they carry, the more they may feel the need to get a head start on losing weight. Losing weight *fast* becomes the object of their immediate plans. Who has the patience to follow a plan that allows you to eat well but lose only a few pounds per month? Maybe other people can afford to take that time but not me! I need to lose weight now (that is, before summer, before school starts, before the reunion, before the wedding, etc.)!

Remember Jan who struggled with a sudden weight gain of fifty pounds between eighth and ninth grades? She practiced *every* quick-weight-loss program she could find during high school and college (that is, she dieted in between ravenous seasons of eating copious amounts of junk food). I said that she now enjoys a healthy weight without dieting. She isn't plagued mercilessly by wild cravings. She doesn't worry about food anymore. She eats what she wants when she wants it. How did she manage it?

Jan fell in love during her sophomore year in college (no, the weight didn't disappear because she was in love!). She weighed 155 pounds at the time, and her beau weighed a whopping 120 soaking wet (he was five nine). (Visions of Mr. and Mrs. Jack Sprat suddenly appear.) Through the help of a nutritionist who suggested a diet of all natural foods, Jan brought her weight down to 145. She was still trying to diet and not eat "too much" of the natural foods. The bingeing slowed down some as well. When Jan became engaged to be married, she decided that she needed to take drastic measures to lose weight. She followed a "purifying diet" prescribed in a "health magazine" and then took to periodic ten-day juice fasts, drinking only fruit and vegetable juices. She would lose weight during the fasts, then put it all back on within a month. As the wedding approached, she became more determined. She decided on a complete fast, drinking only water. She was going to try to fast for twenty-one days, following the advice of various books on the virtues of fasting. (I do not recommend this practice. Anyone considering a fast of any length over one day should do so only under the supervision of a medical professional.)

A month before the wedding, weighing in at the same old 145 pounds, she stopped eating. After ten days she had lost 17 pounds. On the eleventh day she had a glass of fresh fruit juice (it was at her wedding shower!) and gained back a pound. She continued to gain back weight, while not eating anything for another nine days. At the end of the nineteenth day she was very hungry and very discouraged. She weighed 135.

At that point she reached a decision. Maybe she was just predisposed to be fat forever! Her new husband assured her that he would love her no matter what shape she took. So, she gave up on dieting for good. She says, "I decided that I had done everything humanly possible to lose weight, and it didn't work. I accepted that I couldn't be responsible for what my body did with the food I ate. I could only be responsible for eating a healthy natural selection of good food and trust the rest to God. At that point I threw away my bathroom scales and focused on other concerns."

An amazing thing happened once she gave up dieting and committed herself to a healthy balanced diet; she ate only natural foods and eliminated all white sugar, white flour, and processed junk foods. Within a few months her weight dropped down to around 115 pounds. Okay, at that point she did retrieve the scales and take a peek, but she never went back to dieting. She has maintained this weight for over twelve years (except during three pregnancies). She has even allowed herself occasional junk foods and sugar in moderation, but the intense cravings and binges are a thing of the past.

Imagine how tragic it would have been if she had concluded that she was just born to be fat and yet continued to try dieting out of guilt and shame? If we are to learn any lessons from her story, they would be as follows:

1. We may not be responsible for what our bodies do with the food we eat, but we are responsible for eating a healthy balanced diet.
2. We can give up fad diets and at least try feeding ourselves only the good food nature provides.
3. We can eliminate junk food that may wreak havoc on our delicate internal balance.
4. We can give ourselves some time for our bodies to adjust and regulate themselves to a healthy new life-style where they are not forced to go hungry in a land of plenty.
5. We can spend time with people who are committed to loving us, regardless of what our predispositions may be.

6. Dealing with the Theory That Predisposition Alone Is the Cause of Obesity

Health care professionals agree that several elements affect the problem of obesity. We will be hard-pressed to find a doctor who will tell us that we are obese simply because our bodies are set on it and there is nothing we can do.

DOING ALL WE CAN

Our search for the cause and solution to our problem might be compared to that of people trying to identify allergies that cause them to have terrible reactions. They need to systematically isolate the problem by suspecting *all* possible allergens. They eliminate all suspected substances from the system, then reintroduce them one by one until they get a reaction. We need to begin by suspecting that *all* the theories regarding the causes of and solutions for obesity may apply to us and exhaust the possible remedies for each of them before we can responsibly opt to conclude that we are just destined to be obese.

Since all of the suggested solutions are basically healthy choices, we will not be any worse off if we apply them in our lives and they were unnecessary. If we strongly feel compelled to avoid one of the areas under consideration, that may be a sign of the need to look most closely at that particular area. For example, if we have a strong aversion to looking into the emotional aspect of obesity, we may be getting close to something very painful that we desperately want to avoid. If our obesity were really part of a coping mechanism to help us avoid dealing with some traumatic emotional injury, it would follow that the pain would make us want to keep away from exploring that area. As with physical injuries, in the emotional and spiritual realm, sometimes the pain—and not wanting anyone to touch us there—tells the doctor where to operate.

We need to *thoroughly and systematically* work through the prescribed treatment programs discussed. It should be a long-term goal, giving ourselves plenty of time to work through each area (but not allowing ourselves a long time to avoid working through the programs). We will likely find something to help us with our obesity. However, if we have diligently and thoroughly exhausted all possible solutions, we can at least be free of some of the guilt and self-condemnation we've lived with. If we can look ourselves in the mirror and say that we have done our best, we have done all we can do in regard to our obesity. Then we can turn our attention to making the best of the lives we have. We may find comfort and a strategy for living in Reinhold Niebuhr's Serenity Prayer: God, give us grace to accept with serenity the things that cannot be changed, courage to change the things which should be changed, and the wisdom to distinguish the one from the other.

Just because we are obese does not mean that our obesity is the definition of who we are. Think of many of the great people of our time who have lived with excess weight and yet are not thought of primarily in terms of their obesity. Think of Luciano Pavarotti, Beverly Sills, Sandi Patti, Orson Welles, Elizabeth Taylor, John Candy, Dom DeLuise, Oprah Winfrey, and others who have struggled with excess weight. We think of them in terms of the great talents they have shared with others, not primarily in terms of their size. Like them, we all have inherent talents. We can turn our attention toward the positive contribution we can make to the lives of others and set about developing our talents.

Perhaps we need to learn to look at our genetically inherited size range as a part of the wonderful combination of perceived strengths and weaknesses each person inherits. These set up the limits within which we are challenged to learn to live happy and productive lives.

Notes

1. Elizabeth Taylor, "A Star Is Reborn," *People Weekly,* Jan. 18, 1988, pp. 81–82.

2. Lee Willerman and David B. Cohen, *Psychopathology* (New York: McGraw-Hill, 1990), pp. 509–10.

3. Henry E. Adams and Patricia B. Sutker, *Comprehensive Handbook of Psychopathology* (New York: Plenum, 1984), p. 663.

4. Adams and Sutker, *Handbook of Psychopathology,* pp. 663–64, and "Opiate Antagonist Counters Obesity," *Science News,* Feb. 14, 1981, p. 103.

5. Lawrence J. Hatterer, *The Pleasure Addicts* (South Brunswick, N.J.: A. S. Barnes, 1980), p. 15.

6. Hatterer, *Pleasure Addicts,* pp. 15, 16, 24.

7. Carin Rubenstein, "The Moral Weight of Fatness," *Psychology Today,* July 1980, p. 42.

8. Catherine Houck, "Programmed to Be Fat?" *Cosmopolitan,* June 1987, p. 58.

9. Nelly Edmondson, "Are You Destined to Be Fat?" *Weight Watchers Magazine,* Feb. 1989, p. 66.

10. Goldblatt, Moore, and Stunkard (1965), in Adams and Sutker, *Handbook of Psychopathology,* p. 653.

11. "As Seventy Million Americans Try to Shed Weight," *U.S. News & World Report,* Dec. 22, 1980, p. 61.

Chapter 14

◆

FREEING OUR CHILDREN FROM OBESITY

The TV talk show set consisted of eight chairs on a carpeted raised platform. Every other chair was occupied by a thin, attractive woman appearing to be in her thirties or early forties. Beside each slender woman sat a teenage son or daughter who was visibly overweight. The topic was something along the lines of "Skinny Moms, Fat Kids," although I didn't catch the exact title. Each mother was a weight-conscious dieter who had struggled throughout her son's or daughter's childhood to keep the child thin . . . to no avail.

Zabrina was one of the girls. She was sorry to disappoint her mom and was disgusted with her own body. She talked about a life of always dieting, trying hard not to eat. Her mom ran a fitness-dance studio and Zabrina tried going to class, but she felt out of place. She was only eight at the time, and it was an adult class. She said it was kind of hard on her, comparing herself to all those lithe and limber dancer types. She had been chunky for as long as she could remember. After a while her mom excused her from class, but her attempts at dieting continued.

When the camera turned to Zabrina's mother, you could see the family resemblance, the same bright green eyes, the same delicate nose sprinkled with sand-colored freckles. The only difference was that while Zabrina's face was full and round, her mom's face was thin and glowing with health. You could see the consternation all over those lovely features. She confessed that she had always feared her daughter would be overweight, even before she was born. When Zabrina first reached eagerly for that slice of pizza, at eighteen months of age, the fight was on. Zabrina grew up dieting and gaining back more weight than she lost.

Now Mom wonders where she went wrong. She's hounded by a nebulous sense of guilt and shame. Her worst fears were realized in spite of the fact that she did everything in her power to thwart them. Some theories suggest that they were realized *because* she did everything in her power to limit her child's diet.

Where is the help for Zabrina and the other kids like her? Was she predisposed to gain weight, and her intuitive mom just sensed it? Or could she have been predisposed to react to the insufficient food supply her body had endured by storing extra fat? Is this her body's predisposition to protect her in an environment where food is always scarce? Are the periodic binges more than just a child's rebellious nature in response to strict parental control? Could she be responding to the body's physiological demands for nourishment to make up for recurrent seasons of chronic hunger? The approach taken to view the problem will influence the approach needed to solve it. Since traditional diet and exercise techniques have failed, what can be done to help Zabrina and those like her? What can these well-meaning parents do (that they haven't already tried) to finally free their children from the misery of obesity? The answers may surprise you, but there is tremendous hope.

According to the most recent studies, one out of every ten children ages ten to fourteen is considered obese (weighing 20 percent or more above ideal weight). However, most health care professionals agree that except in extreme cases (where the child is 50 percent or more above a healthy weight for a prolonged period of time), children should *not* be placed on a low-calorie diet. Children grow and develop at their own individual rate and should not be judged by some arbitrary standard that their parents adopt.[1]

Ricardo Uauy, M.D., of the Center for Human Nutrition at the University of Texas Southwestern Medical Center, says that many factors may cause a predisposition for childhood obesity—genetics, a fat-promoting home environment, and a low level of physical activity. He also warns that parents should not badger their children about dieting and losing weight. He says, "This could lead to a preoccupation with weight, which may develop into eating disorders. Instead, parents should try to keep their kids' weight steady and allow normal growth—height and stature—to catch up to their weight."

In an article in *Good Housekeeping* magazine, Dr. Uauy advises, "Avoid putting children on strict, lean diets, which may not provide all the nutrients needed by growing bodies. Rather than having kids diet, get them physically active—walk with them to the store rather than driving; start a new hobby with them that keeps them moving while keeping their mind off food."[2]

BABY FAT FEARS

Casey was a beautiful baby girl. At birth she weighed eight pounds and measured twenty and one-half inches. At seven weeks she had grown to thirteen pounds nine ounces. The pediatrician said she was "a bit chunky," but it was nothing to worry about. By six months she was weighing in at twenty-six pounds, and her mother was beginning to worry. The doctor had a height-weight chart that compared the child's weight to the average weight of other children the same age. Casey had soared off the chart . . . on the heavy side! Mom had always dreamed of her baby being exceptional, but that wasn't exactly what she had in mind!

Casey's mom was experiencing growing concern that her baby was born to be fat. She felt guilty because her diet consisted solely of breast milk. Mom felt solely responsible. She feared that her little girl would go through life abnormally fat. That was a terrifying thought since Mom had experienced her own bout with obesity and knew the devastation it wrought.

Fortunately, Casey's pediatrician was Dr. Robert Hamilton of St. John's Hospital in Santa Monica, California. He had a great deal of confidence in the way God had designed little bodies to grow and adapt in response to nature's provided diet of breast milk. He was able to alleviate Mom's fears and convince her to trust her baby's body to develop to a healthy weight, even though for the moment she seemed "abnormal." No baby is "normal" per se. Babies are specially designed (via genetic predisposition) to grow at their own rate.

Dr. Hamilton says that young children will eat as much as they need. As long as they are provided a good variety of healthy foods, there is no need to limit the amount they eat. Casey's mom took the good doctor's advice, and it proved to be correct. By about age three, Casey's weight dropped down into the "normal" range on the height-weight scale. At age six, she is a beautiful, healthy little girl who stays on the thin side of the "normal" range. She is physically active and has a positive self-image. She grew up being taught to see herself as unique, not seeing herself as prone to be fat.

BABY FAT FACTS

How can we be sure that the baby's fat is normal and not caused by something we're doing wrong? There are only a few ways parents might cause a baby to gain additional weight beyond normal baby fat. If we're worried, we may want to follow these guidelines:

1. Breast-feed the infant *if* that is possible. (Although breast milk is the ideal baby food, plenty of children have grown up healthy without it.) Even working moms can rent an electric breast pump and leave nature's perfect baby food available when Mom is not.
2. Be careful not to give the baby foods with added sugar or to introduce the baby to junk foods that lack real nutrition. Plenty of great child care books offer healthy guidelines about when and how to introduce healthy solid foods.
3. Rich formula doesn't thin out the way breast milk does, so if the baby needs to be on a formula, consult with the pediatrician regarding the baby's feeding schedule and the amount of formula to use.
4. Don't assume that every cry is a cry of hunger. Check to see if the baby is thirsty (in which case, the child would accept a bottle of water) or just wants to suck on a pacifier.
5. Don't force-feed the baby on the parents' schedule. A baby's appetite changes in keeping with the baby's changing needs. If the baby refuses the breast or the bottle, check to see if something else is needed.

Babies Need to Be Fat

Jean Antonello is an obesity and eating disorder specialist in Minneapolis, Minnesota. She explains that babies are fat because they *need* to be:

A baby's survival depends on fat for several reasons. Babies are helpless, totally dependent on others for food, body warmth, stimulation, and protection. Their baby-fatness between birth and age two or three is adaptive because of complete dependency.

They need insulation from temperature changes when they kick off their blankets. They need a substantial internal source of food if they get hungry during the night and no one hears them cry or they don't wake up. This same internal source of food must supply their bodies' needs during illness when they cannot or will not eat for several days.

Babies also need padding for those inevitable falls. Unquestionably, babies need to be fat. So they generally are.[3]

A PARENT'S POWER

One of the most basic principles of sociology states that persons will see themselves in the same way the most important person in their lives sees them. From the children's viewpoint, the parent or primary caregiver is the most important person in their lives. The view we hold of our children has powerful influence in terms of how they see themselves. If we view them as fat or we are consumed by a fear that they will grow up to be fat, our children will grow up with an image of themselves as fat. This negative definition of who they are can lead to all sorts of emotional problems and has been shown to contribute to the development of various types of eating disorders, including obesity. If we are consumed with a fear of fat, we need to get professional help for ourselves and not impose our fears on our children.

"SHAME ON YOU!"

Another thing we can do to free our children from the damaging effects of obesity is to reduce the level of shame in their lives. Shame is more than guilt over wrong behavior. Shame is the belief that there is something defective in the person as a human being. Guilt says, "I blew it. I made a mistake." Shame says, "*I* am a mistake!" If we adopt the belief that our children are predisposed to obesity and our view of obesity is that it's a horrible defect, our children may conclude that they are horribly defective persons. That is a grave danger.

Counseling professionals working in the area of addiction cite that shame tends to fuel the addictive cycle. Shame breeds discouragement. It leads children to believe that there is no use in trying to make a change. They are just defective. This is not what it means to be predisposed to obesity. We may feel this way about ourselves and convey our deep sense of shame to our children. Shaming our children for the way they look or their eating habits will do nothing productive to help them. In fact, if their eating is tied in to an emotional need for comfort, the increased shame will send them back to their source of immediate comfort (in this case, food).

It is understandable that parents want to spare children the health risks, pain, and misery associated with obesity. That may be especially true if we already suffer from obesity. The first and best thing we can do for them is to get help for ourselves and provide them with a model for victory over a troubling problem. If we are not obese, we need to stop enforcing our own low-calorie diet plan with our children. Children are created to respond to their bodies' appetite cues to tell them what they need to eat. They are not yet programmed to adjust their appetites to the artificial demands of our culture. We can help them by reinforcing the true fact that each one of us develops at a different pace and that our bodies will adjust over the course of growing up. We can provide them with plenty of healthy foods and replace junk food with great tasting natural treats. Most vitally, we can give them a view of themselves that says, "You are a special, unique person! You have a lot going for you! There is a great deal more to your value than how you appear during any one phase of growth."

Notes

1. Ricardo Uauy, "Born to Be Fat?" *Good Housekeeping,* June 1988, p. 181.

2. Uauy, "Born to Be Fat?" p. 181.

3. Jean Antonello, *The Anti-Diet Book: How to Become Naturally Thin by Eating More* (St. Paul, Minn.: Heartland Book Co., 1989), p. 152.

Section 4

◆

ALCOHOLISM

Chapter 15

◆

ALCOHOLISM: DISPELLING THE MYTHS

I was raised with some very common views about alcoholism and alcoholics. I saw alcoholics as some people see those who battle depression, suicidal tendencies, and obesity: I felt they were morally or spiritually feeble. I thought they were simply weak-willed people who had given up on life and hid behind the bottle like mice in a cereal box. I had no regard for them other than to believe that if they wanted to change, they could; all they had to do was pull themselves together. I viewed alcoholics as those folks who spent time on skid row, and if they weren't there yet, they would be one day. It was just a matter of time. I was without compassion for one of the most pervasive problems in America. I could have cared less how alcoholics got that way or if any of them ever decided to change. In my opinion, they were just living out the results of their irresponsible behavior. Obviously, my insight was limited. I'd never considered the possibility of other factors, certainly not predisposition. That would soon change.

The first graduate school I attended was a seminary where I studied counseling. I had the good fortune of being allowed to sit in on doctoral seminars the first year. The seminars I attended focused on the various self-help organizations and twelve-step groups such as Alcoholics Anonymous. From those early days of discovery I was beginning to sense that my views were not entirely accurate. When a recovering alcoholic came to speak to us, he wasn't exactly what I had anticipated. First of all, *he* was a *she*. She was the wife of a minister and the farthest thing I could imagine from a skid row bum. As she told her story, I could tell that the problem was not all a result of weak-willed people who had abandoned God for the bottle. I had no idea that introduction to alcoholism was the beginning of a life working with alcoholics.

As my graduate studies in counseling continued, my frustration with my course of study increased. I was restless during my practicum counseling sessions. My supervisors told me I vacillated between being overly directive and detached. I couldn't have agreed more. It was frustrating because the folks with problems never told me the real problem. They gave me a presenting problem that often had nothing to do with their actual struggle. It seemed that although they had asked for help, they were determined to look good and put up as good a front as possible until I could break through to the real problem. I did not do too much breaking through. It was a boring process for me to sit in a little room and listen to two people lie to me and each other. I can't tell you how much I respect marriage counselors as a result of unsuccessfully trying to be one.

I went to my professor and told him my dilemma. I was frustrated and wanted to work with people who had severe problems. I was tired of the pretense and wanted to go where people had come to the end of themselves and were trying to find a way out. He told me it sounded like I wanted to work in a psychiatric hospital, but he explained that since I had no license or degree or other credentials, it would be impossible. Within two weeks I was working in a psychiatric hospital as an orderly on the night shift twice a week. If I could raise a family on an orderly's wages, I would be one today. It was the greatest job I had until I found the one I have today. When I say, "I never had a job I didn't hate," there was one exception, and that was it. Even cleaning bed pans was not so bad because of all of the other wonderful experiences of having direct contact with people in trouble.

It was not the same as it is today. Very few people sought help at a psychiatric treatment center fifteen years ago. The people were severely mentally ill. I remember Betty who jumped out the second floor window in a suicide attempt. She landed in the grass, which hurt her neck a bit, got back up, came inside, and told the ward clerk she had tried to kill herself. There were the identical twins who didn't know which one was which. The psychiatrist tried to clear up the confusion with electroconvulsive therapy, which I watched on several occasions. I think it only added to their confusion. A lot of the people on the ward liked to take their clothes off in front of others. It was amazing how quickly some of the people responded to their treatment. It was also sad that some left us for the back ward of a state mental hospital. Nothing could get through to them, or at least nothing seemed to.

Another group of patients came in and left on a regular basis. They were alcoholics. They entered the hospital sick, trembling, and often hallucinating. They were the worst of the worst alcoholics because in a place like Fort Worth, Texas, fifteen years ago, people didn't stop drinking until there was absolutely no other option available. What was so surprising about them, almost every one a man, was that within about five days, they looked like they didn't have a problem in the world. With the amount of medication the psychiatrists put them on, they probably didn't care much about anything. They came in dependent on liquid from a bottle, and they left with many prescriptions to nonliquid mood elevators out of a bottle. Not much good happened in their lives other than they were well-fed, so they could go back out and drink again—at least until they died. We regularly got reports when one of them did die. Either cirrhosis of the liver or a car crash usually was enough to end a life of drinking. Sometimes they just bumped into something or hit their head against a curb and died of a subdural hematoma. Each death was as sad as the one before. After working with those wonderful people, I was developing compassion. I discovered that alcoholics were real people who needed help—help they weren't getting.

I will never forget working those night shifts. Well, actually, I was sleeping through most of them. Sometimes I would set my chair in the middle of the hall so if anything happened, I would be instantly awakened. I did that one night, with my legs wrapped around the front legs of the chair. The fire alarm went off, and the patients rushed out of their rooms in time to see me stand up, or attempt to, and fall flat on my face with a bloody nose. If laughter is therapeutic, they were all a lot better off emotionally that night.

On another night I positioned my chair in the same place and dozed off as usual. I was awakened by a 240-pound ex-marine running by me and then going straight through a plate glass door. He didn't even stop. My supervisor called the police to inform them who was out on the street. He was experiencing delirium tremens and hallucinating. The police were not too happy with their assignment. I remember thinking that there was no hope for the man. He was too sick for anyone. I was wrong. They found him, bleeding and scared. They brought him back, but he was not the same man. It was as if when he went through that plate glass door, he went through another door, the door to reality. He made an incredible recovery after seeing just how sick he was and how destructive the drinking could be. His ability to come back to the real world gave me a new sense of who alcoholics are and the potential each one has. Back in those days, when the treatment was minimal for alcoholism, his recovery was the exception. Most did not make it.

After working at the hospital for a while, I received word that the owners wanted to change things. They were converting the hospital from a psychiatric treatment center to an alcohol and drug treatment center. I was fortunate enough to go out to California for training. We were all full of excitement and fear. We were excited because we knew how many alcoholics were not being helped. We were afraid because we did not know what to expect when we started working with alcoholics beyond our old favorites who regularly came and went.

The training taught us how to be more directive. It taught us how a team works together to implement treatment and that psychiatrists no longer determined everything about the care of the patient. It also taught us how to implement the principles of twelve-step recovery. There was a program manual written by Muriel Zink, and I read every word of it. Through that manual she was my first teacher about alcoholism. She was the first to help me see alcoholics as normal human beings with an abnormal ability to drink. I have been indebted to her ever since.

Fifteen years ago I learned that there is hope for alcoholics. I learned that they could be an impulse away from death and come back and recover their self-esteem, families, and jobs and restore their relationships with God. I was amazed to see people who hung out at the Fort Worth stock yards almost every night until 3:00 A.M. drinking come in for treatment, and two years later, still sober, they would bring their wives to the hospital for the quarterly alumni potluck dinner. It was a rich time for a twenty-three-year-old. I became addicted to working with addicted people and people with emotional problems. In some way I have done that all of my professional life.

In the beginning I was a narrow-minded helper who had his own ideas about alcoholism, its causes, and how people recover from it. All of those ideas were counterproductive in working with alcoholics. I had to learn a new way of thinking. I did learn to think differently, and it changed my life. I no longer believed that alcoholics could be or should be shamed into sobering up. I discovered real people, creations of God with as much potential as young graduates coming out of Harvard or Yale. The people who were starting out on a life of recovery were graduating from a tough school of reality, and they were qualified to handle almost anything that came their way since they had overcome the biggest obstacle of their lives, themselves.

WHAT ARE THE MYTHS?

The false information I had was in the form of myths concerning drinking, alcoholism, and alcoholics. I have listed the most destructive ones and presented the reality that counters them.

Myth #1: Alcohol affects everyone in the same manner.

At the heart of predisposition theory is the reality that alcohol does different things to different people. Everyone's system and metabolism are different. Tolerance varies for alcohol. One drink makes some people wildly intoxicated, but for others, it produces little or no effect. Some alcoholics can drink a case of beer and feel no intoxicating effects. Not being able to hold liquor is not a sign of weakness; it just means that the body cannot handle it. Being able to hold liquor is not a sign of personal strength, either; it is a sign of an alcoholic.

I have worked with thousands of alcoholics, and all have had one thing in common. It's not wealth or weakness. It's not beauty or brains. Every alcoholic has the ability to drink vast quantities of alcohol and still feel very few of the effects normal drinkers feel. This "gift" of consumption is applauded in our society. If we were acting on accurate information, we would not look so highly on those who drink people under the table. We would pity them because sooner or later, they will feel the effects and see the result of alcoholism in their lives.

One of the more interesting studies completed on the effects of alcohol on different groups was conducted by Marc A. Schuckit, M.D., professor of psychiatry at the University of California, San Diego, School of Medicine. He compared the effects of alcohol on young boys taking their first drink. He compared boys with alcoholic fathers to boys with nonalcoholic dads. After the drink he had the boys perform certain skills to determine how well they functioned. The boys with alcoholic fathers did much better on the tests than those who did not have alcoholic dads. Even before the first drink, the children of alcoholics have a higher chance of developing tolerance and addiction to alcohol than those who do not inherit genes with alcoholic predisposition.

Understanding this concept is important because people must be able to drink a lot of alcohol if they are to become addicted to it. The tolerance allows the addiction to develop, and then the addiction pulls the alcoholics into drinking behavior that results in eventual devastation. If people do not have this ability, they may develop all sorts of emotional problems and other addictions, but they will not become alcoholics.

Most people relate alcoholism to drunkenness. They are two entirely different problems. Anyone can decide to get drunk at any time, and it is clearly wrong to do so. But it is not a sign of alcoholism; it is a sign of problem drinking. Problem drinking can be stopped with counseling or a mere decision to no longer get drunk. Alcoholism cannot be stopped that easily.

Many alcoholics never get drunk. They drink below their tolerance level and never become intoxicated. I have heard many families register shock at the thought of a family member being an alcoholic because that person could hold liquor so well. They tell stories of a father or mother who drank all day but never lost control. Only in the latter stages do many alcoholics lose control and experience repeated drunkenness. The people did not become alcoholic overnight; they were just following a predictable progression of alcoholism into the late stages.

Myth #2: Alcohol is just another drug.

Alcohol is a very unique drug that affects each person differently. It is selectively addictive because most people have automatic limiting mechanisms that prevent them from drinking enough to become addicted to it. Only about 20 percent of the population can drink enough alcohol to experience its addictive effects. The rest of the population will get too sick or too drunk or pass out before they can ingest enough alcohol to develop alcoholism. Those who appear to be too weak to hold their alcohol are just born different. Fortunately for them, they have a built-in protection from alcoholism.

Persons who are protected from alcoholism are not protected from repeated drunkenness, however. They can become intoxicated, but they will not be dragged through the addiction progression of alcoholism because of the selectivity of alcohol's addictive properties.

Most people who use heroin will become addicted to it. Most people who use crack or cocaine will become addicted to it. The mood-altering drugs of choice like these and Valium are fairly universally addictive. Alcohol's selective addictability makes it unique. It is also the reason there is so much confusion around it since it does so many different things to different people who drink it.

Myth #3: People cannot become alcoholics on just beer or wine.

The form of alcohol doesn't matter; one is just as addicting as the other. Most people know that one glass of beer and one glass of wine and one shot of whiskey have the same alcohol content. The question is, How much of each kind does the person drink?

When I talk with people, I focus on two things: "How much could you drink when you first started drinking, and how much do you drink now?" It doesn't matter what kind of drinking they did; it only matters how much. By the time they have gotten to me, most are drinking amounts large enough to kill a normal person. There are varying opinions about the definition of a heavy drinker or a person at risk for alcoholism. One that is fairly acceptable is someone who consumes five drinks three or more times a week. A person involved in that much drinking of any sort is likely an alcoholic, even if no problems have surfaced yet.

Myth #4: People who can control their drinking are not alcoholics.

Most alcoholics can control their drinking for an extended period of time if the motivation is strong enough. When an alcoholic does control the drinking, it is not a sign of normal drinking; it is a sign of controlled alcoholic drinking. If a wife says to a husband that she thinks he is an alcoholic, he can probably get her to change her mind with a test. He will promise not to drink for one month; if he does drink, he will get help. He may have severely white knuckles trying to hang on to his abstinence, but he most likely can pass the test.

The reality is that only alcoholics would ever need to probe the ability to control drinking. Normal drinkers are under control, never lose control, and have nothing to prove. If people have a need to prove they can control their consumption, they have one of the key indicators for alcoholism.

Myth #5: Alcoholics drink for relief; everyone else drinks just to be sociable.

Everyone who drinks, alcoholic or not, is drinking for the same reason. Some say they drink for the taste, but plenty of beverages taste good without alcohol. No-alcohol beer and no-alcohol wine have the taste of the real thing. Some may say they drink to be sociable. But people have been drinking for thousands of years because of the effects of alcohol. People at happy hour are there to relieve stress and escape through the effects of alcohol. They do some very unsociable things under the influence.

There are not two classifications for drinking, noble and not so noble. There is only one classification, and that is drinking to feel less of the pain of life. When the social drinker does it, he returns to normal, and his life is little affected. When the alcoholic does it, it begins a process of adaptation to the chemical and the development of an addiction. Two people of equal emotional and spiritual strength end up at different places not due to different reasons or needs to drink. They end up at different places through drinking because of their bodies, not their minds.

Myth #6: People become alcoholics because they have some form of mental illness.

Alcoholics start out as very normal people with a very abnormal body in its tolerance of alcohol. Mentally ill people and alcoholic people are two entirely different populations.

Those with emotional problems are often normal drinkers. Their drinking neither helps nor hurts their situation. They often remain with their emotional problems throughout their lives if their mental illness is chronic. Alcoholics start out normal, but the drinking and the addiction cause terrible emotional and social problems. Once they enter a recovery process, their personalities change dramatically, and the emotional problems go away. They do not linger and crop up throughout their lives. It is a completely different progression of the problem and the healing process.

Often alcoholics get the idea that they have a mental illness, and if they can just become mentally strong enough, they can lick their problem. It doesn't work that way. Alcoholism destroys emotions, the ability to think, and the spiritual life. The sooner alcoholics accept that they cannot overcome their problems with trying harder or emotional healing, that it is body and not mind, the sooner they will accept what they have and begin to recover from it. They may develop a new mind, but they will never develop a new body to drink with.

This mental illness myth is a close cousin to the myth that alcoholics have an addictive personality. There is no evidence to support a group of personality characteristics that lead to alcoholism. Alcoholics are extremely diverse in character and personality. Once on the path of alcoholism, they develop similar characteristics because the progression of alcoholism is predictable in each alcoholic. Once a person enters into a process of recovery, the personality similarities diminish as the force of addiction diminishes.

No one has been able to pinpoint a specific mental condition that leads to alcoholism. Alcoholics have only one thing in common, the ability to drink a lot of alcohol.

Myth #7: Alcoholics can return to social drinking once the sources of internal conflict are identified and resolved.

Thousands of alcoholics attempting to return to social drinking and failing over and over again prove this theory wrong. Once again, the body developed the problem that eventually produced internal conflicts. People may develop a new way of thinking, but they will not develop a new body. Alcoholics may have an extended period of controlled drinking, but it will eventually give way to the addiction and once again spin recklessly out of control. When alcoholics are in a solid recovery process, there is no need to experiment with what they can get by with. They are so busy experiencing the lives they have been missing, they don't desire to drink. Those who are not in a solid recovery program are the ones who attempt to control their drinking and fail.

Myth #8: Alcoholism is a secondary problem. There is a deeper primary problem that must be resolved.

Alcoholics have frustrated psychologists and psychiatrists for years. They come into the counseling session once or twice a week to gain some insight into the deeper problem that has supposedly manifested the alcoholic drinking. Although some methods may produce short-term results, this approach only delays the recovery process.

Alcoholics need treatment and support so they can exist one day without alcohol. They need to put enough sober "todays" together so the brain can clear out the toxic chemicals that result from heavy drinking. Insight doesn't do that for alcoholics. And insight does very little good if one hour after it is developed, they are drunk.

Myth #9: From a biblical standpoint, alcoholism is a sin.

The Bible does not address alcoholism. Many believe that a drunkard is an alcoholic, but that is not true. Anyone can be a drunkard. Not just anyone can become an alcoholic. The Bible is quite clear on the issue of drunkenness. It is a sin, can never be rationalized, and should be avoided at all costs. Its consequences are both spiritual and emotional.

On the issue of drinking, the Bible is not so clear as it is on the issue of drunkenness. Some interpret Scripture to forbid drinking, and others interpret it to allow drinking in moderation. The view sometimes depends on the way a person was raised. The drinking-sin debate is one that will not be resolved here, but it has no bearing on the alcoholism-sin issue.

Alcoholism is not a sin any more than high blood pressure is a sin. People predisposed to high blood pressure could be sinning by not watching their diet and eating too much salt. But the result would not be the sin. People predisposed to alcoholism would be sinning if they drank. The behavior would be the sin. Alcoholism is not a behavior; it is a condition. It is also a condition that leads to other sinful behavior as persons lose the ability to judge properly what is appropriate behavior and what is not. Also, toward the end of the progression the personalities of alcoholics so radically change that they are capable of doing just about anything, no matter how horrible it might have seemed a few years earlier. This deterioration in morality is often the process that leads alcoholics to seek help and recover. The immorality is not the cause of the alcoholism; it is a result.

Myth #10: There are many different types of alcoholism.

There is only one type of alcoholism, but it has many different stages. What appears to be a unique brand of alcoholism is merely a person stuck in one particular stage. People vary in how fast they go in and out of a stage. No matter how fast it progresses, it eventually results in out-of-control drinking. If we know alcoholism in all its stages, we do not have to wait for a person to reach the last stage before offering assistance.

Myth #11: Alcoholism is a slow form of suicide.

Alcoholism is not a slow form of suicide; it is a sorry means of survival. Alcoholics don't choose to drink themselves to death. They are trapped in addiction, so they drink to make it through another day.

Alcoholics have lost the ability to make choices because the addiction is so powerful it takes choices away. The hope for them is for someone to intervene and help them out of the death trap.

Myth #12: Alcoholics must either hit bottom or want help before they can be helped.

Before effective intervention techniques were developed, the only way an alcoholic found treatment was to lose everything, hit bottom, and beg for help. That is no longer the case. We do not need to sit by and watch a person self-destruct before we reach out and offer hope and help. If we do that, we wait until the person has lost family and job and self-esteem, the three things that motivate most alcoholics to recover. Those who repeatedly relapse do so because they have little to stay sober for. The sooner we intervene with the help of a professional intervention counselor, the greater the chance for the alcoholic to experience long-term recovery.

Two forces prevent alcoholics from making a rational decision to recover. One is the mood-altering effects of alcohol. It distorts reality and removes the ability to make good decisions. The other destructive force is addiction. It is so powerful that it requires daily treatment. The only treatment available to the alcoholic is more of the chemical. The chemical temporarily treats the problem, but eventually, the short-term cure for the obsessions and compulsions of addiction leads the alcoholic deeper into addiction.

Myth #13: Treatment programs help drinkers reach the maturity level of nondrinkers and social drinkers.

Social drinkers often drink to ease the stress and tension of everyday life, but recovering alcoholics, who must remain abstinent, do not have the option of seeking an external means of easing stress and tension. Alcoholics must learn to cope with stress and anxiety, free of alcohol and drugs. In addition, they must stay sober and cope with stress with a central nervous system that has been damaged by saturation with alcohol and subsequent withdrawal. Further, after going through treatment, alcoholics have come to see clearly all the devastation their drinking has caused, a realization that many social drinkers can avoid.

Treatment has confronted alcoholics with all of their failures, mistakes, and missed opportunities. They must deal with normal pressures and with all the dismaying reality of the past drinking years—and do it free of chemicals available to social drinkers. For all of these reasons, alcoholics must surpass the level of maturity of nondrinkers and social drinkers.

Myth #14: Relapse is an indication of failure.

Relapse is a predictable part of the recovery process. When a second heart attack occurs, we consider it a part of the heart disease process. We do not blame the patient or the doctors. In alcoholism it is different. We are angered by the relapse, and our uncontrolled emotions often make it difficult for alcoholics to recover from it. We need to see relapse as a new beginning point. The persons have validated with the relapse that they will not be able to return to normal drinking and to try is useless. We need to reinforce our desire for them to resume recovery and assist them in doing so.

Myth #15: Recovering alcoholics are persons who have stopped drinking.

Many alcoholics have stopped drinking but never started recovery. Sometimes stopping drinking produces worse symptoms than continuing to drink. Overwhelming guilt, anger, and depression can result. Recovery is not just stopping a destructive behavior; it is entering into a process that improves every area of the individual's life.

Recovering alcoholics are dramatically different from nondrinking alcoholics. Their lives exude a natural and attractive serenity. It is so attractive that it motivates us to improve our lives, also. Recovery is not a difficult process for survival; it is a rewarding life-style that enhances the lives and relationships of those who are close. Those who have stopped drinking and remain miserable need our help to enter the recovery process.

CONCLUSION

Often when confronted with new information that challenges the old, we balk. We are threatened and find it hard to reconsider long-held beliefs. I know because mine were very entrenched. The important consideration is, What results do our old ways of thinking produce? My view of alcoholics as weak-willed certainly made me feel better about myself, but it didn't do anything for the alcoholics I came in contact with. Seeing alcoholism for what it is—a problem with physiological roots—is very freeing for alcoholics. It removes the shame that often drives them back to the alcohol. The results from this new view are very rewarding as we watch people stop trying to get good enough to drink again and start working their recovery program.

If alcoholism is truly influenced by genetics and physiological roots, there must be solid evidence for it. The following chapter makes the case for biological predisposition.

Chapter 16

◆

THE CASE FOR PREDISPOSITION

Emmet and Hazel Ross embodied contradiction. He was frail and thin; she, large and weighty. He was nervous, volatile, detached. She was strong-willed, overbearing, intrusive. Both were traveling evangelists and Scotch-Irish by birth. Moving frequently with their four young boys, they traveled the midwestern backcountry tent circuits of the forties, fifties, and sixties, preaching with zealous gusto and great emotion of the fires of hell and the benefits of heaven and the expediency of salvation. From sermon to altar call, they seemed two of a kind. But before the sermon and after the altar call, Michael recalls, they had a single overwhelming commonality—they drank a lot of alcohol. From sermon to altar call, a strange lull of sobriety overcame them. All else was chaos and ruin. They argued harshly and constantly. Much later they divorced. Each remains an ailing alcoholic. Neither will admit to alcoholism. To their sons, they have so far left only a legacy of violent addiction.

Of the sons, not one has escaped the plague. Josh, the oldest, married at sixteen and fathered two children. At age twenty-three, depressed, alcoholic, and unemployed, he ended his life in violent suicide. Kevin, the youngest, fled the country at age thirty after an alcoholic rage during which he assaulted his best friend, crippling him for life. The remaining sons, now middle-aged, are identical twins whose lives inscribe parallel paths to ruin. Both have shown signs of alcoholism since adolescence. During the high-school years, drink followed drink, violence followed violence, and the circuits of addiction beckoned and burned without mercy. With belligerent, antagonistic, reckless abandon, they made the rounds with drink after drink.

One remarkable observation followed Michael and Matthew through their high-school years and into adulthood. After each had had a case of beer, and long after their friends were drunk, asleep, or heeding a warning high, the brothers still had an iron grip on control. They "held" their drink but not their tempers. A glance at Michael's girlfriend while he was drinking might result in fury. His fists found their mark without weaving. Obsession, delusion, physical and verbal abuse—those were visible marks of a problem, but the line Matthew and Michael walked did not blur or waver or weave.

Michael was young when he married, just out of high school. He had possessed Dana, body and soul, since their early teen years. He has depended on her and abused and imprisoned her all these years, refusing her access even to her own family. She has never protested. Four sons and a daughter, rebellious, impulsive, agonized, eye the ruins and begin their own alcoholic pilgrimage. Michael says nothing is wrong.

Matthew, much later, married a college sweetheart. Less violent than his brother, he uses deception where his twin uses force. Drinking, followed by promises, followed by drinking, followed by reassurances, followed by more drinking and then verbal abuse, has ended in loss of home, loss of job, loss of driving privileges, loss of family, loss of a clean legal slate, loss of reality, and nearly loss of life. His wife, disheartened, has filed for divorce. Two small daughters are heartbroken. According to Matthew, nothing is wrong.

Neither Michael nor Matthew will admit to alcoholism. Neither believes he needs help. In their wake, they leave fire and ruin, pain and broken lives. As an inheritance, they leave what they received—the charred circuits to ride.

FACTS ABOUT ALCOHOLISM

This story is about a particular sort of addiction. It is about a condition that plagues "everyone else" and "someone else's" children. Our society, in twentieth-century America, may well be the most addiction-driven society in history—and the most prone to deny the evidence. But the evidence is here. Day after day, we all see it. The tragic consequence of driving with a nervous system impaired by alcohol or drugs. Or the pain of abused and deeply wounded children from an alcoholic household. Or the indifferent violence of narcotics users and dealers. The waste of minds and bodies and spirits greets us brazenly on highways, in schools and churches, on playgrounds, in offices, on sidewalks, in parks, through the condominium walls and windows, and even, for many of us, in the place we know best—the home.

In 1984, 56 *million* American families experienced alcohol-related problems within their own four walls. Those problems cost our nation's citizens $116 billion and accounted for about half of all hospital admissions. Every day of the year, Americans were drinking 1.2 million gallons of hard liquor (enough alcohol to significantly intoxicate 26 million people). In addition, Americans drank 28 million six-packs of beer, took 30 million sleeping pills, smoked the equivalent of a small house made of marijuana, and snorted a bathtub full of cocaine for every day they lived.[1] Fifty percent of the total consumption of alcohol in the United States is attributable to 10 percent of the nation's drinkers.[2]

In 1989, for alcohol alone, Americans spent a total of $88.5 billion. (Compare that with the $12 billion we spent on snack foods or the $10 billion on fruit juices and drinks.)[3] Approximately 10 million Americans are estimated to be addicted to alcohol, and another 7 million are designated as abusers.[4] Together, they have cost additional billions of dollars in impaired productivity.[5]

Seventy percent of all persons police arrest each day display evidence that an illegal drug is currently in their systems. Fifty percent of them test positive for alcohol intoxication. And every day, five thousand more people, young and old, try cocaine for the first time.[6]

Kara is ten years old and in the fifth grade. She has grown up in an upper-middle-class home. She is well adjusted and bright. The neighborhood in which she lives, the school she attends, and even the sort of parents she has mark Kara as matched to our society's prototype for "child most likely to succeed." Yet, 39 percent of the children in Kara's grade are already feeling pressured to drink alcohol. Within four years, 75 percent of her classmates will feel the same pressure. Kara is three times more likely than not to be among them.[7]

ALCOHOLIC HOMES

According to current estimates, 22 million of today's adults have grown up in an alcoholic home. Seven million children under age eighteen are currently affected by an alcoholic parent.[8]

In the United States, 188 children and adolescents will abuse alcohol every thirty minutes. During the same thirty minutes, 685 teens will use some form of narcotic.[9] By the time Kara's class has graduated from high school, probably between 85 and 95 percent of the class will have experimented with alcohol and drugs.[10] Their first taste of alcohol will have occurred, on average, at age twelve. Many, even as preteens, will have serious problems with substance abuse,[11] and their early drug abuse will predispose them to an increased risk of experiencing other sorts of problems later in life.[12] It is unrealistic, even for parents like Kara's, even for responsible and loving Christian parents, to think that their child will remain unaffected.

In 1988, the National Council on Alcoholism reported that signs of serious alcohol-related problems were evident in approximately 3.3 million drinkers ages fourteen to seventeen.[13] *Newsweek* reported that 66 percent of teens who were asked to identify the greatest problem faced by their age group named alcohol and drugs as that problem.[14] Yet adult Americans continue to deny the severity of the problems of substance abuse and addiction.

In a survey of six hundred high-school seniors and their parents, Emory University in Atlanta, Georgia, reports that 35 percent of the parents interviewed believed their children to have consumed alcohol in the past month, while according to their children, 70 percent had done so.[15] Ninety-two percent of pastors surveyed in one study agreed that substance abuse was a major problem among their community's young people. Only 13 percent believed that the problem existed in their own churches. Statistics drawn from the same study, comparing "churched" with "unchurched" young people, showed that only 3 to 8 percent more of the unchurched youths than churched youths had drunk beer (8 percent more), used tobacco (7 percent more), or tried cocaine (3 percent more), while 9 percent *more* churched young people had tried marijuana than had their unchurched peers.[16] Time and again, we Americans have been all too ready to deny the prevalence of substance abuse and addiction problems in our society. We American Christians are apparently just as guilty of denial as is the rest of our society.

We have only glimpsed the magnitude of the problems of abuse and addiction. However, our purpose here is to investigate what factors may predispose certain people to the addiction we call alcoholism. Over 50 percent of American families are affected by such problems, but almost 50 percent are not. Why? What can we do if our own families are among those who suffer because of alcohol addiction-related problems? How can we help other families to overcome them? What can we do to prevent them in the future? These questions are at the heart of the exploration we are about to begin, but the first question we must answer is, What is addiction?

WHAT IS ADDICTION?

In the past few years especially, controversy has raged over what one may legitimately call an addiction. To some counselors and ministers, both professional and lay, it has often seemed useful to describe a wide array of human problems as addictions. In their critics' opinions, this tendency has appeared irresponsible and, on the whole, to disregard or selectively regard many of the conclusions of current research. To complicate matters, popular demand for this approach to counseling and personal growth help has increased dramatically, and a sizable industry has arisen to provide for this demand. Some critics accuse addiction treatment specialists of cultivating fads to create new markets for themselves, thereby victimizing the vulnerable and naive among those who believe they need help.[17] Proponents of the addiction approach to treating certain problems often argue that they are seeing dramatic results in the treatment of such problems. Both critics and proponents number among themselves many highly respected scientists, counselors, priests, nuns, ministers, and clients. Who is one to trust? Trust the ones who are getting results in working with addicts.

It seems obvious that at least some sort of generally recognized definition of addiction should be helpful, though not conclusive, in identifying those who are to be legitimately considered addicts for both treatment and research purposes. I include here guidelines that are generally accepted as adequate measures for the assessment of addiction.

Let's review the four clinical symptoms recognized as diagnostic measures of both the presence and the severity of addiction:

1. *Preoccupation* with a substance, when that preoccupation is prolonged and compulsive;
2. *Tolerance* of the substance: larger and larger doses are needed in order to produce the same results that formerly required a smaller dose;
3. *Dependency:* withdrawal symptoms, either physical or psychological, are experienced when use of the substance is abruptly discontinued;
4. *Debilitation:* both physiological and social (e.g., family, job) functioning is significantly impaired.[18]

These criteria, though easily descriptive of those who are still using a substance such as alcohol, are less successful in describing those who are in a period of abstinence but cannot truly be considered recovering. For many addicts, alcoholics among them, recovery is a lifelong proposition. Most of those who treat alcoholism recognize that, though currently free of these clinical features, an alcoholic will remain with an "addicted" body throughout life. That is, the body of the alcoholic will continue to respond to the drug in such a way as to cause return to the observable addictive patterns should drinking be resumed.

Also, with reference to these criteria, many counseling professionals believe that addictive behaviors may develop apart from abusing a particular physical substance but may involve chemical reactions in the brain when engaging in certain behaviors such as sex or gambling. Two psychologists, who published a text on psychopathology, explain, "Pathological gamblers display virtually all the features of addictive behavior. They are compulsively preoccupied with the excitement of gambling to the point where their personal and occupational functioning becomes impaired; they must continually increase the stakes in order to sustain excitement . . . and when prevented from gambling, they may experience psychological withdrawal symptoms such as agitation and depression."[19] Despite objections, however, the definition of addiction provided here should serve as at least a general guideline for identifying addiction problems.

DEFINING ALCOHOLISM

Much of the confusion and controversy that surrounds discussions on the causes of alcoholism stems from the lack of a clear definition. The problem extends to much of the scientific research we are about to discuss. It centers on the necessity to distinguish alcohol *abuse* from alcohol *addiction,* or alcoholism. When considering a genuine addiction to alcohol, we must remember that something other than a problem of moral character, environment, or personality has been observed. The body is physiologically, as well as psychologically, tied to continued use of the addictive substance, whatever the initial reason for abusing it. However, *abuse* is not necessarily *addiction.* Many people abuse alcohol, but not all of them are alcoholics. How do we know the difference?

A remarkable fact about alcohol addiction, as with addictions to many other familiar drugs, is that tolerance for the drug varies greatly from person to person. Many drink alcohol regularly, even daily, without becoming addicted. Others are hooked for life from their first drinking experience. Human bodies vary dramatically in their ability to absorb and metabolize alcohol. For this reason, it is often extremely difficult for even an informed person, unaware of a drinker's patterns of drinking over long stretches of time, to distinguish between a drinker and an alcoholic. Perhaps the key, which is often overlooked for other signs and symptoms, is the amount the person can consume. The higher the tolerance, the greater the chance that alcoholism is present.

The National Council on Alcoholism (NCA) gives the following definition of alcoholism: *alcoholism* is a "chronic, progressive and potentially fatal disease." It is characterized by "repeated drinking that causes trouble in the drinker's personal, professional or family life. When they drink, alcoholics can't always predict when they'll stop, how much they'll drink or what the consequences of their drinking will be."[20] The NCA offers the following major physiological criteria for a diagnosis of alcoholism:

1. Physical symptoms of withdrawal evidenced when consumption is decreased or discontinued
2. Tolerance, indicated by a blood alcohol level of 0.15 percent without signs of intoxication
3. Alcoholic blackouts
4. Any major illness that is alcohol-related (e.g., alcoholic hepatitis or cirrhosis of the liver)

Here are behavioral indicators: (1) drinking persists after a doctor's advice to stop, (2) social problems are evidenced (e.g., marriage, employment), and (3) the drinker appears to have lost control of the drinking.[21]

In the recent revision of the *Diagnostic and Statistical Manual (DSM III-R)*, the American Psychiatric Association sketches three different "typical" patterns encountered in those who abuse alcohol and may depend on it: (1) large amounts of alcohol are consumed daily and regularly; (2) large amounts are consumed on weekends only; and (3) extended periods of sobriety are broken by binge drinking, which may last for long periods of time (weeks or months). *DSM III-R* also warns, however, "It is a mistake to associate one of these particular patterns exclusively with alcoholism."[22] Complicating matters still further, it notes that alcohol addiction is often found in company with other drug abuse or addiction, or as secondary to some form of psychopathology. *DSM III-R* lists nine symptoms, similar to those mentioned previously, three of which must be present to indicate a diagnosis of alcoholism.[23]

How should the average person, attempting to understand and recognize alcoholism, interpret all of this? Some people who may abuse alcohol periodically—enough to cause occasional conflict in their families or even kill someone while driving drunk—are not necessarily alcoholic.

Abusive drinking may, indeed, be almost entirely a result of problems in character or environment, learned behavior, or destructive patterns of thought. That does not seem to be true for alcoholism. Alcoholics are trapped in an escalating and devastating progression and may not have any idea that they are addicted to alcohol. What symptoms can those of us who watch from the outside, and who are in the best position to intervene, hope to identify? It is of utmost importance that we distinguish between alcohol abuse, or problem drinking, and alcoholism, not only in attempting to understand what causes alcoholism but also in treating *both* conditions.

RECOGNIZING ALCOHOL ADDICTION: THE PROGRESSION

Alcoholism winds its way into persons' lives the way some beautiful wisteria vines, hanging lavish clusters of flowers across the outer wall of a house, end up penetrating and destroying the house they adorn. The first and most subtle sign of alcoholism is increasing tolerance. The beauty of it is this: people who have high physiological tolerance to alcohol *look,* to everyone around them, as if they are completely unaffected by the substance. They look stronger—as if they have extraordinary self-control. They may drink most people under the table or may simply feel no intoxicating effects after one, then two, then three glasses of wine. Still more insidious, these same people may, in their first experiences with drinking alcohol, feel the same pleasant effects normally associated with a social drink or two. As they continue to drink "normally," however, they find that these effects are no longer felt with just a drink or two. In short, they are (perhaps very quickly) developing a tolerance for the drug. All seems well, but the body has already begun its slow progression of dependency and demand.

Until they pass middle age, these same people may continue to drink unbelievable quantities of alcohol, still able to "walk a straight line" afterward. Meanwhile, their nonalcoholic companions continue to exhibit built-in limitations as to how much they *can* drink. After a fairly consistent maximum quantity is consumed, they fall asleep, grow nauseated, or get uncontrollably drunk so that further consumption, which would eventually produce permanent changes in the body, is automatically cut off.

Increasing tolerance, then, observed over a period of time, is the major distinguishing factor between a social drinker (however abusive he or she might be when under the influence of alcohol) and an alcoholic.[24] Tolerance is not a sign of greater physical or moral strength. It is a sign that something is not normal in a person's physical response to alcohol. It is not cause for praise. It is a sign that progression toward disaster has begun. This progression is not present in the "normal" drinker.

In crossing the North Atlantic by plane at high altitudes and during the daytime, one sometimes sees bright white patches scattered across the ocean surface. When someone sees this for the first time, the response is often predictably, "Icebergs!" It takes moments or hours to realize that the current season and latitude of the flight render the visual identification of icebergs improbable. Inquiring, one is told sheepishly, "Oh, that's garbage," and the vision grows dark. Alcoholism is something like the sheets of floating suds and garbage—by the time people get close enough to see what is really there, they likely have ended up in the middle of it. Once they are in the middle of alcohol addiction, doing what is necessary to extricate themselves may be the most difficult thing they will ever do, whether they are alcoholics or members of an alcoholic's family. Most assuredly, they will not be able to do it without help —from family, from friends, probably from trained medical and counseling professionals, and certainly from God. When the deed is done, they will know, as the psalmist did, what it means to be plucked out of deep waters—and they will know what it will take to stay afloat.[25]

By the time the next stage of the alcoholic progression is reached, the body of the alcohol-tolerant person is already showing signs of definite physical addiction. In addition to drinking for the usual reasons, this person also begins to drink to relieve physical and psychological pain. Many of these painful symptoms are the direct physical result of withdrawal from the addictive substance. Physical craving for alcohol is present, and while periods of abstinence are still possible, they are increasingly difficult to maintain. Loss of control over drinking, emotions, and responsibilities is characteristic of this stage, and the addicted person, struggling to regain it, is finally aware that there is a serious problem. Rather than admit to the problem and seek help, most alcoholics continue to drink and, at times, to try desperately—and unsuccessfully—to bring their lives back under control.[26] Crying help at this stage is not like pulling oneself up by the proverbial bootstraps. It is the deliberate relinquishing of still more control until responsible decision making is again possible.

But the alcoholic's body has, by this time, reached a point of dependency, producing the energy necessary to function in daily life more easily and efficiently from alcohol than from food, and it therefore demands alcohol in ever increasing quantities. Alcohol will make the alcoholic feel normal, and without it the person will feel unimaginably miserable. As quantities consumed increase, alcohol acts as a poison to the alcoholic's body, which is less and less able to "detoxify" itself, to rid itself of the poisonous qualities of the drug. Toxins (poisonous substances) accumulate in the cells of the body, causing problems in many organs, including the brain. As brain functions are affected, rational thinking and normal inhibitions deteriorate. The alcoholic has reached the stage of "toxicity"—the poisoning of the body by the addictive substance—which cannot be reversed without causing symptoms of withdrawal. The more severe the addiction, the more severe the withdrawal. Even after the addicted person is sober, these effects persist, sometimes for months or years.[27] Some research indicates that evidence of the parent's alcoholism may be inherited by the alcoholic's offspring even after ten years of parental abstinence from alcohol.[28]

Seven American authors, to date, have won the Nobel Prize for literature. Four of them were indisputably alcoholic (Sinclair Lewis, Ernest Hemingway, Eugene O'Neill, and William Faulkner), and a fifth, John Steinbeck, is a good bet. That amounts to 71 percent of our nation's most honored writers of this century. The list could go on and on, from F. Scott Fitzgerald to James Thurber to Tennessee Williams and, as one author puts it, "kegs-full of others."[29] Is it any wonder our twentieth-century American imaginations are suffused with vivid images of drunks and drunkards, from the disillusioned of the Great War to the disenfranchised of the Great Depression to the bankrupt homeless of the Great City's Bowery? Not only our daily experience (remember, more than 50 percent of families) but even our stories reel and stumble and die stripped to the bone. Yet, just as with depression, despair, and poverty, we Americans often think of drunkenness as a stage that will pass—either of its own accord or with a little help from its host. We acknowledge that when the stress of life drives many people to drink heavily, there are always some who do not stop when stress is eased. We think of them as poor souls, bereft of all self-respect and self-control, victims of their own cowardice and lack of character or of some malignant fate —lying beside the railroad tracks, stretched out under newspapers in a gutter, slumped in a chair at the local bar. And so they often seem, though perhaps not for the reasons we name. Yet, it is only in the very last stages of alcoholism that the reality of the disorder may begin to match our imaginations.

Mental disorientation, physiological deterioration, and emotional upheaval mark the last gasps of alcoholism. The addict's body, which after all has its limits, has had enough. Poisoned consistently and increasingly over years or decades, it begins to collapse in earnest. The alcoholic is thrown back and forth between the agony of withdrawal (which can, of its own accord, cause death at this stage) and the agony of watching himself or herself poison the body. The godlike state of tolerance is entirely gone. The person is trapped. Serious damage manifests itself in the liver, heart, lungs, and intestines. Malnutrition overtakes a body starved of good food. Unless someone cares enough to intervene, the whole progression is sure to end in intense suffering and untimely death, for the alcoholic is no longer capable, at this stage, of choosing between the consequences of withdrawal and the consequences of continuing to drink. Detoxification of the body must come first, carefully and quickly. Even so, much of the physical and psychological damage may never be undone. But even at such a desperate stage, something can be done to help. The alcoholic, perhaps enslaved throughout most of adult life or longer, may yet live, with the right kind of help, to be free of addiction—free to live one day at a time truly *deciding* not to drink.

RAPID PROGRESSION IN TEENAGERS

Adolescents often progress through the stages of alcoholism more rapidly than adults. While adults take from five to ten years or longer to manifest the full range of the disease, adolescents may take as few as one or two years. Teenagers often use other substances along with alcohol. This may accelerate the progression of alcoholism.[30]

THE NATURE/NURTURE CONTROVERSY

Controversy over the nature and origins of some human ailments has whirled incessantly since recorded time began. On the surface of things, the issue is this: Does the problem develop because the afflicted person has learned certain behaviors to cope with a poor environment? Is it the result of inadequate development of the person's moral character? Or is the problem directly connected with physical abnormalities, with inborn propensity toward developing the problem regardless of environment? Beneath these superficial questions lurk the questions we are really asking. Like those who questioned Jesus about the man born blind, we ask, "Who sinned? Was it this man or his parents?" (Is it our fault? Is it their fault? Is it his fault?) What we mean is, "Who is responsible for this?" and "Who is responsible to fix it?" and "Is it fixable?"

These are important questions. By virtue of being human, we want to believe that all problems, especially when they bring great pain into our relations with one another or with ourselves, are "fixable." This hope is never "wrong" in itself (in fact, it is fundamental to all real faith and moral character), but it can sometimes be misused. It may be rooted in an unrealistic expectation that all of life's suffering (especially our own) can, with enough human effort (usually someone else's), be relieved. It is a particularly American trait to believe that with enough individual fortitude and effort on the part of someone with a problem, the problem can be solved (especially if the "someone" is someone else).

Such a prevailing attitude works against all real hope for healing and change, and it is an attitude to which many American Christians are, sadly, not strangers. But it is Christian heresy to believe that people can, solely by the strength of individual effort, solve either their own or anyone else's problems. Christian faith fundamentally affirms that human beings were not created to go it alone. The value systems of the frontier —or of corporate America—do not bear fruit in the healing of persons.

However, we are not absolved from taking appropriate responsibility. Even when the process of overcoming a problem such as addiction involves an abnormality that has at least some of its roots in the formation of one's physical body or in the experiences of infancy and early childhood, out of memory's reach and seemingly impossible to reverse, each individual must assume some level of responsibility. Sometimes the first step in accepting such responsibility is seeking or accepting help from others. Eventually, it will always involve being willing to do whatever is necessary to promote recovery and growth. The meaning of the Latin root word from which our verb *to accept* is taken includes the idea of "holding on tightly" to something. We must all go on "holding on tightly" to appropriate responses (responsibility), however small, if recovery and growth are to proceed in and around us.

The questions of nature versus nurture are significant ones, but as we go on to present evidence of what seem to be predisposing factors involved in becoming addicted to alcohol, it will be good to remember that these questions are more important for shedding light on *how* we can best take up the scalpels of appropriate responsibility and loving action, whether for ourselves or for someone we love, than for determining who or what is to blame or for deciding whether there is hope of recovery. Whatever the cause of an alcoholic's problems, there *is* always something that can be done to help—if we are all willing to do whatever it takes. There is always hope.

WHAT CAUSES ADDICTION TO ALCOHOL?

In Plains, Georgia, the family of James Earl Carter, Sr., has been involved with peanut farming for many years. Its members have eaten many of the same foods, breathed the same air, walked the same ground, and lived in much the same way for much of their lives. Most of them have also died the same deaths. James Earl, Sr., his two daughters, and one of his two sons have all, tragically, died at a young age—and all from pancreatic cancer. Former President Jimmy Carter is the lone survivor among the four Carter siblings. The Carter family, defying the odds even for known genetic disease transmission, is one family being studied by researchers in hope of finding what causes pancreatic cancer.[31]

In 1955, Dr. Americo Negrette noticed something strange on the outskirts of the Venezuelan town in which he was a university professor. There were people—lots of them—weaving back and forth across the streets. They were not drunk, as he thought at first, but suffering from a strange illness. "The dancers," as he called them, lived by the scores in the vicinity of Lake Maracaibo and were all descendants of a single afflicted woman. The more than ten thousand members of the afflicted family became the subjects of a study conducted to identify the gene or genes that cause Huntington's disease, a fatal neurological disease that begins by affecting balance and progresses to the destruction of mental as well as physical abilities. As a result of the research, a gene was found, and a test has been developed to identify whether the disease gene is present in the children of an afflicted parent.[32]

In the Ross family, as we have seen, a terrible pattern has devastated at least two generations. It is already entrenched in part of a third. Of the many millions of alcoholics in the United States, a large percentage belong to families like the Rosses. In the last three decades, more and more researchers have been trying to solve the riddle—just as they continue to try, with the Carter family, to unlock the secrets of pancreatic cancer and, with the "dancers" of Lake Maracaibo, to identify the culprit genes of Huntington's disease.

Alcoholism runs in families. That is no secret, no innovation of twentieth-century research. Over two thousand years ago, Aristotle observed that alcoholic women often had children who followed in their drunken footsteps. Although he might have had the genders confused (male children of alcoholic men may have the highest risk of developing alcoholism),[33] he was certainly on the right track in observing that alcoholism sticks close to home. Many others throughout history have sounded similar alarms, and they are proving to have been worth the listening.

Modern research techniques have taken up this age-old observation and put it to the test. The result? Alcoholism runs in families.

But what causes alcoholism? Even though alcoholism runs in families, the most common presumption concerning alcoholics has usually been that the person's family environment, moral upbringing, personality, or own moral choices cause the person to be a slave to alcohol. As we will see, however, little current research will support these ideas about alcohol addiction, and much will cast doubt on them. Environmental, psychological, and spiritual factors are certainly involved in why people do or do not drink either normally or problematically. But they are less likely to be central to the process of addiction to alcohol once drinking, for whatever reason, begins. Anyone may *decide* to drink normally or abusively, but no one *decides* to become an alcoholic.

It may be helpful if we stop for a moment and think about why, under normal circumstances, a person—any person—drinks alcoholic beverages in the first place. After all, it is impossible to become alcoholic without first ingesting alcohol. Why do we take that first drink? Why do we continue—sometimes in spite of negative effects, such as headaches or nausea, or in spite of distaste? I can think of three primary reasons: (1) pleasure; (2) relaxation or relief of stress, discomfort, or pain; and (3) social acceptance. Research supports each possible reason for starting and continuing to drink "normally."

For example, increasingly large doses of alcohol are increasingly successful in relieving stress and anxiety.[34] Researchers have found that injections of alcohol result in exaggerated stimulation of a part of the brain that produces sensations of pleasure by raising levels of the neurotransmitter dopamine in the synaptic spaces between nerve cells.[35] In the human brain, areas associated with relief of distress are distinct from areas associated with the experience of pleasure.[36] Drugs or drug components that produce extremely intense pleasure act in a different way and on a different part of the brain, then, from those that produce relief from discomfort and pain. Either effect might certainly encourage one to drink. Although the specific effects of alcohol on the brain are not completely clear, it is believed that in most individuals, alcohol acts on both the distress-relief area and the pleasure-producing area, giving substantial incentive to drink and keep drinking.

As for the social impetus behind drinking alcohol, testimonies of the effects of peer pressure abound. One study of American Indians confirms those effects. Although American Indians have inherited a physiological deficiency in the metabolism of alcohol, which is associated with Asian peoples and which has elsewhere resulted in decreased rates of alcoholism,[37] their rate of alcoholism soars. The rate of alcoholism for American Indians is among the highest in the world.[38]

Despite strong incentives to drink and keep drinking, something different must happen in the bodies of alcoholics to enable them to continue drinking long past the point where normal drinking is forced to stop. Remember, even problem drinkers—who habitually and to their detriment drink to the point of drunkenness but do not exhibit the signs of addiction, such as withdrawal—reach a point where their bodies force cessation of drinking. At the extreme, most drinkers pass out before saturating their bodies with alcohol to the point of toxicity. Alcoholics do not—not until tolerance disappears in the late stages of alcoholism. And most of us stop drinking long before passing out. We have experienced sufficient relaxation or pleasure or approval to satisfy us. Or we have experienced unpleasant side effects that sufficiently deter us. That is not true of alcoholics. Because physical tolerance is higher, drinking can and must continue beyond normal levels in alcoholics to produce effects equal to those the rest of us experience with much, much less.

Alcoholism is not a simple condition, and there are no easy answers to what causes it. But as we review the results of research performed in the last two decades to examine the causes and nature of alcohol addiction, we will find growing evidence that *susceptibility* to alcoholism is likely to be at least partly, and perhaps largely, inherited—without an inherited factor, alcoholism would be unlikely or impossible. Since much controversy turns on whether this is true, and since in our own consideration of research and our personal observations of many alcoholics, we are led to believe that it is true, we will concentrate on evidence that involves *biological* predisposition to developing an addiction to alcohol.

Genetic research on the subject is aimed at finding out if alcohol addiction is passed in some measure from generation to generation by means of a gene or group of genes. Three general sorts of testing are used: (1) twin and adoption studies, (2) animal studies (where animals are *bred*—not trained—to exhibit a certain trait common to the disorder being studied), and (3) studies using DNA markers or biological markers. Genetic researchers proceed on the basis of clues derived from family studies or from studies of the nature of a disorder in a large group of affected people. Some clues lead to potential marker traits, or signposts. One clue for alcoholism, as we have noted, is the presence in alcoholics of a tolerance for abnormally large quantities of alcohol. Another clue is that alcohol stimulates the increased production of dopamine, a neurotransmitter, in the nerve cells of the brain.[39] Still another is the discovery that preteen sons of alcoholics have a higher percentage of abnormal brain wave responses than do preteen sons of nonalcoholics.[40] We will discuss these subjects more fully as we go along.

Most people are unaware of the startling way in which alcoholism runs in families. At least 31 percent of alcoholics have a parent who was also an alcoholic. (For most, the parent was the father.) This rate represents 2.5 times the prevalence rate of alcoholism among relatives of nonalcoholic psychiatric patients, and 6 times the prevalence of alcoholism in a normal control group.[41] Even though alcoholism, for some people, is considered secondary to another form of disorder (e.g., depression or antisocial personality disorder), children from families marred by social disorders have one-fourth the risk of alcoholism associated with children of alcoholic fathers, even when the latter were adopted and raised in families whose social functioning was normal.[42]

THE FACTORS OF PREDISPOSITION

In the 1940s, researchers at Harvard University began a forty-year study of six hundred male teenagers. Psychiatrist George Vaillant analyzed the results in 1983, concluding that the major factors apt to predispose one to developing an addiction to alcohol were (1) having a parent who is alcoholic and (2) being raised in an ethnic background that condones adult drunkenness. He also concluded that antisocial behavior, depression, and other emotional problems are results of alcoholism rather than causes.[43]

Some people seem to be born with a higher tolerance for alcohol. Sadly, those whose family history includes alcohol dependency and who already indicate a higher tolerance for the substance may not realize the danger in continuing to drink until they are far down the road and already addicted. Before alcoholism becomes clinically evident, heavy drinking will likely have continued for quite some time. In 1956, the *American Journal of Psychiatry* reported that the only characteristic common to all alcoholics is the ability to drink too much.[44]

In his book *Is Alcoholism Hereditary?*, Dr. Donald Goodwin notes,

By 1980, at least a dozen groups of investigators were studying the children of alcoholics—nonadopted as well as adopted and comparing them with children of nonalcoholics. These were the findings:

1. Children of alcoholics have a higher tolerance for alcohol than do children of nonalcoholics.
2. Children of alcoholics underrespond to certain stimuli recorded on electroencephalograms (EEGs).
3. Children of alcoholics generate more alpha activity on the EEG.
4. Children of alcoholics are more often hyperactive than other children.[45]

TWIN AND ADOPTION STUDIES

The majority of families share environments as well as genes. This fact causes difficulty in distinguishing whether genetic factors play a primary role in the development of a problem or whether environmental factors play a central role in precipitating a condition such as alcoholism. For this reason, twin and adoption studies have been used for many years to help scientists determine whether a problem is more likely to be inherited than environmentally caused.

Studies of identical twins can provide more accurate information concerning whether a problem is genetically transmitted. Identical twins, who are known to have identical genetic makeup, are compared with each other to determine whether the experience of one is concordant with the experience of the other. The concordance rates of identical twins are then compared with those of pairs of fraternal twins (whose genetic makeup is no more similar than other siblings). If a high percentage of the identical twins of a group of alcoholics also develop alcoholism, they are said to be concordant for alcoholism to that extent. In studies of alcohol addiction in identical twins, most earlier studies reveal that they are about twice as concordant as are fraternal twins. This finding indicates that a genetic component is present in developing an addiction to alcohol. Some studies also show concordance in identical twins for both quantity and frequency of drinking.[46] This is good evidence that genetic factors may be involved in developing alcoholism, even though several recent studies either do not confirm the results or limit the results to more severe (longer than ten years) forms of alcoholism.[47]

To further test the results of family and twin studies, researchers conduct adoption studies. Adoptees are compared with both biological and adoptive families to yield even more accurate information about whether a trait is better viewed as inherited or as caused by environmental factors or both. They enable researchers to assess the prevalence of both genetic and environmental causes for developing a disease by comparing traits of the adoptee with traits and environment of both biological and adoptive relatives, and then comparing the results with data from the general population. If a child who is adopted at birth is more similar to a biological parent or parents than to adoptive parents, genetic factors are assumed to be involved. If similar results are found with whole groups of such adopted children, there is substantial evidence for at least some genetic origin for the traits being examined.

In 1973–74, Dr. Donald Goodwin reported that though raised apart from their biological parents, the adopted sons of alcoholic biological parents were nearly four times more likely to become alcoholic than were the adopted sons of nonalcoholic biological parents. He also discovered that sons of alcoholic parents who were raised by those parents were no more or less likely to become addicted to alcohol than were their brothers, who had been adopted in infancy. In other words, the length of exposure to the alcoholism of the parent had no effect on the development of alcoholism in the child. In addition, Dr. Goodwin noted that the severity of alcoholism in the biological parent corresponded to the eventual severity of the addiction in the sons.[48]

In 1978, Remi Cadoret and Ann Gath found that a biological background of alcoholism was the only significant predictor of alcohol addiction in the adoptees they studied. Other factors considered were socioeconomic status of the adoptive parents, psychiatric disorder in the adoptive family, age of the adoptee at adoption, and time spent in foster care before adoption.[49]

Also in 1978, Michael Bohman studied adoptees and their biological and adoptive families. Using state criminal records and other official records, he failed to find any correlation between biological parents and criminality in the adoptee. However, he observed a significant correlation between alcoholism in adopted sons and alcoholism in the biological parents.[50]

A 1980 study of adopted children raised apart from their biological parents found that neither environmental factors (of the adoptive environment) nor the socioeconomic standards of the adoptive parents increased the risk of alcoholism among the adoptees. Alcohol addiction occurred with much greater frequency in those whose biological parents were alcoholic, even in the absence of any subsequent contact with one another. Three general conclusions were drawn: (1) environmental factors are less apt to explain increased risk of alcoholism than are biological factors; (2) when taken into consideration alongside biological factors, environmental factors do not increase liability for becoming addicted; and (3) there is no evidence to support the theory that environmental and biological factors interact in those with a family history of alcoholism to increase risk.[51] Although details of these conclusions have been justifiably challenged more recently, many researchers continue to conclude, while noting that some environmental factors are likely to be involved as well (remember, not *all* sons of alcoholics develop alcoholism), that genetic factors are probably integral to the development of alcoholism.

Dr. Robert Cloninger and his colleagues studied Swedish men and women who had been adopted at an early age. Using government records, they compared information about the adoptees with information on their biological and adoptive parents. They identified those among the adoptees and parents who were addicted to alcohol by the number of times they had been registered with the Swedish county temperance boards for drunkenness. The reports were generally registered following public abuse of alcohol, driving offenses, or family violence.

In 1981, in addition to noting that children whose biological parents were alcoholic ran an increased risk of becoming alcoholic, Cloninger's group described two types of persons who seemed to be predisposed to alcoholism. The two types were differentiated by both biological and environmental factors. Type one alcoholism was identified in the majority (75 percent) of alcohol abusers. It was found in both sexes after the age of twenty-five and was linked to a family history of alcoholism. In addition, four environmental risk factors were determined. Type one alcoholics (1) had been raised for more than six months by their biological mother, (2) were older at the time of adoption, (3) spent more time in the hospital before adoption, and (4) had an adoptive father with a lower economic status. Type two alcoholics were less common and were sons of alcoholic fathers. Alcoholism had often developed in type twos during adolescence and seemed not to be influenced by environmental factors. Type twos tended to be aggressive, rebellious, impulsive, and emotionally detached; type ones tended to be anxious, shy, reflective, and emotionally dependent.[52]

Several researchers have criticized Cloninger's study on a number of grounds, not the least of which is the manner in which he determined whether his subjects were alcoholic. Many subjects so designated were as likely to have been alcohol abusers as alcoholics. Other factors, such as the adoptive family environment and whether the biological mother drank heavily during her pregnancy (known to result in personality problems such as hyperactivity and problems in learning), were not considered at all.[53] Subsequent studies have not consistently confirmed the type one and type two distinctions;[54] however, most studies confirm the linkage of alcoholism in adoptees with a family history of alcoholism in the birth family but not in the adoptive family.[55]

In 1986, an American adoption study reported that adoptees of both sexes with alcoholic biological parents were more likely to develop alcoholism than those with nonalcoholic biological parents.[56] Previously, many studies had agreed that heritability of alcoholism was either much weaker or nonexistent for female children of alcoholics.[57] This finding has yet to be consistently confirmed.

Despite some valid criticism of certain conclusions formed solely on the basis of any of the methods of study described here, most researchers will tend to agree that general conclusions are both possible and necessary. In the case of addiction to alcohol, more and more researchers tend to conclude that certain people are predisposed to becoming alcoholic by virtue of being biological members of families in which the condition has been observed repeatedly. The majority of them will also affirm that some people seem to *inherit* a liability for, or predisposition to, alcoholism. (Note that one inherits not alcoholism but a liability for developing it. Cultural/environmental factors may play a significant part in whether a person who is predisposed ever becomes addicted. An Islamic woman and a Mormon man are unlikely to become alcoholic, even if inheriting a predisposition to become so, since their religions prohibit the drinking of alcoholic beverages. No one can become alcoholic unless alcohol is both available and consumed in large amounts.)

NO MATCH FOR ACCESSIBILITY

Accessibility of an addictive substance can play a major role in addiction, even when the substance is accessible to those who have a high level of previous understanding of the consequences of addiction. In England, 15 percent of all opium addicts are professional medical personnel—doctors and nurses.[58]

In a 1990 issue of the *Journal of the American Medical Association,* an editorial states, "Research during the last two decades has provided strong evidence that at least part of the vulnerability to becoming alcoholic *on exposure to alcohol* is inherited." Most researchers will also note that, as yet, no conclusive proof, such as the identification of a certain gene, has been evidenced. The article continues, "Genetics accounts for only part of the vulnerability to alcoholism. Understanding how genes and environment interact to produce alcoholism in any individual is the larger challenge to both genetic and psychosocial research."[59]

ANIMAL STUDIES

Much of our knowledge of the effects of alcohol and alcoholism has been gained through experiments with animals. Some have produced surprising results related to alcoholism as an inherited condition. Rats and mice have been bred across many generations to produce certain families who prefer to drink much larger amounts of alcohol, even with food and water always available, than other rat and mouse families who have not been specially bred for alcohol preference. These heavy alcohol consumers also show high tolerance for the drug, just like their human counterparts.[60]

Other similarities between human and animal alcoholism are also evident in animal studies. Theodore Cicero and David Wozniak conducted an experiment, reported in 1990, that suggests alcohol can cause mutations in sperm that will affect future offspring. Fifteen male rats drank themselves continually drunk on a diet of 6 percent alcohol that lasted thirty-nine days. After weaning from the alcohol diet, and a waiting period of two weeks, the young male rats (equivalent in age to a human adolescent) were mated with female teetotalers. The resulting offspring (only males were tested) looked just like normal rat pups, gaining weight on schedule and performing routine physical and perceptual chores with abilities equal to a group of control pups. But when eventually placed in a maze (with food waiting for those who could solve the puzzle), those babies took 50 percent more time to claim their dinner than did their normal counterparts. Correspondingly, researchers examining the sons of human alcoholics have found that they have more hormonal abnormalities and more difficulties with learning than sons of nonalcoholics or even their own sisters. Cicero and Wozniak had previously found that sons of alcoholic male rats had hormonal problems not evidenced in their sisters.[61]

Just as strains of rodents have been bred to prefer large quantities of alcohol, some strains have been bred to have a pronounced distaste for the substance. Small amounts of the chemical THIQ (tetrahydroisoquinoline) were injected into mice bred to be repelled by alcohol. After the injection, the mice began to prefer alcohol. The greater the amount of injected THIQ, the greater the craving for alcohol. During cancer re-

A WORD ABOUT THE WOMEN

In the majority of studies exploring the genetics of alcoholism, researchers have found that daughters of alcoholics are at less inherited risk of developing an addiction to alcohol than are their brothers. A January 1990 report may shed some light on the mystery. Apparently, there are significant differences between the sexes in the ability to metabolize alcohol. The primary location for alcohol metabolism is in the liver, and a preliminary stage of metabolism (first-pass metabolism) occurs in the gastrointestinal tissue. When twenty men (six alcoholics) and twenty-three women (six alcoholics) were measured for the amount of alcohol metabolized in first-pass metabolism, males showed 59 percent metabolized, while females showed only 23 percent. In order, from highest to lowest rate of first-pass metabolism, were (1) nonalcoholic men, (2) alcoholic men, (3) nonalcoholic women, and (4) alcoholic women (in whom metabolism was almost nonexistent). The study concluded that female alcoholics have increased risk of physical complications.[62] Increased side effects due to slowed metabolism may deter most women from drinking heavily.

search conducted on alcoholics who had died the previous night, Virginia Davis found a highly addictive substance in their brain tissue. Thinking at first that her subjects had also been addicted to heroin, she later found that the addictive chemical was THIQ. Further research indicated that the body of an alcoholic metabolizes alcohol much differently from the body of a nonalcoholic.[63]

RACIAL CONNECTIONS

Different ethnic groups have differing rates of alcoholism. Inherited physiological differences are thought to explain at least some of the differences in rate of alcohol addiction. For instance, most Asian people have a very different response to alcohol exposure than do most Caucasians. Asians are more likely to experience accelerated heartbeat, flushing, dizziness, and other less pleasant effects of alcohol consumption. The reason is apparently a lack of an enzyme present in the liver, known as ALDH. ALDH I and ALDH II are responsible for breaking down a by-product of alcohol metabolism, acetaldehyde. Many Asians have a deficiency of ALDH I, causing the toxic acetaldehyde to break down more slowly and producing unpleasant side effects in drinkers. The rate of alcoholism among most Asian people has been extremely low. However, an increase of alcoholism in third- and fourth-generation Japanese-Americans, perhaps reflecting greater genetic variety, has been recently reported. [64]

In another animal experiment, a group of macaques, all having the same father but different mothers, were placed under stress through separation from their social group. They were given free access to alcohol, and when they were stressed, their alcohol intake increased. But some animals, who were unusually prone to stress, drank much more than the others. The stress-prone macaques were shown to have different baseline levels of 5-hydroxyindoleacetic acid, a metabolite of the neurotransmitter serotonin, and the trait was inherited through the father. Corresponding human research by Markku Linnoila of the National Institute on Alcohol Abuse and Alcoholism found that among fifty-four violent offenders and arsonists, forty-four had blood relatives who were alcoholic, and thirty-five had alcoholic fathers. The latter were more impulsive and had lower average concentrations of 5-hydroxy-indoleacetic acid in their cerebrospinal fluid.[65]

YOUNG MALE ALCOHOLICS

In a subgroup of male alcoholics who were clinically diagnosed as alcoholic before age twenty, and who have been found to have reduced availability of the neurotransmitter serotonin, researchers at the Veterans Administration Medical Center in New York City have observed a higher incidence of physically violent crime, attempted suicide, and clinical depression. The men were more likely than a control group of later onset alcoholics to have alcoholic fathers. Just after withdrawal from alcohol, the early onset group also had significantly lower blood levels of tryptophan, an amino acid that helps in the production of serotonin.[66]

OTHER STUDIES

Much other evidence presented in the past two decades increases the likelihood that alcoholism is at least partly an inherited condition. One striking piece of evidence involves the brain wave patterns of sons of alcoholic fathers. Primary alcoholics report higher levels of hyperactivity and distractibility in childhood.[67] These traits are often found in those who have abnormal brain wave patterns. In response to stimulus, sons of alcoholic fathers consistently displayed brain waves that were less organized and were smaller than those of sons of nonalcoholic fathers, even though they had never been exposed to alcohol. The same type of brain wave pattern is observed in alcoholics in a period of abstinence.[68] When alcohol is administered to these high-risk sons of alcoholics, it results in brain waves associated with feelings of relaxation. Many researchers feel that this phenomenon may indicate that some alcoholics drink to "normalize" their experience by normalizing inherited tension-and-arousal-producing brain waves.[69] Whether or not this is true, it seems that brain wave patterns are highly heritable (alcoholics who have been abstinent for over ten years can still pass the abnormal patterns to their children),[70] and the brain wave type common to prealcoholic sons of alcoholics may be considered a biological trait marker of alcoholism.

Another trait marker found in alcoholics is a lowered activity response to stimulation of their platelet adenyl cyclase, an enzyme. When the tested alcoholics abstained, this trait persisted.[71] Dr. Ivan Diamond has taken these studies a step further. Lymphocyte cells taken from alcoholic subjects showed a less-than-normal response of adenyl cyclase to adenosine, even after the lymphocytes were cultured in alcohol-free media for five or six generations.[72]

Marc Schuckit, of the University of California, San Diego, School of Medicine, has identified traits by which he can distinguish biological sons of alcoholics based on four different lowered responses to alcohol (subjective feelings after a high dose of alcohol, prolactin level after a low dose, and cortisol levels at two different times after a high dose).[73] This decreased sensitivity supports the assumption of high inherited tolerance in alcoholics.

Although the results need to be confirmed in other studies, Kenneth Blum and his colleagues have come up with a first and promising piece of concrete evidence for the conferrence of genetic susceptibility to alcoholism. In April 1990, they reported finding a certain form of the dopamine D2 receptor gene in 69 percent of the brain samples of deceased alcoholics. The same gene was absent in 80 percent of the nonalcoholic brain samples that served as controls.[74]

We have already noted that many common beliefs about alcoholism are misconceptions. Results of some studies have given us information about what alcohol addiction is not.

A prevalent but probably mistaken notion concerning alcoholics cites an addictive personality as being responsible for the addiction. Observation has often confirmed certain addicted personality traits, but no particular personality type has been found to be common to all, or even most, pre- and postalcoholics. In 1983, *Alcoholism Report* published the results of two studies—both conducted by the National Research Council of the National Academy of Sciences—that found no support for the belief that a particular personality profile prefigures addiction.[75] Confusion seems to have arisen because of certain predictable behavior in persons already addicted to alcohol. Some of these personality patterns include low tolerance for frustration, compulsive behavior, and violent anger. More often than not, they represent a dramatic change in the preaddicted personality and a distinct contrast with the personalities of alcoholics in recovery.[76]

However, a certain set of inherited personality traits in childhood may indicate predisposition to alcoholism later in life. Dr. Cloninger, in his continuing research on the heritability of alcoholism, recently noted three personality traits that are identified with increased risk for alcoholism. Comparing four hundred adopted and nonadopted children of both alcoholic and nonalcoholic parents, Cloninger reports that children possessing the following traits by age ten are more likely to have developed an addiction to alcohol by age twenty-eight. The more intense the traits by age ten, the more likely alcoholism will have developed by age twenty-eight. High-risk traits are as follows:

1. The children need to be constantly occupied and challenged and are easily bored.
2. The children compulsively avoid any negative consequences of their actions.
3. The children crave immediate and external gratification as a reward for their efforts.

(Dr. Cloninger's suggestion to parents whose children may have these traits is that they create an environment full of challenge but also highly structured, and that they surround children with plenty of personal support, security, and strict, consistent discipline.)[77]

Hyperactivity is commonly noted in children born to alcoholic mothers, and as noted above, sons of alcoholic fathers have been shown to have brain wave patterns associated with high levels of arousal and tension,[78] indicating that some hyperactive or frustrated children who demonstrate related personality traits may be predisposed to alcoholism genetically or biologically.

Other studies have suggested a relationship between antisocial personality disorder and alcoholism, but no causal relationship has been established.[79] Alcoholism is often found in company with depressive disorders, but once again, no causal relationship has been determined.[80] In the absence of long-term studies that examine personality traits of large numbers of children and adolescents, and then follow them through thirty or forty years of adulthood, conclusions concerning predisposing personality are not possible. However, says one investigator, "It is unlikely that the key to alcoholism will be found in personality."[81]

Personality traits that develop in response to a person's environment may play a key role in why that person drinks, but there is not substantial evidence to indicate that this type of personality trait has a role in the development of alcoholism. In the same way, spiritual weakness, neediness, or corruption may play a significant role in a person's motivation to drink, but there is little reason to believe that they cause alcoholism. The person who drinks to fill a spiritual void does not necessarily become an alcoholic, and this fact alone does not predispose him or her to developing an addiction to alcohol. Likewise, a person who drinks in response to demonic spiritual influence may never develop the symptoms and characteristics of alcoholic disease, and deliverance from demonic spiritual bondage to drinking does not, of necessity, include the physical healing necessary for deliverance from an alcoholic's need to say no to alcohol, one day at a time, for the rest of his or her life.

CONCLUSION

Evidence for genetic and biological roles in susceptibility to alcoholism is increasingly compelling, but why should it be important in helping alcoholics recover? Although it is only part of the picture of recovery, understanding that alcoholism involves genetic factors enables alcoholics and those who aid them to place the demands of recovery in proper *perspective*. Realizing that addiction to alcohol involves biological components is essential for the physical *safety* of alcoholics during the withdrawal phase of recovery.

Alcoholics often feel trapped—that the condition is inevitable because there is nothing to be done. All their efforts to control the problem have met with failure. They must first realize that the condition with which they are hampered is triggered by a physical substance in a vulnerable body. Most people *can* drink moderately, but alcoholics cannot. Realizing that they have more than the average temptation to deal with should release them from false guilt concerning the inability to "handle" the problem as others do. Realizing that something can be done physically to help, and understanding what it will involve, will communicate hope and encourage responsibility. It should encourage persons to admit the problem of alcohol addiction and to have hope that recovery really is possible. At the same time, it should impress on alcoholics that they have the ability to respond to the condition of alcoholism by initially seeking and accepting available and effective help and that they will be in a position to act in such a way as to prevent continued slavery to addiction. Knowledge of inherited susceptibility has the potential to remove the illusion of "aloneness" in the struggle with alcohol addiction. Others are fighting the same battle, and many are winning.

Notes

1. Tom Parker, *In One Day: The Things Americans Do in a Day* (Boston: Houghton Mifflin, 1984), p. 31, in Stephen Arterburn and Jim Burns, *Drug-Proof Your Kids* (Pomona, Calif.: Focus on the Family, 1989), pp. 11–12; hereafter referred to as *Drug-Proof.*

2. Bruce Bower, "Alcoholism's Elusive Genes: It Runs in Families and Ruins Lives, but Is Alcoholism Inherited?" *Science News,* July 1988, p. 75.

3. Alcohol Research Information Service, *Monday Morning Report* 14 (Jan. 28, 1991).

4. Bower, "Alcoholism's Elusive Genes," p. 75.

5. M. E. Chafetz, *Alcoholism and Alcoholic Psychoses,* in Lee Willerman and David B. Cohen, *Psychopathology* (New York: McGraw-Hill, 1990), pp. 509–10.

6. Parker, *In One Day,* p. 31, in Arterburn and Burns, *Drug-Proof,* pp. 11–12; and Chafetz, *Alcoholism and Alcoholic Psychoses,* in Willerman and Cohen, *Psychopathology,* p. 517.

7. Ken Barun and Philip Bashe, *How to Keep the Children You Love Off Drugs* (New York: Atlantic Monthly Press, 1988), p. 4, in Arterburn and Burns, *Drug-Proof,* p. 28.

8. Gail Gleason Milgram et al., *The Facts About Drinking* (Mount Vernon, N.Y.: Consumers Union, 1990), p. 70.

9. Youth for Christ, "Report to the People," Dec. 1985, in Arterburn and Burns, *Drug-Proof,* p. 23.

10. Lorch and Hughes, "Church Youth, Alcohol," p. 15, in Arterburn and Burns, *Drug-Proof,* p. 42.

11. *Facts on Alcoholism and Alcohol-Related Problems* (New York: National Council on Alcoholism, 1988), p. 6, in Arterburn and Burns, *Drug-Proof,* p. 12.

12. "What Drugs Do and Don't Do to Teens," *U.S. News & World Report,* Aug. 1, 1988, p. 8, in Arterburn and Burns, *Drug-Proof,* p. 16.

13. *Facts on Alcoholism and Alcohol-Related Problems,* p. 6, in Arterburn and Burns, *Drug-Proof,* p. 12.

14. Jerry Adler, "Hour by Hour Crack," *Newsweek,* Nov. 28, 1988, p. 67, in Arterburn and Burns, *Drug-Proof,* p. 13.

15. Barun and Bashe, *How to Keep the Children You Love Off Drugs,* p. 50, in Arterburn and Burns, *Drug-Proof,* p. 22.

16. "Alcohol Use and Abuse in America," *The Gallup Report,* Oct. 1987, p. 3, in Arterburn and Burns, *Drug-Proof,* p. 5.

17. Tracy Weber, "New Breed of Counselors Helps 'Addicts' Break Grip of Religion," *Orange County Register,* March 17, 1991, pp. 1, 26.

18. Willerman and Cohen, *Psychopathology,* pp. 509–10.

19. Willerman and Cohen, *Psychopathology,* p. 509.

20. Bower, "Alcoholism's Elusive Genes," p. 75.

21. Milgram et al., *The Facts About Drinking,* p. 74.

22. Bower, "Alcoholism's Elusive Genes," p. 75.

23. Milgram et al., *The Facts About Drinking,* p. 75.

24. Stephen Arterburn, *Growing Up Addicted* (New York: Ballantine, 1987), pp. 110–12.

25. Psalm 18.

26. Arterburn, *Growing Up Addicted,* pp. 123–25.

27. Arterburn, *Growing Up Addicted,* p. 118.
28. Alcohol Research Information Service, *Monday Morning Report* 14.
29. Ryan Ver Berkmoes, "The Bottle and the Bard: A Physician Explores Why Writers Drink," *American Medical News,* Feb. 3, 1989, p. 27.
30. Milgram et al., *The Facts About Drinking,* p. 86.
31. Marlene Cimons, "It's All in the Family," *Los Angeles Times Magazine,* Feb. 10, 1991, pp. 8, 9, 33.
32. Cimons, "It's All in the Family," pp. 11–12, and Nancy Wexler, "Life in the Lab," *Los Angeles Times Magazine,* Feb. 10, 1991, p. 31.
33. Frederick K. Goodwin and Emily M. Gause, "From the Alcohol, Drug Abuse, and Mental Health Administration," *Journal of the American Medical Association* 263 (Jan. 19, 1990): 352.
34. Hull (1981), in Willerman and Cohen, *Psychopathology,* p. 522.
35. Willerman and Cohen, *Psychopathology,* p. 516.
36. Wise (1988), in Willerman and Cohen, *Psychopathology,* p. 516.
37. Wolff (1972), in Willerman and Cohen, *Psychopathology,* p. 518.
38. Hanna (1976), in Willerman and Cohen, *Psychopathology,* p. 519.
39. B. Tabakoff and P. L. Hoffman, "A Neurobiological Theory of Alcoholism," in Enoch Gordis et al., "Finding the Gene(s) for Alcoholism," *Journal of the American Medical Association* 263 (April 18, 1990): 2095.
40. Gabrielli et al. (1982), in Willerman and Cohen, *Psychopathology,* p. 524.
41. T. C. Harford, M. R. Haack, and D. L. Spiegler, "Positive Family History for Alcoholism," *Alcohol Health & Research World* 12 (1987–88): 138–43, in Willerman and Cohen, *Psychopathology,* p. 525.
42. Willerman and Cohen, *Psychopathology,* p. 521.
43. Bower, "Alcoholism's Elusive Genes," p. 75.
44. F. Lemere, "The Nature and Significance of Brain Damage from Alcoholism," *American Journal of Psychiatry* 113 (1956): 361–62, in Arterburn, *Growing Up Addicted,* p. 60.
45. Donald W. Goodwin, M.D., *Is Alcoholism Hereditary?* (New York: Ballantine, 1988), p. 4, in Arterburn, *Growing Up Addicted,* p. 59.
46. Arterburn, *Growing Up Addicted,* pp. 60, 61, 65, and Gordis et al., "Finding the Gene(s) for Alcoholism," p. 2094.
47. Willerman and Cohen, *Psychopathology,* p. 525.
48. Goodwin et al., in Arterburn, *Growing Up Addicted,* p. 54, and in Willerman and Cohen, *Psychopathology,* p. 525.
49. Remi J. Cadoret and Ann Gath, "Inheritance of Alcoholism in Adoptees," *British Journal of Psychiatry* 132 (1978): 252–58, in Arterburn, *Growing Up Addicted,* p. 53.
50. Michael Bohman, "Some Genetic Aspects of Alcoholism and Criminality," *Archives of General Psychiatry* 35 (March 1978): 268, in Arterburn, *Growing Up Addicted,* p. 53.
51. Cadoret, Cain, and Grove (1980), in Arterburn, *Growing Up Addicted,* p. 51.
52. Bower, "Alcoholism's Elusive Genes," p. 74.
53. J. S. Searles, *Journal of Abnormal Psychology* (May 1988), in Bower, "Alcoholism's Elusive Genes," p. 74.
54. Marc A. Schuckit, *Archives of General Psychiatry* (April 1990), in Bruce Bower, "Gene May Be Tied to 'Virulent' Alcoholism," *Science News,* April 21, 1990, p. 246.
55. Gordis et al., "Finding the Gene(s) for Alcoholism," p. 2094.
56. Cadoret et al., in Willerman and Cohen, *Psychopathology,* p. 526.

57. Willerman and Cohen, *Psychopathology,* pp. 525–26.

58. Jaffe (1965), in Willerman and Cohen, *Psychopathology,* p. 511.

59. Gordis et al., "Finding the Gene(s) for Alcoholism," pp. 2094–95.

60. T. X. Li et al., "Rodent Lines Selected for Factors Affecting Alcohol Consumption," *Alcohol Alcohol* Suppl. 1 (1987): 91–96, in Gordis et al., "Finding the Gene(s) for Alcoholism," p. 2094, and in Willerman and Cohen, *Psychopathology,* p. 525.

61. John Horgan, "When Dad Drinks," *Scientific American* 262 (Feb. 1990): 23.

62. Mario Frezza et al., "High Blood Alcohol Levels in Women: The Role of Decreased Gastric Alcohol Dehydrogenase Activity and First-Pass Metabolism," *New England Journal of Medicine* 322 (Jan. 11, 1990): 95.

63. Arterburn, *Growing Up Addicted,* pp. 57–58.

64. Stoil (1987–88), in Willerman and Cohen, *Psychopathology,* p. 518.

65. Goodwin and Gause, "From the Alcohol, Drug Abuse, and Mental Health Administration," p. 352.

66. Bruce Bower, "Early Alcoholism: Crime, Depression Higher," *Science News,* March 25, 1989, p. 180.

67. Jones (1968); Tarter et al. (1977), in Willerman and Cohen, *Psychopathology,* p. 524.

68. Gabrielli et al. (1982), in Willerman and Cohen, *Psychopathology,* p. 524, and Henri Begleiter, in Goodwin and Gause, "From the Alcohol, Drug Abuse, and Mental Health Administration," p. 352.

69. Propping (1978), in Willerman and Cohen, *Psychopathology,* pp. 523–24.

70. Henri Begleiter, in Alcohol Research Information Service, *Monday Morning Report* 14.

71. Boris Tabakoff et al., "Genetics and Biological Markers of Risk for Alcoholism," *Public Health Report* 103 (1988): 690–98, in Goodwin and Gause, "From the Alcohol, Drug Abuse, and Mental Health Administration," p. 352, and in Gordis et al., "Finding the Gene(s) for Alcoholism," p. 2094.

72. Ivan Diamond, in Goodwin and Gause, "From the Alcohol, Drug Abuse, and Mental Health Administration," p. 352, and in Gordis et al., "Finding the Gene(s) for Alcoholism," p. 2094.

73. Schuckit, in Goodwin and Gause, "From the Alcohol, Drug Abuse, and Mental Health Administration," p. 352.

74. Kenneth Blum et al., "Allelic Association of Human Dopamine D2 Receptor Gene in Alcoholism," *Journal of the American Medical Association* 263 (April 18, 1990): 2055–60.

75. Arterburn, *Growing Up Addicted,* p. 50.

76. Milgram et al., *The Facts About Drinking,* p. 70, and Arterburn, *Growing Up Addicted,* p. 50.

77. Alcohol Research Information Service, *Monday Morning Report* 14.

78. Willerman and Cohen, *Psychopathology,* p. 523.

79. Milgram et al., *The Facts About Drinking,* p. 70.

80. Arterburn, *Growing Up Addicted,* p. 50.

81. Milgram et al., *The Facts About Drinking,* p. 70.

Chapter 17

---- ◆ ----

FREEING OURSELVES FROM ALCOHOLISM

HELPING SOMEONE ELSE

Nothing has the capacity to so completely destroy every area of a person's life like alcoholism does. Spiritually and emotionally, it leaves everyone—alcoholic, family, and friends—devastated. Yet the alcoholic goes on drinking, goes on denying that there is a problem or that there is a need for help. Those close to the alcoholic are often sucked into the enabler role and find themselves doing all the wrong things for the right reasons. If they ever break the cycle of enabling, which goes from trying hard to feeling guilty to trying harder, they may be able to help the drinker stop drinking.

We must remember why alcoholics do not want to admit that there is a problem or that help is needed. They deny because of the stigma. They do not want the label of alcoholic. They also deny because they do not believe anyone can help. Each of us must win the battle for credibility and show the alcoholics that we understand and we do not judge. If we show understanding, compassion, and a sincere desire to help, we have a good chance of being allowed to help. As we do, we must always be careful not to be manipulated by the alcoholics.

When I work with an alcoholic, I always think of each person as two people. Down inside there is the healthy person, the real person who wants to be free. But more prominently displayed is the sick person, who is addicted. At times I will hear the healthy person reach out for help, only to be overcome by the unhealthy addicted person trying to sabotage attempts to stop the addiction. I have to be careful that I do not listen to the addicted person. And I constantly remind myself that the longer the person is off alcohol, the stronger the healthy person will grow, and the weaker the addicted will become. If I continue to remind myself of the two dimensions of an addict's character, I am better able to persevere in trying to help the person.

Setting the Stage for Help

If we are intent on helping a person stop the alcoholism progression, we need to set the stage first. John Wallace, in *Alcoholism: New Light on the Disease*, gives the following seven rules that are helpful in setting the stage:[1]

1. *Do not be misled by the alcoholic's excuses.* The reasons for drinking are not valid and should not be accepted or considered appropriate. We must see each excuse as a hurdle that the alcoholic is asking us not to jump while hoping that we will care enough to jump over. The addicted side says, "I don't need help," while the healthy side knows something must be done and hopes we are persistent enough to follow through.

2. *Understand that alcoholism has a physiological basis and that no one is to blame.* Even if someone were to blame, this would not be the time to discuss it. No alcoholic has ever been shamed into recovery. It only drives the person back to the bottle to find some kind of relief from the intense guilt. Hope is the only thing that will motivate the person to get help.

3. *Do not deny the problem.* The people around the alcoholic should not cover up the consequences of the alcohol problem; instead, we should point out to the alcoholic the results of the drinking. If we have been covering up and now start to present the alcoholic with consequences, it will cause a change in behavior. The person may realize that we will no longer allow ourselves to be manipulated, and the person may become angry or depressed. Those reactions are indicators that we are doing something courageously right.

4. *Seek help.* In seeking help, the spouse and family realize that no one except the alcoholic can control the alcoholism and keep sober. Outside help provides the necessary support when the alcoholic is finally ready to accept aid. We must be careful who we receive help from. There are many who would divert our loved one down a path of pseudospiritual growth. We must be sure the treatment center we choose is in perfect agreement with our values.

5. *Timing is crucial.* We should not try to reason or argue with the

alcoholic when he or she is intoxicated. The time to confront is at the point of the least amount of alcohol ingested. We can't expect a miracle, either. This huge monument of denial must be chipped away slowly.

6. *Examine our own drinking and drug use, explore our reasons for use, and examine our patterns of behavior.* I have been in intervention sessions that seemed to be going well until the alcoholic was able to point to the out-of-control behavior of the one doing the confronting. We must clean up our acts before we ask someone else to clean up his or hers.

7. *Do not become obsessed with the alcoholic.* Family members must break free of their obsession with the drinking; they cannot "control" the alcoholic out of the problem. To enable change, growth, and development, each family member needs to assume responsibility for his or her own life.

Most important, we must prepare spiritually before trying to help. We need to spend time in prayer and Bible study. We may want to get away to a secluded place for prayer and fasting. We can only do so much, and asking God to do what we cannot will free us from feeling overly responsible. It will also call into the situation the power of God, which is needed in countering the power of addiction.

Addiction is extremely powerful, and we cannot deal with it alone. If we try to fix the person, we will fail as we have failed many times before. For that reason we must obtain professional help from someone with our values. Someone who does nothing but work with addiction problems every day will provide us with the greatest chance for change in the person we love.

HELPING OURSELVES

Perhaps we are concerned about ourselves and our own drinking problem. We have plenty of reasons to be optimistic about the future. We did not cause this condition, but we are the only ones who can fix it and we are responsible to fix it as soon as possible. If we have been trying to fix ourselves, we know it is a waste of time. We know it has always resulted in failure. There is no need to struggle any longer. All we have to do is admit to the situation, the pattern, and the history. We have to admit that we do drink differently, more than most others. Then we must humble ourselves to make a phone call and ask for help. When we do, we enter into a new world of hope and solutions. We abandon the struggle to cope for a new world of freedom.

Our journey of recovery has found only a starting place. It must continue for a lifetime, founded on reality, faith, decision, continued honesty, and support. We can do it with the help of God and the support of people who care deeply about us and want the best for us.

CONCLUSION

If we or someone we love has a drinking problem, there is only one reason not to get help. It is the killer disease of denial. We must see the reality of the problem and break through all of the emotional reasons to deny what is there. We must accept our responsibility to deal with the situation before us. God will provide us with the strength we need. The pain of change is never greater than the pain of looking back with regret on lost opportunities and wasted lives when it is too late to do anything.

Note

1. Quoted in Gail Gleason Milgram et al., *The Facts About Drinking* (Mount Vernon, N.Y.: Consumers Union, 1990), pp. 104–5.

———————— ◆ ————————

Chapter 18

FREEING OUR CHILDREN FROM ALCOHOLISM

Over the past few years there has been a decline in the use of drugs by most segments of the adolescent population. That would appear to be good news to most parents. Sadly, it is not. With the decline in drug use in general has come a dramatic increase in alcohol use in particular. What is even more alarming is that kids do not drink like they used to. Today they drink to get drunk. They see no reason to drink if it is not to completely obliterate reality with a drunken stupor. Not all of these kids are alcoholics and not all of them will be, but every one needs help before there is loss of life or limb. Now more than ever parents need to reach out to their children and help them stop drinking before the devastation gets even greater.

The following tips offer the greatest hope available of initiating change within our children and our families. Each one relates to either preventing the problem or arresting it once it has started.

STARTING WITH OURSELVES

Our attitudes and actions play an important role in children's decisions to use or abstain. If we are heavily involved with the drugs of our culture, we have no credibility when asking children to avoid the drugs of their culture. If we reach for a Valium or a drink when under pressure, we must change our behavior to set the best example.

If there is evidence of alcoholism and heavy drinking on the family tree, we have to provide special education to our children. They need to know that a high tolerance may be a family trait that has led to many others being involved in alcoholic drinking. We must do our best to see that heavy drinking is *not* portrayed as a virtue.

Additionally, we must examine our behaviors of excess. If we are overweight or workaholics, we send a message that excess is okay. We may need to obtain professional help for our obsessions and compulsions before we can adequately help our children with a compulsive drinking problem.

BUILDING A SOLID FOUNDATION

Every treatment center, even the most secular, discusses the vital role God plays in the recovery process. Alcoholics and drug addicts can't recover without turning their lives over to the One who created them. If God is so vital in treatment and recovery, surely God is essential in the prevention of a problem. Raising our children to know that God deeply cares about every decision they make is the strongest foundation we can provide.

In our society we see drugs and alcohol filling a values vacuum. Some kids are raised not knowing the difference between right and wrong. It is no wonder we have lost this generation to rampant immorality. We as parents must do what the government cannot. We must provide a foundation of morality that is a guiding force in each thing our children do. If we do not have a strong faith in God, there is little chance our children will. The strongest motivator of kids who remain abstinent is their belief that God created them and their bodies and their desire to do only those things that bring honor to God.

BUILDING SOLID CHILDREN

Children who search for meaning, acceptance, and self-worth easily succumb to peer pressure. We need to provide these things for our children so they won't seek them from someone else. If parents are negative, critical, and rejecting of children, they will turn to peers who will be positive and affirming, or they will do anything to get praise from those potentially negative peers. It is only natural that rejected children will drink if that brings a feeling of acceptance.

To avoid this setup, we must encourage our children. We can emphasize the positive, catch them in the act of doing something right, and let them know we are deeply concerned about each decision made and hope that each decision will produce positive results. We can let them know that our love is not conditional, that whatever they choose, we will be there for them with love and acceptance.

TEACHING OUR CHILDREN

Too often parents leave education to someone else. When that happens, it is usually someone from the street. We must start early teaching children the dangers of drugs and alcohol. We must teach, starting at kindergarten, the harmful effects of alcohol and the harmful effects of all irresponsible behavior.

If we wait until they are in junior high, we are probably waiting too late. Children will make the decision of whether or not to drink between the ages of ten and twelve. I think those ages are getting younger every year. That is why we must start early, so when the children choose, it will be an informed decision.

MOTIVATING OUR CHILDREN

Short-term rewards and short-term restrictions are the best prevention tools. Children will not refuse to drink because of the possibility of cirrhosis of the liver. But tell them that if they're caught drinking, the driver's license and the car go away, and we'll tell them something that will have an impact. Being able to tell a peer that parents will take the license away provides an excuse to say no. It is not the cure-all to the problem, but as one component, it provides an added edge.

IDENTIFYING ABUSE EARLY

Any parent actively involved in a child's life will be able to notice evidence of drinking. Experiencing radical mood swings, hanging around friends who drink, smoking tobacco (ten times greater chance of smoking marijuana), defending the use of drinking by others, and possessing strange paraphernalia are all symptoms of drug use and drinking. If children are doing some sort of drug, there is a 99 percent chance of drinking, heavy drinking, to go along with it. The natural thing is to deny the problem exists and try to cover it up. But we must break through the denial, see the reality, and act on it. The sooner we see it, the sooner we can stop it. Remember, we must be involved with our children to see the need for change.

INTERVENING EARLY

Intervention is the process of confronting children with consequences of alcohol use, abuse, and alcoholism. We may come to a point where we have to make a serious decision. In extreme circumstances, we may have to decide whether we will continue to act as suppliers or ask them to move out unless they are willing to obtain treatment. It is very tough to confront, but the alternative is to enable the problem to grow and addiction to set in deeper. The fear of sending children out into the streets must be overcome by the fear of being primary enablers of a growing addiction that will eventually kill them.

FINDING THE BEST TREATMENT RESOURCE

Wars are won because people seek wise counsel. Treatment involves waging war on addiction. But not all resources are equal. A center with a strong reputation for quality care, a place that goes out of the way to help us face the problem, is the place for us. A quality center will always involve the family in treatment. Each family member must make adjustments if treatment is to be effective. The least we can do is call and discuss what kind of program is available.

At New Life Treatment Centers we have a journey program for kids. It is a fifty-two-day wilderness program that enables kids to experience the consequences of the behavior immediately. This program is staffed with a field team and therapists. If children do not wear dry socks to bed, they experience cold feet that night. If they do not prepare their own food, they do not eat. The consequences are immediate and sure. This program has changed lives more intensely than any program I know of.

SUPPORTING RECOVERY

Tremendous barriers to children's recovery are parents who do not support the recovery process. Parents must forgive children for not meeting the expectations of being perfect (or at least wonderful) children. Facing the reality of an addict in the family is hard for many parents to bear. Eventually, children sense the resentment, and they end up in a no-win situation. Feeling the pain of failure, they return to drugs, playing out the feelings of worthlessness perceived from the parents. Parents who have difficulty supporting recovery should seek counseling for themselves.

REACHING OUT

Rather than wonder about our children and drug problems, we should talk to someone experienced in dealing with these problems. We can't afford to hide or deny any longer. If anonymity is important, we can call anonymously. The worst thing we can do is to do nothing. We have the power to change children's lives. The pain may intensify in the short term, but the long-term rewards of healthy children will be worth the price of the pain.

CONCLUSION

There aren't many things worse than parents on a guilt trip. I certainly have not wanted to put parents on one. I hope we will feel the need to accept responsibility to do everything we can to help our children. That means we will have to do the painful thing of helping ourselves first. Too often parents don't help their children because they are too lazy to help themselves. Please accept the challenge of creating a better generation to follow. Accept the challenge to free our children from some of the pain we have had to endure because we did not know the truth.

Whatever things are true, whatever things are noble, whatever things are just, whatever things are pure, whatever things are lovely, whatever things are of good report, if there is any virtue and if there is anything praiseworthy—meditate on these things.

—Philippians 4:8

CONCLUSION

◆

PRINCIPLES FOR LIVING LIFE ON PURPOSE

OUR SLATE

We do not come into this world as a blank slate. The tablet of our reality has all sorts of stuff already written on it, and some of it is not too helpful to establishing a productive life. These hand-me-down genes, which we did not choose, are often in the act of betraying us before we speak our first word. By the time we are twelve, our slate contains emotional graffiti, secondhand emotions, placed there by well-meaning parents and sometimes even evil parents. With this skewed tablet, we set out on a life that at times seems to be more difficult than we can bear. With our first big challenge we often face our first big regret that we wish we were stronger, better prepared, healthier from the core of our souls to the cortex of our minds. Many spend their whole lives regretting they did not have it better, regretting their heritage, and hating who they are. For those who live in regret, there is little hope that they will find a way out of their pain and into a life where they can feel good about themselves and the relationship they have with the Creator. They compound their predisposition to problems with a meaningless life of foolish choices, each problem stacking up on top of the next, creating a monument to a wasted life.

It does not have to be that way. Each of us can reverse the tide that has cast us upon the shores of self-abuse, revictimization, and pain. We do not have to live a life of depression with the thought of suicide looming in the back of the mind. We do not have to compound our problems by creating more of them because we do not have a plan, because we are not living life on purpose. A classic case of this type of destructive living was found in the life of a woman ironically named Hope. Hope's story is common among those who live with genes and emotions from childhood that predispose them to problems from the beginning.

HOPE'S STORY

Hope's parents were both sick people. Her mother was depressed most of her life, and in the worst of her despair, her anger and hatred spewed out into Hope's heart. Her mother verbally and emotionally abused her throughout childhood. Anytime Mom saw something good in Hope, she tried to stamp it out or push it down so she wouldn't be reminded of how deficient she was. Hope's father was no better. He drank most of the time when he was at home. His mood swings were bizarre. At his worst he would hit and throw things. At his best he would be passed out in the bedroom. He had little time for his daughter. There was nothing she could do to capture his attention—not until she reached puberty.

Often when a mother withdraws into her own world of misery, a daughter is pushed in as a replacement. Hope was demanded to fulfill her father's sexual needs. She was also required to do all of the chores around the house because her mother, lying in bed, could not do them. It was a miserable life up until the age of eighteen. By that time, Hope had further compounded her problems. She ate a lot and weighed about 220 pounds. She had started drinking at age sixteen in an effort to medicate her pain. The weight and the booze deepened her depression and left her with a mind that obsessed over everything. Hope was a sad case but not an unusual case. She was twenty years old before she realized she did not have to be a victim of hand-me-down genes and secondhand emotions.

Hope reached the end of herself when she crashed her car one night driving home from getting her father more beer. She hit her head so hard that it split open, requiring her to be hospitalized for a few days. During that time, she met a social worker who took a special interest in her. As Hope unfolded her life, the social worker saw almost a carbon copy of her own life before she had put the pieces together. She arranged to visit Hope when she left the hospital. Her mission was to create a real human being out of Hope. For two years she met with her, and by the end of that time, Hope was a different human being. Because of a Christian social worker who loved people, Hope was given an invitation to start over, and she took it. In the process she discovered she did not have to revictimize herself. She found that she, too, could live life on purpose. The following principles helped Hope. If we feel we are predisposed to sad and difficult lives, if we have made matters worse through destructive decisions that led us into more pain, these principles will help us, just as they did Hope.

PRINCIPLES FOR LIVING LIFE ON PURPOSE

Purpose Principle #1: Surrender

One of the great mysteries of life is, How do people fix something by giving up on fixing it? Often those who are not familiar with how recovery works wonder why alcoholics must admit they are powerless over alcohol before being able to have the power to stop drinking. On the surface, it doesn't make much sense—especially if we believe that people with problems are weak and they just need to try harder. Admitting powerlessness would seem like the perfect excuse to continue to be weak and not try harder. This lack of insight has confounded many who have watched as people like alcoholics have put their lives back together by admitting they cannot do it under their own power.

The problem with people like you and me is that we try very, very hard. We spend most of our lives trying hard. We use every kind of home remedy imaginable. We believe what people tell us; if we would just work harder, pull ourselves up by the bootstraps, we could conquer this thing. I've pulled on my bootstraps so much throughout my life that they are up around my ears. It never helped. And it's no wonder. As we have seen, many problems are caused or exacerbated by genetic and environmental predispositions. Pulling on our bootstraps doesn't change those predispositions. In fact, pulling on our bootstraps gets us nowhere except looking better for a little while.

In our search to fix ourselves we often find something that will help us cope better and ease the pain for a while. We breathe a sigh of relief because we are convinced we have found the answer. But because we are merely coping, it does not last long. One of the laws of coping is that the coping mechanism of choice will also decrease in its effectiveness over time. Another law of coping is that under stress, the coping mechanism will prove less and less effective as the stress intensifies. Millions of people are going through life with a goal of just being able to cope. That isn't exactly what I call living life on purpose.

Individuals out to fix themselves will pick coping mechanisms that compound the problem. Hope was sexually molested. To deal with the pain and build a protective wall so that no one else would want to molest her, she ate. The eating helped her cope. It made her instantly feel good. It medicated her pain. But where did it get her? It got her a huge body that was painful to look at each time she glanced in the mirror. Her coping mechanism of food was used to medicate the pain and prevent her from feeling it again. But because it was a treatment that dealt with issues on the surface of her life, it produced deeper pain in the deep wounds she felt.

I did exactly what Hope did. When I got a girl pregnant in my first year at Baylor University, I paid for her to have an abortion. The guilt from that incident racked my soul like nothing I had done before. I felt so alienated from God. I was on my own, and I did not know what to do with my pain. I never told one person about the abortion. So in my pain I ate. I had about eighty ulcers eating away on the inside. I was so depressed, it was hard to go to class. The eating got my weight up to 220 pounds; I was so unattractive that no one would want to have sex with me. I medicated my pain with food, and the weight it brought on protected me from the situation that caused the pain. At that point in my life, all I wanted to do was cope. It was the ultimate goal, but it was a goal too low to allow me to enjoy life or have a relationship with the God who created me.

At the depths of my despair—facing depression, obesity, and thoughts of suicide—I believe God placed me in a seminar that literally changed my life. It did not make me perfect and it did not free me from a life of problems, but it changed my way of living so dramatically that I was never the same again. In that seminar I heard something I had heard a million times but did not truly understand. I needed to surrender to the God who created me. I needed to stop trying to fix myself and let the God who loves me fix me. I had come to the end of myself. At that point I allowed God to do what I could not. I allowed Him to heal the guilt and shame I felt.

My life was radically different from that point on. What I had fought to maintain, I lost. Once I gave up on the fighting and surrendered to God, God gave back to me what I lost. I can't imagine how many blessings I would have missed if I had not allowed God to take control of my life. And throughout my life, He has continued to reveal to me that He loves me and cares for me. That was displayed greater than at any other time when in my arms was placed my daughter, born of a young girl who refused to give her up to abortion. What I had destroyed, God gave back, and He wants to do the same for every struggler.

The first step in living life on purpose is to allow the Person who created us to finish the creation. We must stop trying to make ourselves better and submit to the Master Designer. We must put ourselves back on the potter's wheel and let God take all the cracks and breaks and chips and turn them into something more valuable than we ever dreamed possible. Each day we must look to God and let Him know we want His will for our lives. The daily process of total surrender is the beginning of a life full of purpose.

Purpose Principle #2: Connect

We cannot do this alone. We are not trained to evaluate or treat the problems caused by our predispositions. We must reach out to someone for support and professional guidance. To delay connecting with someone who can help is to delay the healing process.

As we mess up our lives through acts of irresponsibility, we feel natural guilt. It is real, and it affects everything we do. Then there are those who take great pleasure in compounding our guilt by shaming us. They make us feel like second-class people, unworthy of God's love or anyone else's. The more guilt and shame we feel, the more we find ways to isolate ourselves from others. We abandon authentic relationships for superficial ones. We lose the ability to look people in the eye and relate to them openly and honestly. To start over is to make a decision to reverse this process.

If we feel all alone, we are in great company. Everyone who travels down the rough road of personal problems ends up there. The longer we live there, the more difficult it becomes to reconnect and reopen ourselves to vulnerability. Treatment is so helpful to counter this because we are thrown in with fellow strugglers who are also trying to overcome the desire to isolate and withdraw. Support groups can also be a powerful place to connect. The only problem is that it is easy to say all the right things in a group and fake it for a while. Sometimes professional help is the only way we can be confronted with our continuing bent toward hiding behind our facade of fake feelings.

Groups, treatment centers, and professional counseling are all practice for the real world. We try out what it is like to be real again in these artificial settings so we can actually be real in the real world. People who don't avail themselves of this kind of help miss one of the most freeing experiences available. These settings appear scary to an outsider, but they are full of loving, caring people who want to help. When we get serious about living life on purpose, we will find a group or a center or a professional to help us come out of hiding.

Purpose Principle #3: Think

Sandy, my wife, and I traveled to Kauai recently and rented a room on the sands of a small bay. It was so remote, we were the only ones on the beach. There were no phones or television sets. It was the perfect place to rest for a few days. The first night we were there, we crawled into bed, and the most incredible feeling overwhelmed me. The wind was blowing through the windows, and the surf was washing up on shore just outside. The air was so cool we had to have a few blankets to keep us warm. I could not believe how wonderful I felt. Something about the wind, the cool air, and those heavy blankets saturated me with a sense of well-being. I wondered why it was so peaceful, causing me to lie there, looking at the ceiling and smiling in the dark.

Then I realized I was reliving something from my childhood that I had experienced many times. When I was growing up, my grandparents had a house on Lake Leon just outside Ranger, Texas. It seemed that no matter how hot it was during the day, the nights were always cool. There was a screened-in porch where the kids often slept. It was my favorite place. At night the winds would whip up the hill off the lake and across the beds on the porch. We needed thick blankets and quilts to keep warm. After a fun day with all the relatives water skiing, swimming, and eating the best barbecue ever made, it was a very secure feeling to curl up in those beds with the wind swooping overhead.

As I lay in bed in Hawaii thinking of those wonderful memories, I did not have an ounce of depression or anxiety within me. I felt happiness, gratitude, peace, and love. I dwelt on those memories, and my life was better because of it. It brought to mind the verse in Philippians that reads, "Whatever things are true, whatever things are noble, whatever things are just, whatever things are pure, whatever things are lovely, whatever things are of good report, if there is any virtue and if there is anything praiseworthy—meditate on these things" (4:8).

There are so many things we do not have control of, but our thoughts are our own. We can choose to avoid recalling all the good times and feelings, or we can decide to think on those things that give us pleasure and joy and relief. That is especially important to do if we are dealing with some very tough issues. We need to balance our resolution of the hard realities of our past with those things that are pleasant and good. Consciously thinking of positive memories can help us overcome our predispositions.

This practice translates into another area, also. As we recover from our problems, we come to accept some of our limitations, which is healthy and allows us to have more realistic expectations of ourselves and others. In becoming realistic, we are forced to face some of our weaknesses. That can be a very depressing process. We need to think about our strengths while we learn to accept our weaknesses. We need to choose to focus on what we can do while we choose to no longer attempt those things that have produced failure.

We can live life on purpose only if we use our heads. Too often we have gotten in trouble because we have allowed our hearts or some passionate moment to direct our paths. We often victimize ourselves because in the absence of our own plans, we just fall into the plans of anyone who comes along. We need to make a decision to turn on the brain God gave us and use it. We have an incredibly powerful tool to improve the quality of our lives if we choose to do so. It is our choice of how we use our brains, to either help us or hurt us. With the decision to help ourselves, with the power of our minds working for and not against us, we can overcome many of the negative predisposing factors in our lives.

Purpose Principle #4: Choose

Few people enter adulthood with the ability to make good choices that have long-term positive outcomes. Many of us had parents who made all of our decisions for us. If we had drill sergeant parents who ordered us around and never allowed us to make decisions and never told us how they made theirs, we were left with two problems in this area. First of all, we were not allowed to develop good decision-making skills, and second, we received the message that we were not competent enough to make good decisions. Authoritarian parents never do us any favors in the decision-making process. They predispose in us a tendency toward bad decision-making.

I have been a terrible decision maker all my life. I think those things that I chose and worked out did so because God intervened. Many of my decisions have been made under pressure and in the midst of tremendous confusion. I am married to one of the all-time great decision makers. She has taught me well in this area. She looks at the long-term view and weighs the consequences of each direction that could be taken. But before she decides, she accumulates as many facts as possible. She takes her time in the beginning; she endures short-term inconvenience for the long-term pleasure of having made the right choice. If we are poor decision makers, we can learn to make good ones. We need to find someone who is a good decision maker and ask for help in developing that skill. That person can help us overcome our predisposition to bad decision-making.

One key to making good decisions is delayed gratification. Most of us want what we want, and we want it *now*. We look at what will make us feel the best in the shortest amount of time. In the long term we suffer because of our shortsighted perspective. The God who created us sees things from an eternal perspective. We see things from a very limited, finite perspective. That is why we often go against what is God's best for us. We need to delay the thrill of the moment and take a few seconds before making a decision and see it more from an eternal perspective than our usual short-term scope.

The basic elements of making good decisions are (1) to get all the facts and then (2) to consider all of the consequences of the decisions, thinking long term rather than short. When we start doing this and considering others as we go, we make our lives easier. We stop having to clean up the messes this year that were caused by poor decisions in previous years. We replace our long-term pain with the short-term inconvenience of taking our time before we decide.

Often we make poor decisions as a self-fulfilling prophecy. We come to accept that we do not have what it takes to make healthy choices so we end up making poor ones. Alone, without God's help, we might mess everything up. But God wants us to call upon His strength, especially if this area is a weakness. God wants to help us make the best of what we have. We need to fight against the thoughts of incompetence and stretch our limitations by asking God to help us. We do what we can with what we have and trust God to do what we cannot. We can become good decision makers.

Purpose Principle #5: Restore

Most likely the worst experience of my life was paying to have a baby aborted. I obsessed over it and wondered what things were like for the girl. With years in between us and that horrible event, I wanted to talk with her, make sure she had forgiven me for my irresponsibility. I ordered a Baylor alumni directory, and when it arrived by mail, I looked her up and made the call. It was a wonderful experience. There was immediate restoration. She understood who I was then and that I am not the same person anymore. She experienced emotional pain over it all, but she did not let it destroy her life. It was a tremendous load off my mind to experience her loving attitude. The restoration process often alleviates years of guilt, shame, and remorse.

There was a time in my life when I needed to make big changes, and as a result of those changes, I called or wrote everyone I had hurt and asked for forgiveness. (If you didn't get a call or a letter and you think you should have, I apologize.) Each phone call or letter back to me lifted another burden of guilt. People were so affirming that we are all in this together. It is amazing how willing people are to forgive if we take the first step toward restoration.

So many people go through life punishing themselves for how they have treated others. They could remove the self-inflicted sentence simply by making the effort toward restoration. That means saying they are sorry to certain people. It may also mean paying back a debt that was not paid. It could mean doing some work for someone without charge because they took a paycheck they did not work for. Restoration and restitution take many forms. But the result is always positive. Even if the person does not forgive them, they can feel good that they made the best effort possible to make things right.

I remember back in my seminary days I had a dry cleaning bill of $75 that I charged up before I took a cruise. When I got back from the cruise, I didn't have any money left so I conveniently forgot to pay the bill. I never went back into that cleaners again. But I did not forget it. It kept coming to mind over and over, and I finally decided to do something about it. I figured up the interest and wrote a check to that cleaners for $100 and stuck it in my wallet. I was going there on business, and when I did, I dropped by the cleaners. I walked in and gave them a check for $100. They had no record of the debt and tried to give the check back. There was no weeping or changed ways because of my visit. But I look back on something that caused me to feel bad about myself, and now I feel good about it.

It takes humility to make restitution. If we attempt it, we soon find that humility is easier to live with than guilt. Humility hurts short term and feels good long term. Guilt hurts short term *and* long term. Restoration removes its poison from our lives and allows us to realign with our fellow strugglers. Rather than just focus on our relationship with God, we need to focus on our relationship with others. The Bible tells us not even to worship God until we have made things right with other human beings. When we feel guilty, we want to look up; God wants us to look to our side for the person we have hurt. Restoration is a wonderful gift to God, to those we have hurt, and to ourselves. It is a way of taking responsibility for our lives—including the harmful effects of problems we were predisposed to. It is living life on purpose rather than continuing to be revictimized by the same problem of years past.

Purpose Principle #6: Forgive

Not only do we need to ask people to forgive us if we have hurt them, we need to forgive those who have hurt us. That is always easier said than done, especially for the person who was sexually abused very young and has lived with the scars of that abuse for many years. As painful as it may be, we need to do whatever it takes to forgive others. The Bible tells us that God will not forgive us of our sins if we do not forgive others of their sins.

In forgiving others we are able to see them as fellow strugglers. We no longer hold ourselves up as near perfect; we see ourselves as no better than anyone else. As we examine our own lives, we see the destructive things we have done to survive. Whether it was abuse of people or chemicals or some compulsive behavior, we all do things to survive that we would not normally do. Someone who has been abused has been victimized by a person trying to survive. If the adult had it to do over, if we could peer down into the depths of the heart, we would see that the adult would never want to hurt the young person in that way.

It is essential that we forgive others. If we do not, we obsess over the abuse and become victimized by the terrible event over and over again. We remain captives to environmental predisposition. Forgiveness frees us from it and helps us move beyond it so that we live on purpose, not in reaction to some predisposing event that happened years ago.

One of the first things we need to do in the forgiveness process is forgive ourselves. We sometimes do not offer forgiveness to others because we do not hold it out for ourselves. We need to see ourselves as broken people who did the best we could at the time. We need to see ourselves as human beings who God loves unconditionally. We also need to let our misdeeds of the past be motivation not to repeat them in the future.

For many of the predisposing emotional traumas that ail us, the healing salve is forgiveness of ourselves and others.

Purpose Principle #7: Love

To come to the seventh principle is to come to a point where the self-obsession must be totally abandoned and given over to unselfish love for others. We need to give of ourselves to someone else. If we do not, our efforts at maturity and development will be wasted. The Bible tells us that we can have the greatest of all there is in the world, but if we do not love people, it will all be for nothing. God is love, and we cannot be part of Him if we do not also love as He does. Followers of God must find a way to love, even if it seems impossible. To better enable ourselves to love others, we can pray a simple prayer, "God, help me to love people more today." If we start each day in that way, we will find ourselves at the center of God's will, and over time, our hearts will once again be open to loving others.

Sometimes we should not wait to feel like doing something before we do it. Sometimes if we do something first, the feelings are sure to catch up. That is certainly the case with love. If we are married to someone who has struggled with us through all our problems, but now we find difficult to love, there is a way to restore that love. We can't wait until the feeling comes; we must act as if the feeling is there. We must do the things we would normally do if we loved the person: become a servant, try to please, take the focus off self, and place it onto the other. Very quickly, feelings of love will return. This principle is especially important for those of us who face the effects of predisposing emotional trauma. The feeling may return a little less quickly for us, but if we act as from love, it will surely come.

We need to turn from our critical nature and find the beauty of God in everyone. Then we need to let that discovery lead us to action. We cannot love if we do not do something about it. When I see Jimmy Carter building houses for the homeless, I am convinced he loves those people. His actions are more important than the intentions of another who does nothing. We need to get busy meeting the needs of others, helping restore hope to others, and helping others feel loved. If we do that, God will give us the gift of loving others. Our purpose and direction will change as we become motivated by the changes we see in others as they respond to our efforts to show them love.

Purpose Principle #8: Persevere

The book of James provides us with great perspective on our temporary miseries. James reminds us to look back at all the suffering that Job endured. In the midst of it all, Job did not lose faith, and God richly restored him. James ends his comments on Job by saying, "You have heard of the perseverance of Job and seen the end intended by the Lord —that the Lord is very compassionate and merciful" (5:11). If we are in the midst of crisis or life has continued to be more painful than we imagined it could be, we must persevere.

God never rewarded anyone for perfection. All He expects of us is perseverance. He tells us those who persevere will receive the crown of life. We know that life will not always be wonderful, but if we trust God, we can be assured that all of the unwonderful moments will work together to form a life of love and accomplishment that can be truly wonderful for us and those who love us. We need to run from the temptation to feel sorry for ourselves and, instead, look to God to help us persevere for His glory and the accomplishment of His will, not our own.

In the midst of Job's struggle he cried out something that has been a battle cry to me in the midst of pain and heartache. Job's words pierced through the pain he was experiencing as he cried out, "Though He slay me, yet will I trust Him" (13:15). That is a great challenge to all of us to maintain our perspective and purpose through our struggles. To be able to say to God that no matter what we must endure, we will not turn from Him, that is the ultimate surrender. It is the ultimate act of humility and love to God. That is all He asks for, an attitude of perseverance with Him, no matter where He leads.

CONCLUSION

The predispositions that we bring into this world or we develop through childhood do not have to become prescriptions for failure. We have the ability, with the help of God, to take what we have and to make an incredible life out of it. Eight simple words are the keys to eight difficult but life-changing principles:

SURRENDER

     CONNECT

        THINK

          CHOOSE

            RESTORE

              FORGIVE

                LOVE

                  PERSEVERE

Each principle is a step along a wonderful journey to finding peace within yourself, peace with those around you, and peace with the God who made you. Before you give up on being happy or at peace or feeling good about yourself, I invite you to take this journey of living life on purpose. I invite you to use all of the insight available—including insight into the affects on your life of hand-me-down genes and second-hand emotions—and to believe that with the help of friends, family, caring professionals, and above all God you can know peace and happiness. God loves you greatly and is waiting to bless your life with all of His eternal goodness. He is waiting for you to take that first step toward Him and all He has to offer you.

RESOURCES

If you would like help with an emotional problem, there are counselors available to talk with you at:

New Life Treatment Centers
1-800-NEW-LIFE
All phone calls are free and confidential.

Organizations that have information on problems with a genetic predisposition:

The March of Dimes
1275 Mamaroneck Ave.
White Plains, New York 10605
914-428-7100

The National Society of Genetic Counselors
233 Canterbury Drive
Wallingford, Pennsylvania 19086

Hereditary Disease Foundation
1427 Seventh Street, Suite 2
Santa Monica, California 90401
213-458-4183

Publications are available from:

National Archives and Records Service
General Services Administration
Room 201
Washington, D.C. 20408

> Genealogical Records in the National Archives
>
> Genealogical Sources Outside the National Archives
>
> Military Service Records in the National Archives of the United States

Superintendent of Documents
U.S. Government Printing Office
Washington, D.C. 20402

Where to Write for Birth and Death Records: U.S. and Outlying Areas DHEW Pub. No. (PHS) 80-1142

Where to Write for Birth and Death Records of U.S. Citizens Who Were Born Outside of the U.S. and Birth Certifications for Alien Children Adopted by U.S. Citizens, HRA 77-1143

Where to Write for Divorce Records: U.S. and Outlying Areas DHEW Pub. No. (PHS) 80-1144

Where to Write for Marriage Records: U.S. and Outlying Areas, DHEW Pub. No. (PHS) 80-1145